GIRLS' LAST TOUR

①

TSUKUMIZU

GIRLS' LAST TOUR

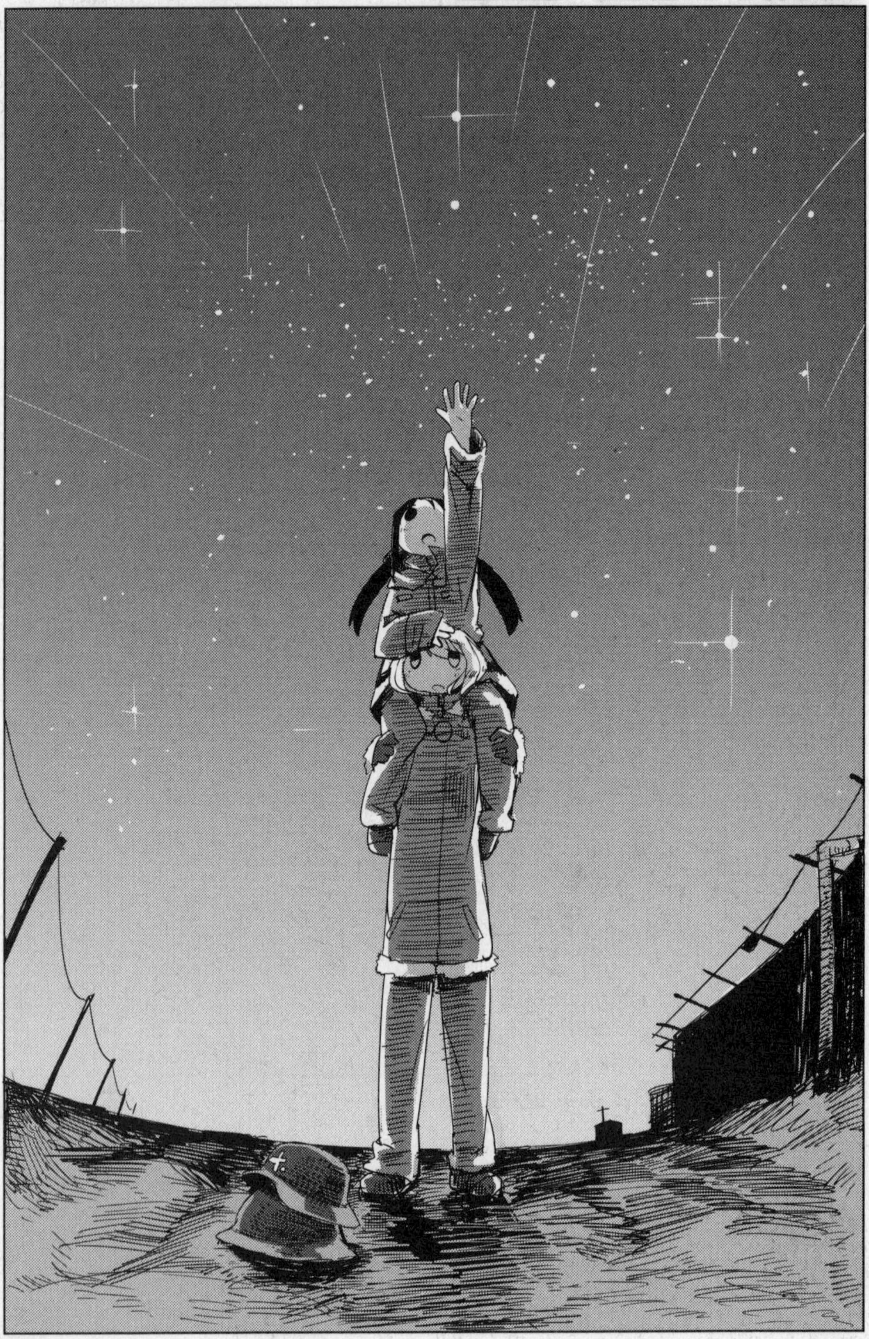

01

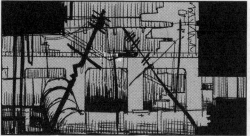

SFX: DODODODODODO (DADRMDRMDRM)

GARA GARA GARA GARA GARA (KLAKA)

DARK.

DODODODODODODODODODODODODODO

DODODODODODO

GATA (RATTLE)

GATA

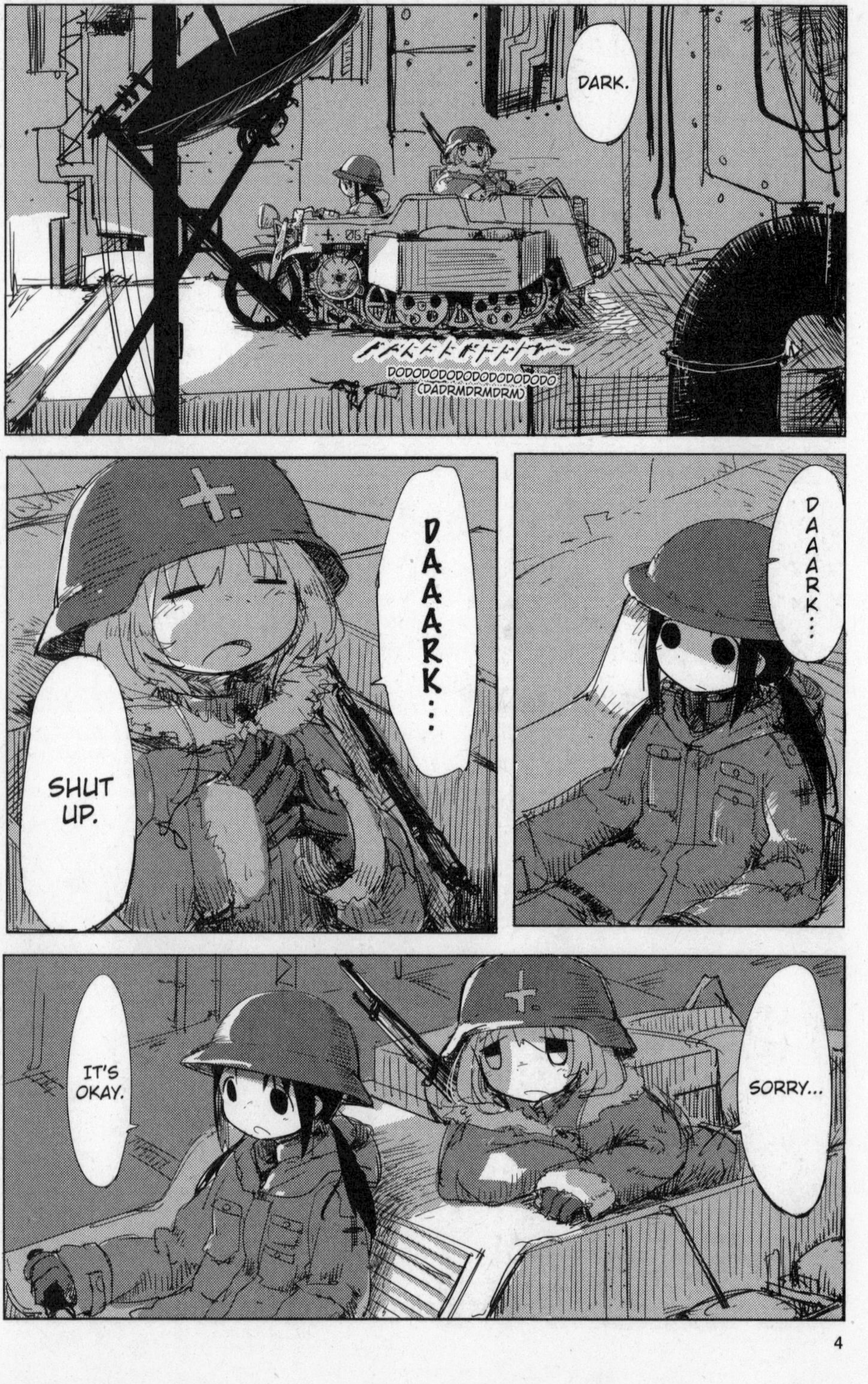
DARK.
DODODODODODODODODODO
(DADRMDRMDRM)
DAAARK...
DAAARK...
SHUT UP.
SORRY...
IT'S OKAY.

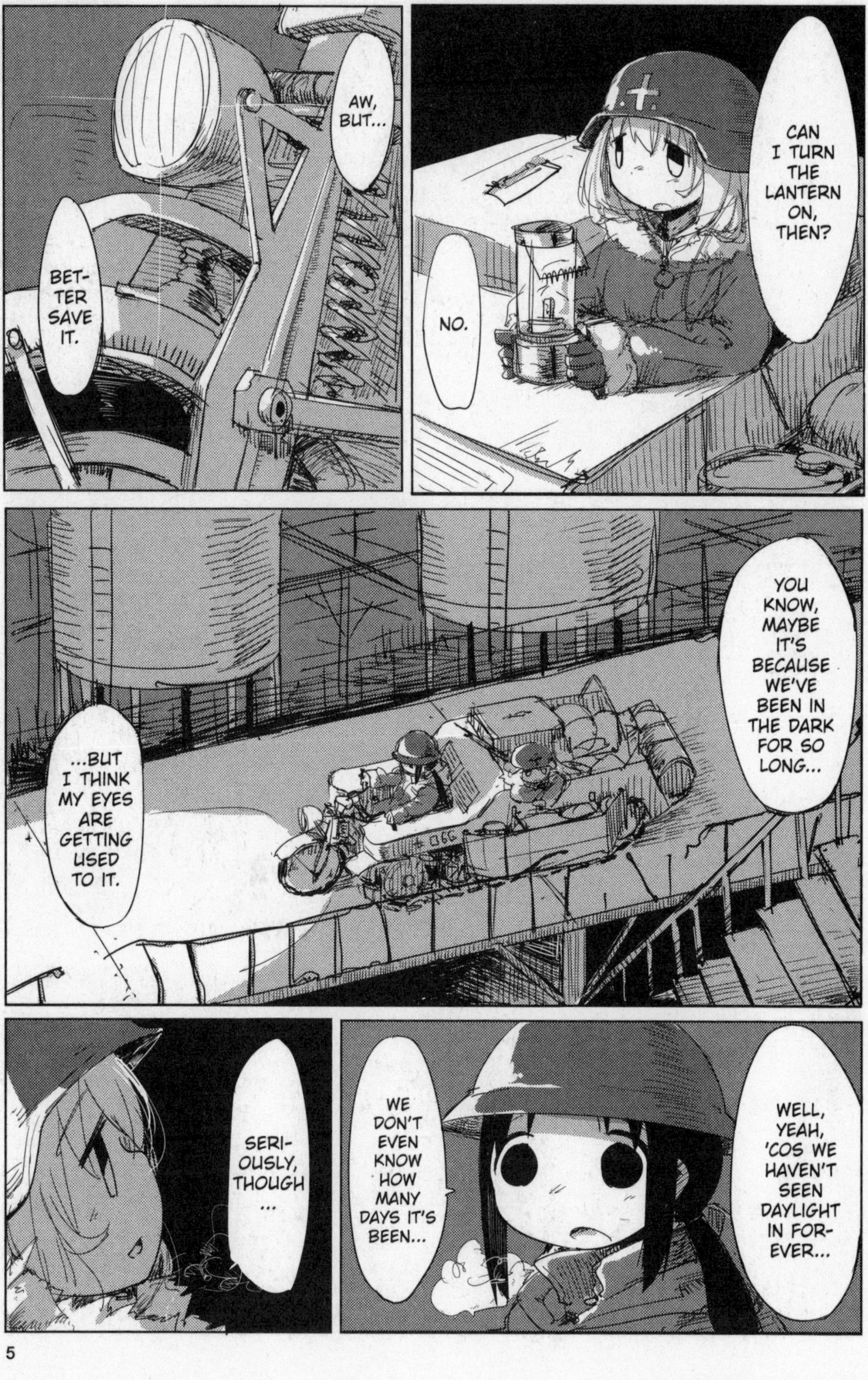
CAN I TURN THE LANTERN ON, THEN?
NO.
AW, BUT...
BET-TER SAVE IT.
YOU KNOW, MAYBE IT'S BECAUSE WE'VE BEEN IN THE DARK FOR SO LONG...
...BUT I THINK MY EYES ARE GETTING USED TO IT.
WELL, YEAH, 'COS WE HAVEN'T SEEN DAYLIGHT IN FOR-EVER...
WE DON'T EVEN KNOW HOW MANY DAYS IT'S BEEN...
SERI-OUSLY, THOUGH ...

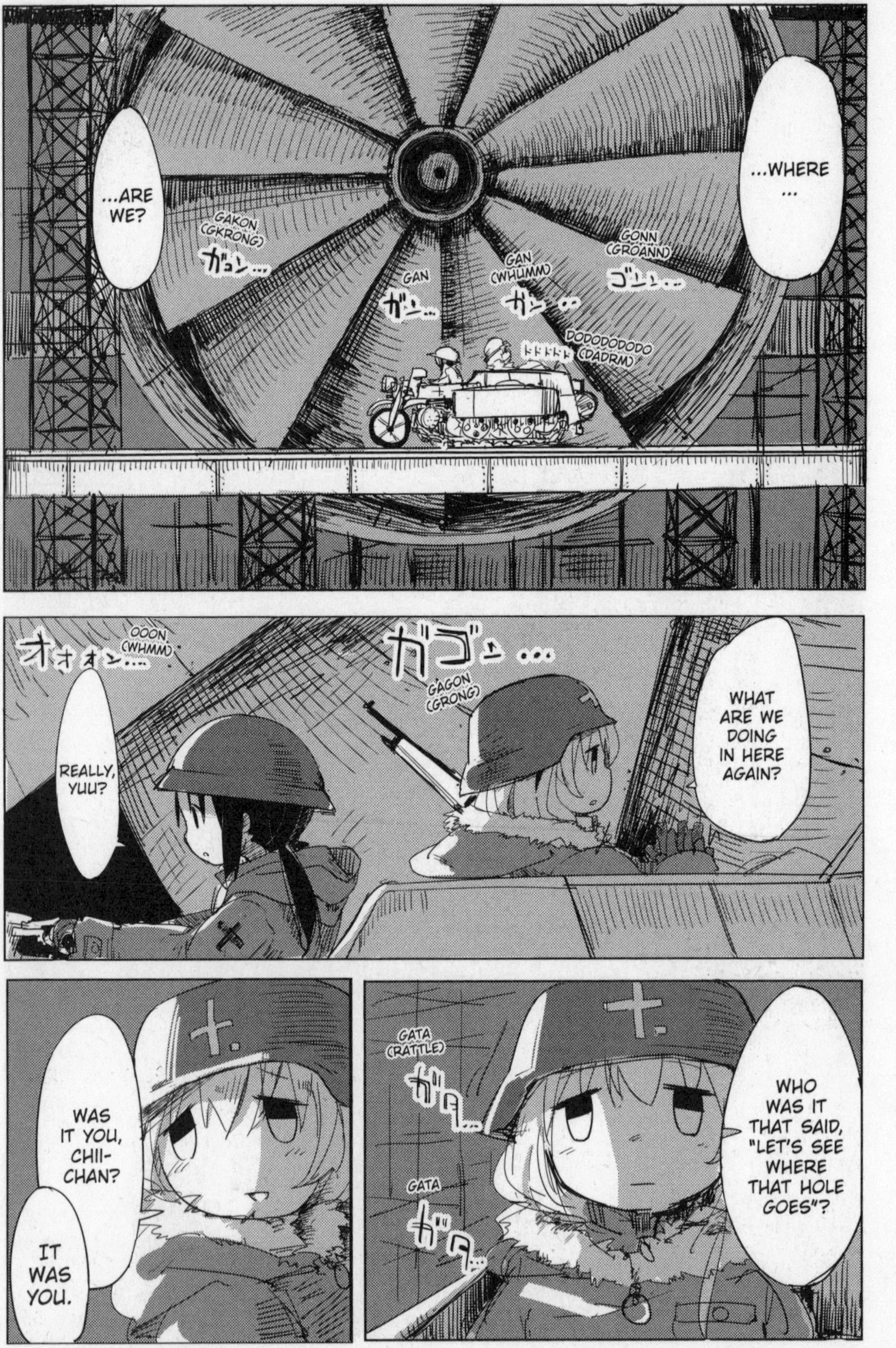
...WHERE ...
GONN (GROANN)
GAN (WHUMM)
GAN
GAKON (GKRONG)
DODODODODO (DADRM)
...ARE WE?
GAGON (GRONG)
OOON (WHMM)
WHAT ARE WE DOING IN HERE AGAIN?
REALLY, YUU?
WHO WAS IT THAT SAID, "LET'S SEE WHERE THAT HOLE GOES"?
GATA (RATTLE)
GATA
WAS IT YOU, CHII-CHAN?
IT WAS YOU.

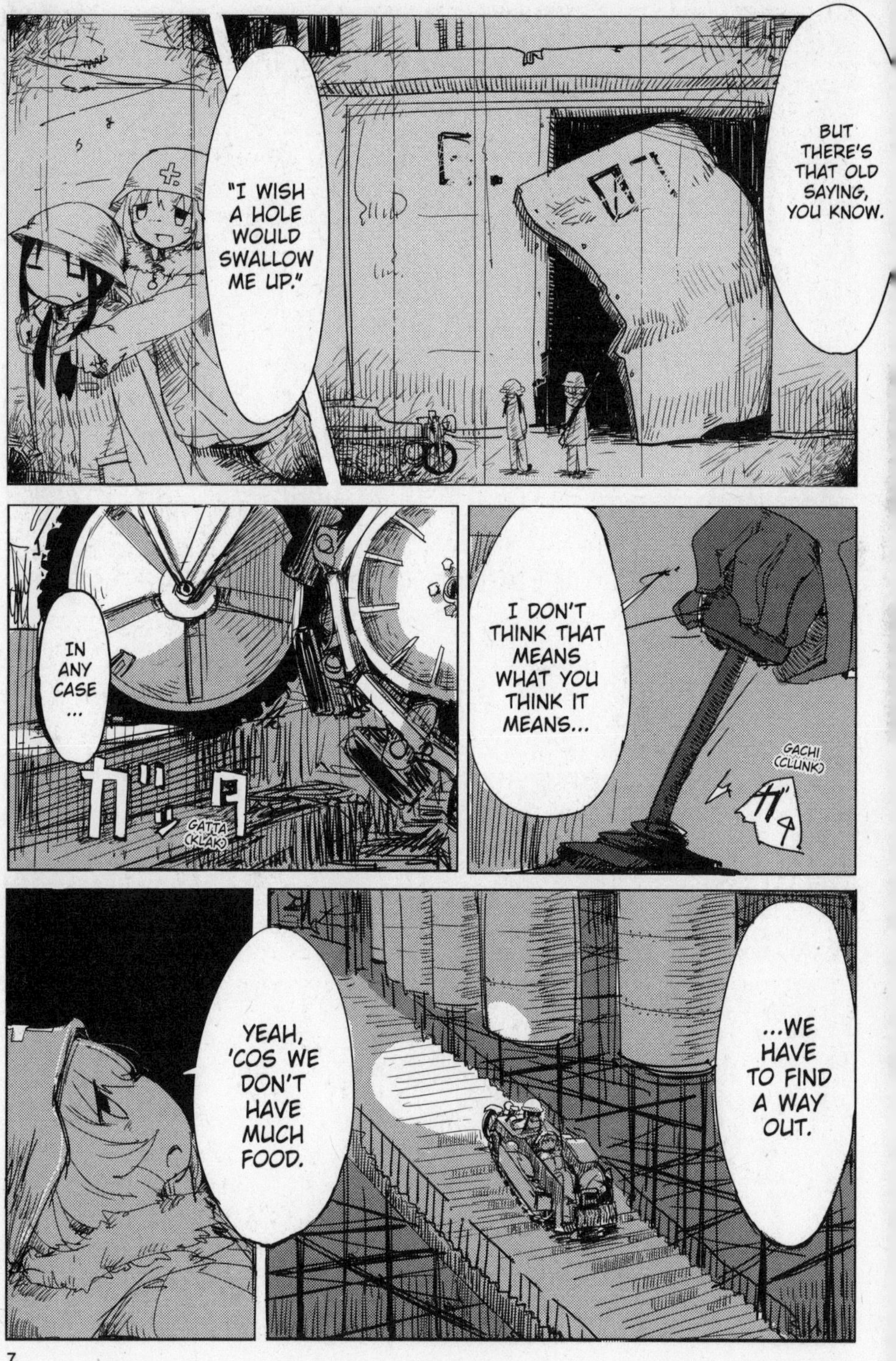
BUT THERE'S THAT OLD SAYING, YOU KNOW.
"I WISH A HOLE WOULD SWALLOW ME UP."
I DON'T THINK THAT MEANS WHAT YOU THINK IT MEANS...
GACHI (CLUNK)
IN ANY CASE ...
GATTA (KLAK)
...WE HAVE TO FIND A WAY OUT.
YEAH, 'COS WE DON'T HAVE MUCH FOOD.

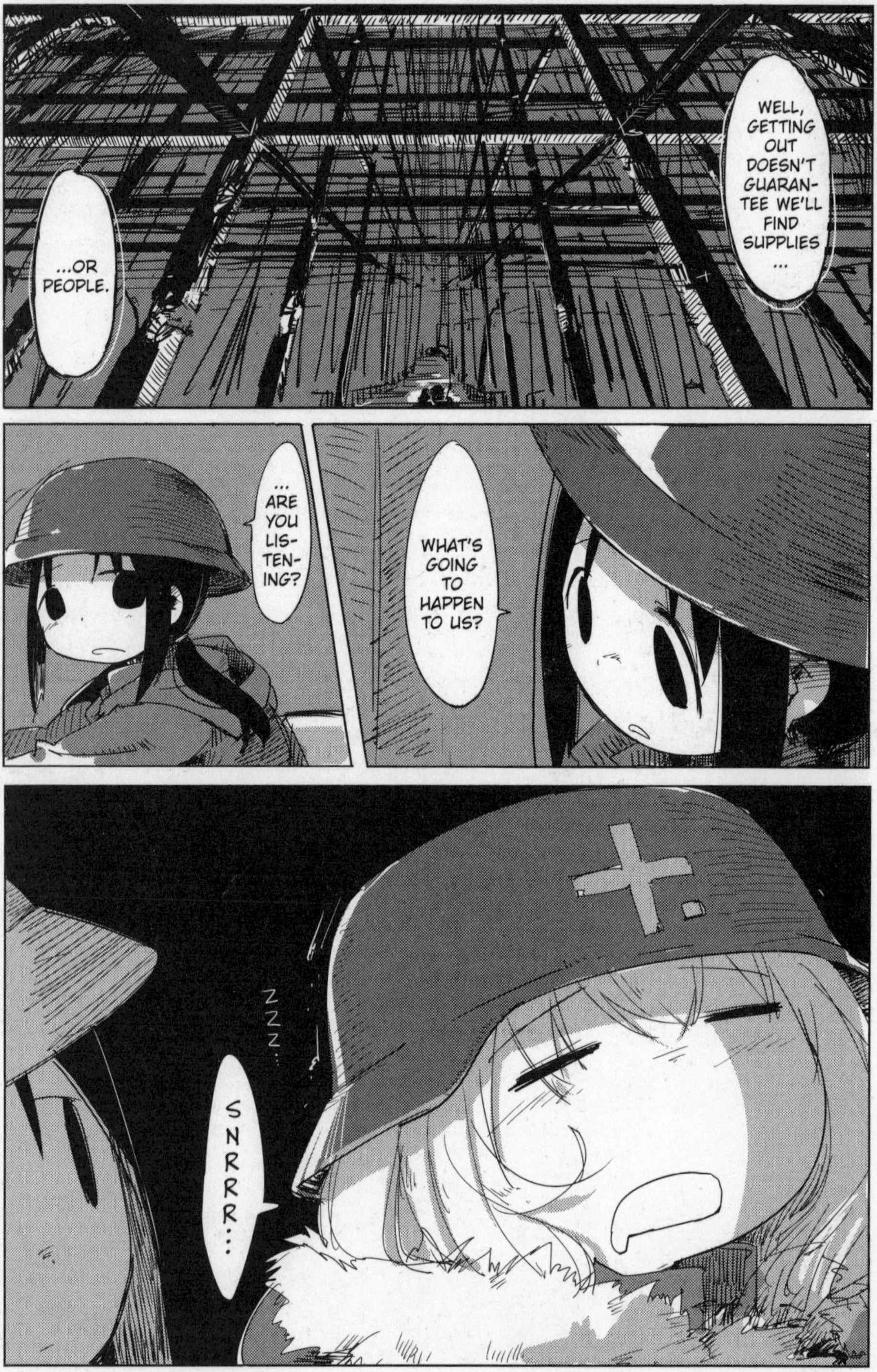
WELL, GETTING OUT DOESN'T GUARAN-TEE WE'LL FIND SUPPLIES ...
...OR PEOPLE.
WHAT'S GOING TO HAPPEN TO US?
... ARE YOU LIS-TEN-ING?
ZZZ...
SNRRR...

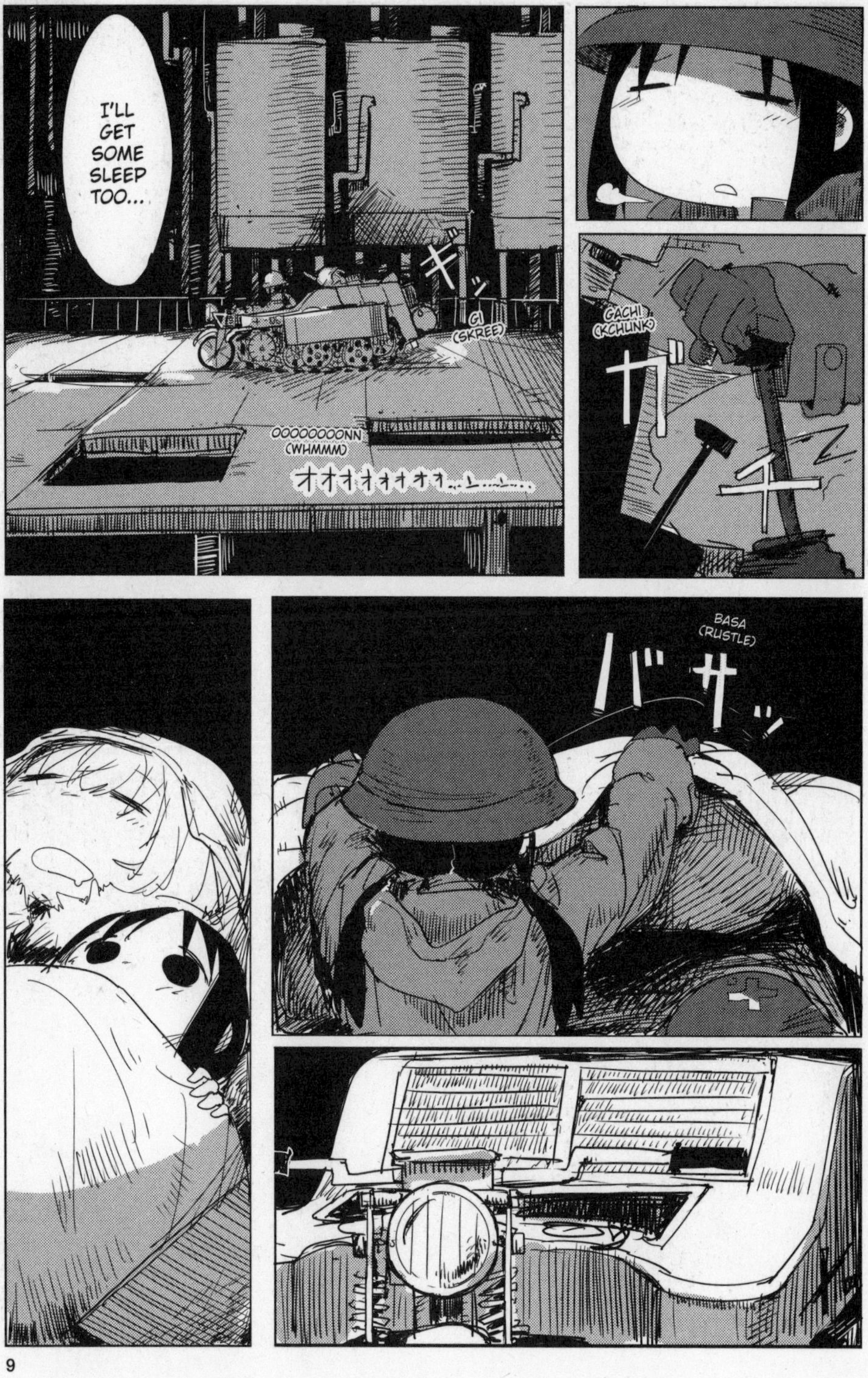
GACHI (KCHUNK)
ガチ
I'LL GET SOME SLEEP TOO...
ギッ
GI (SKREE)
OOOOOOOOONN (WHMMM)
BASA (RUSTLE)
バサッ

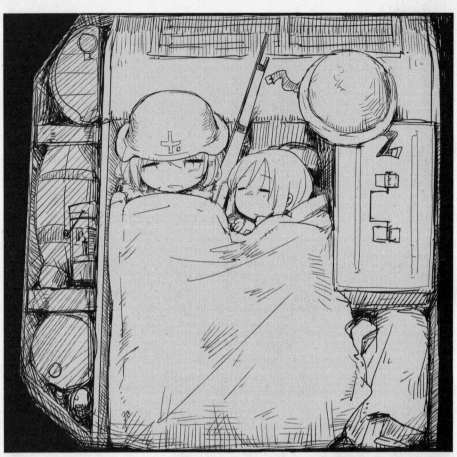

HUNGRY
...

OOOOOOOON
(WHMM)
オオオオ… オオオオ…

MN.

MNN...
MOCCHA
MOCCHA
(MUNCH)

BRR.
BURU
(SHIVER)
ブル
ブル
BURU

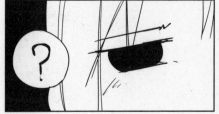
?

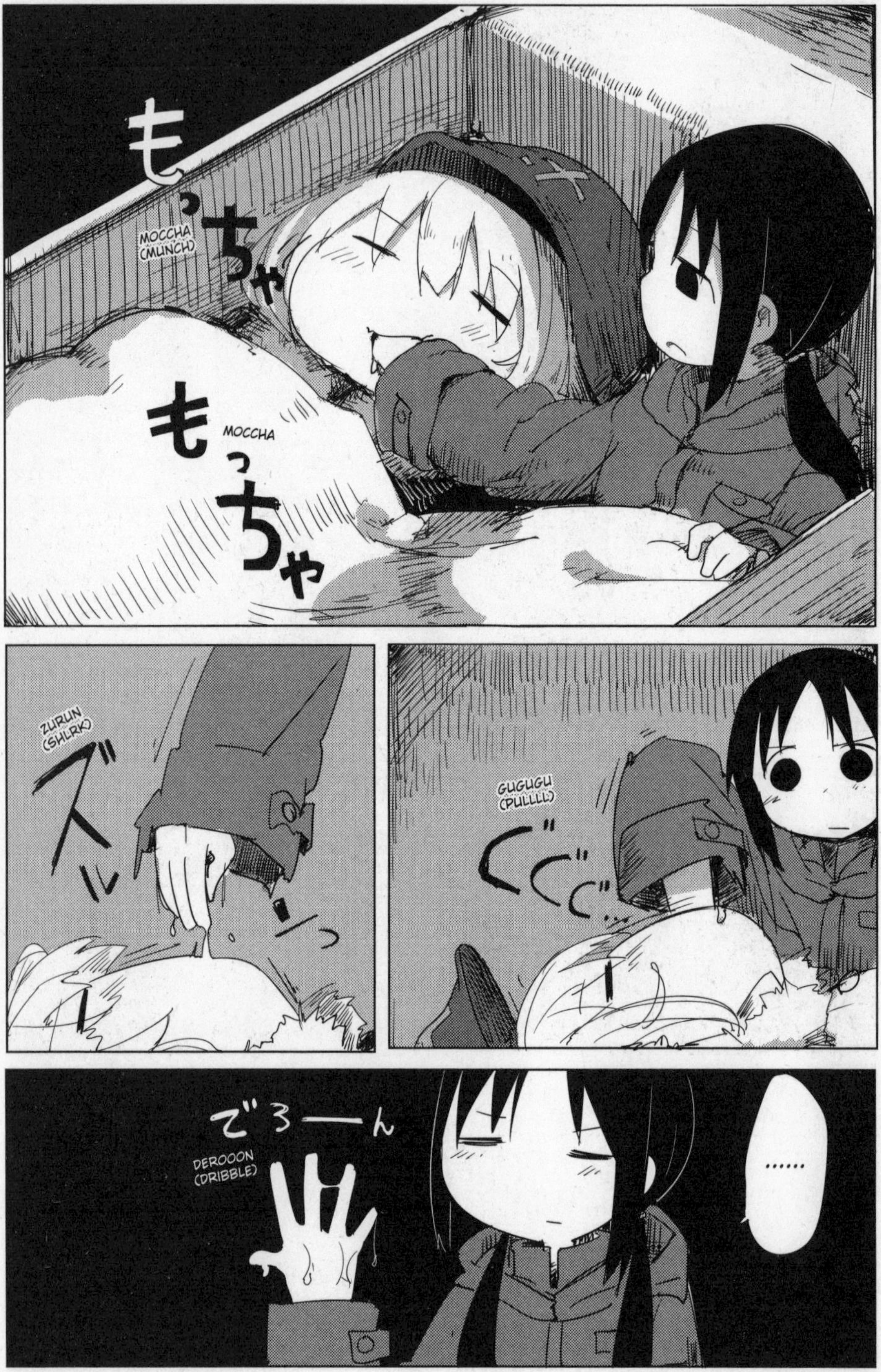
もっちゃ
MOCCHA (MUNCH)
もっちゃ
MOCCHA
ぐぐぐ…
GUGUGU (PULLLL)
ズルン
ZURUN (SHLRK)
……
でろーーん
DEROOON (DRIBBLE)

...AH!

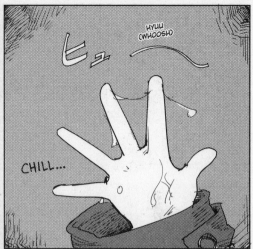

HYUU
(WHOOSH)

CHILL...

WIND...

YUU!

HEY!

PECHI
(SMACK)

PECHI

HEY,
WAKE
UP.

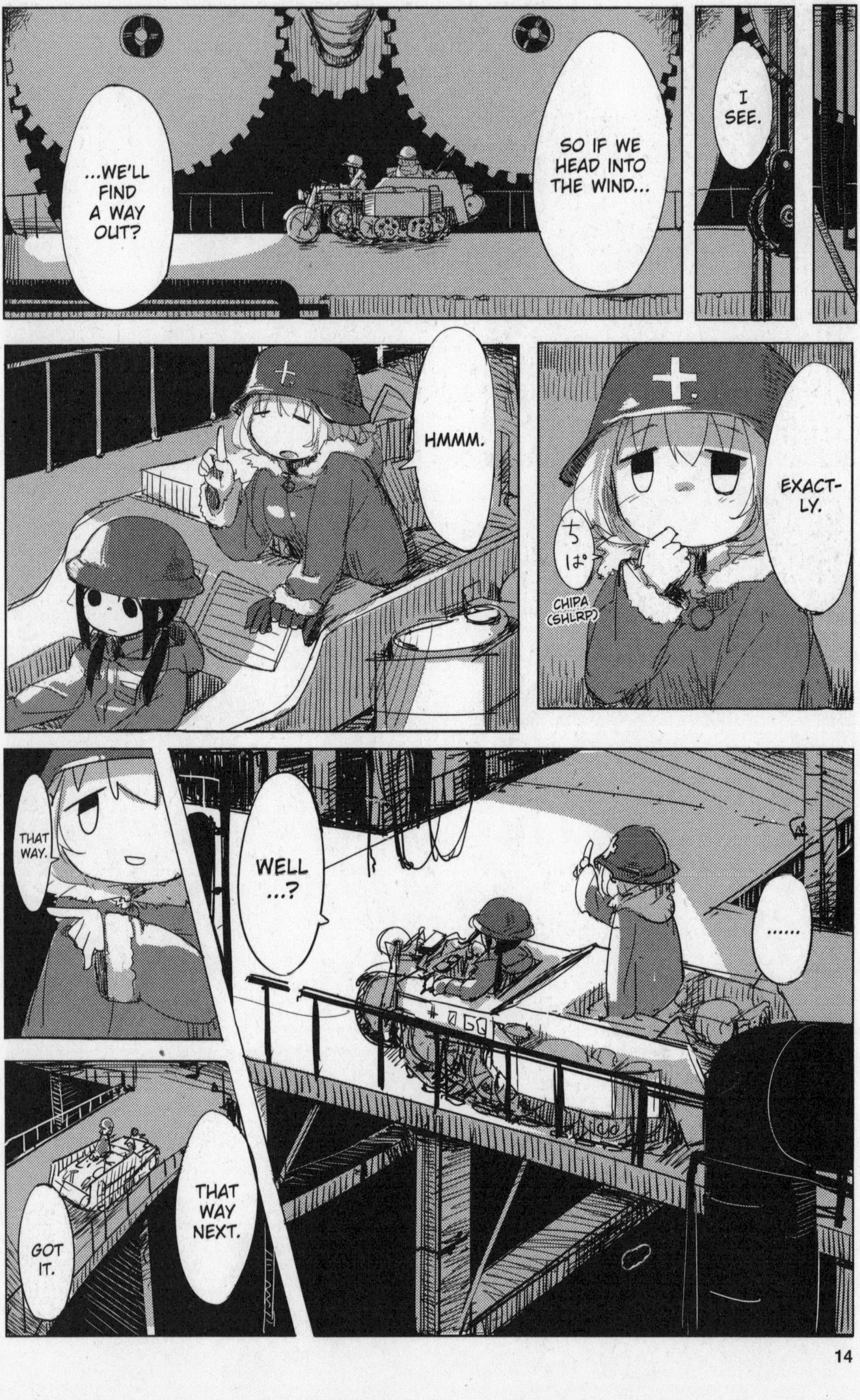
I SEE.
SO IF WE HEAD INTO THE WIND...
...WE'LL FIND A WAY OUT?
EXACT-LY.
ちぱ
CHIPA (SHLRP)
HMMM.
......
WELL ...?
THAT WAY.
THAT WAY NEXT.
GOT IT.

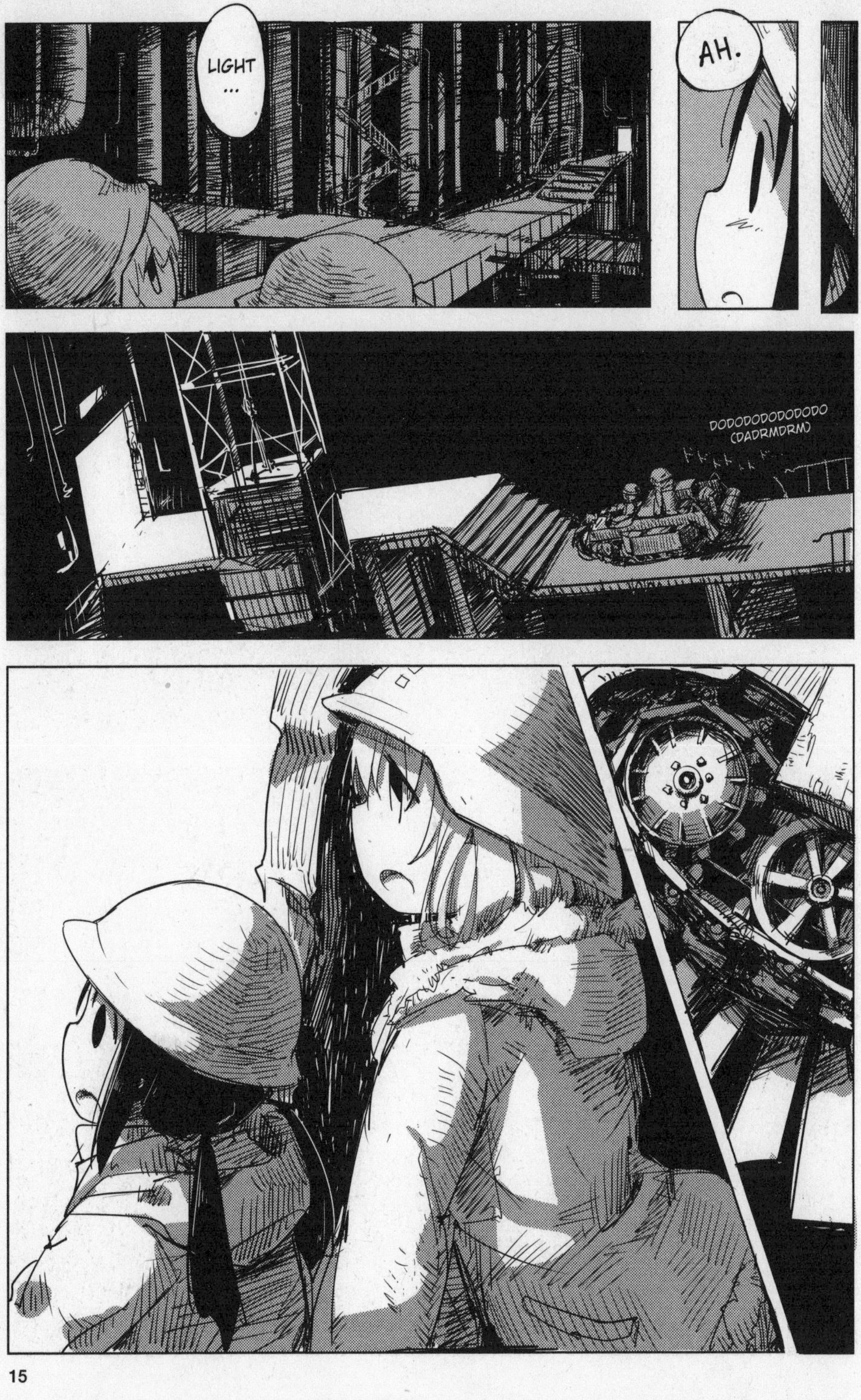
AH.
LIGHT ...
DODODODODODODO
(DADRMDRM)

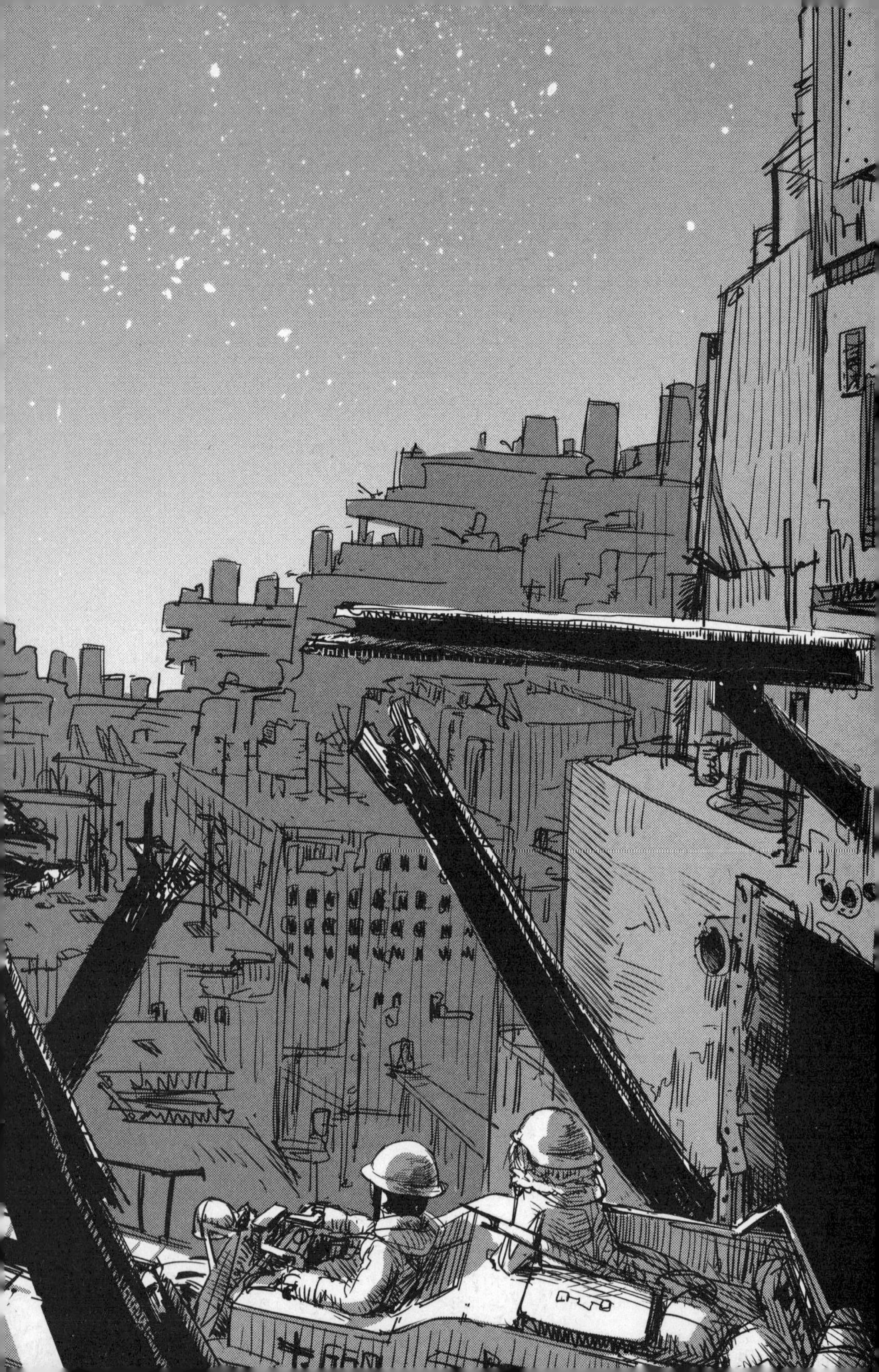

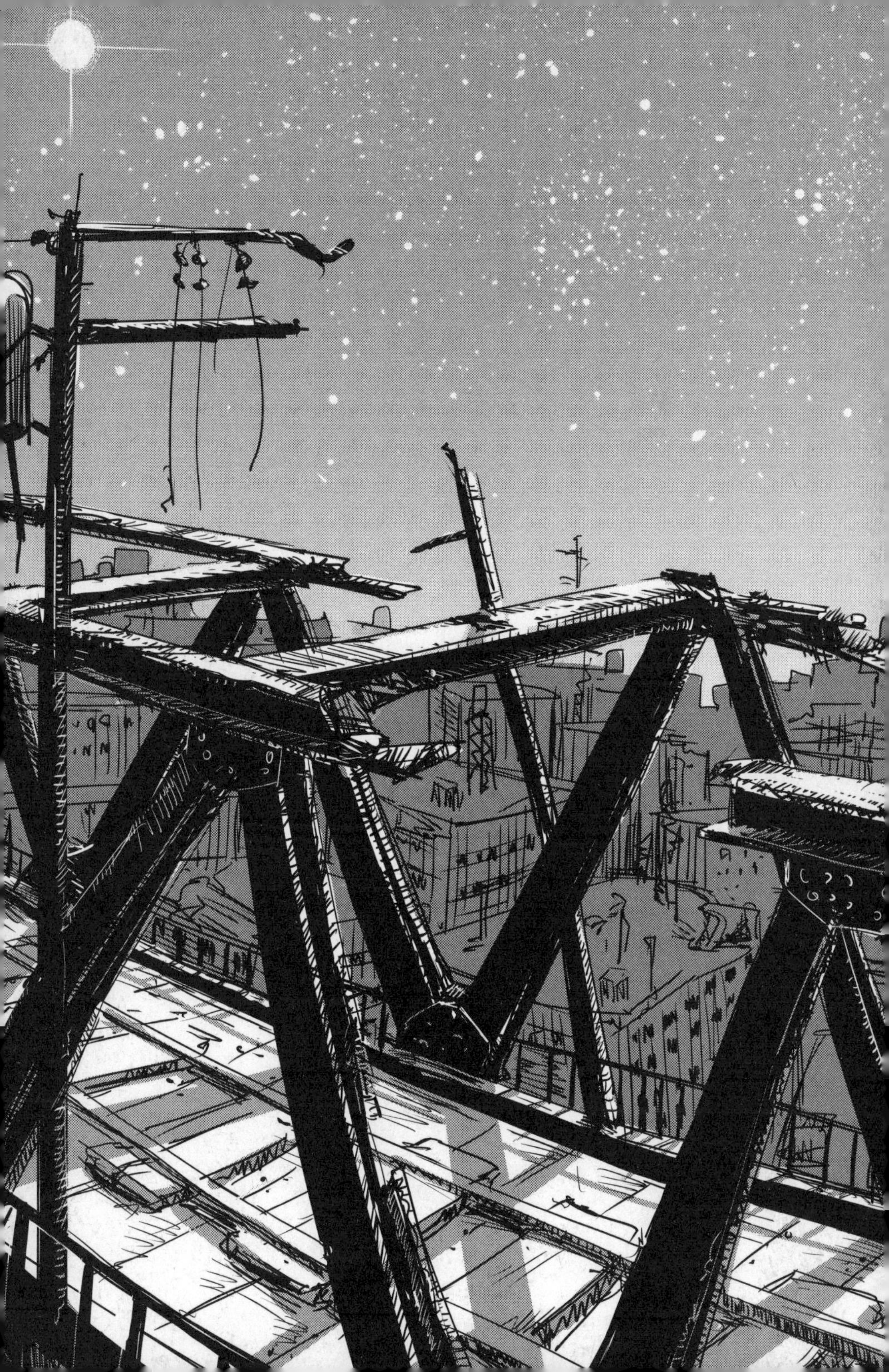

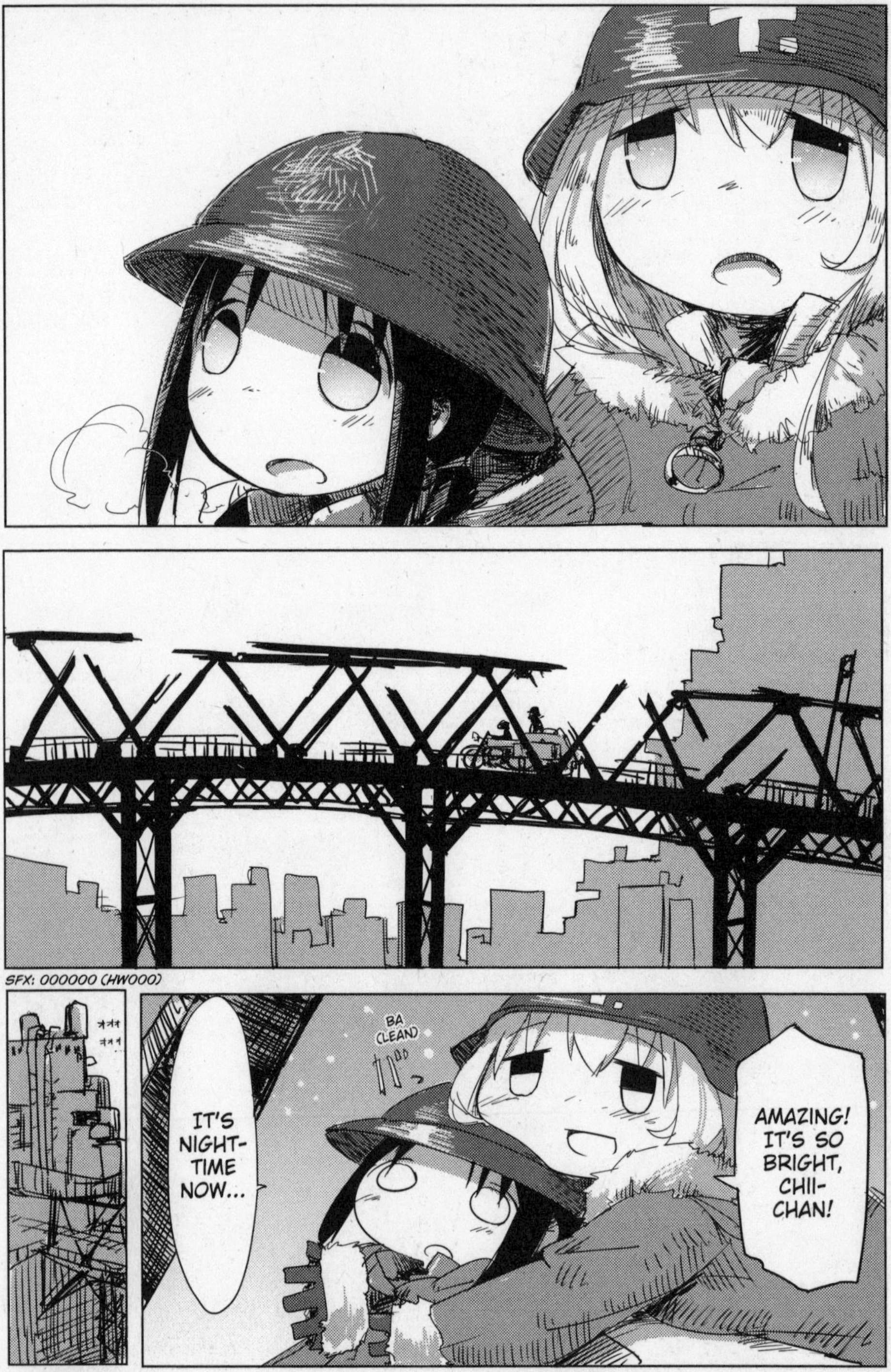
SFX: OOOOOO (HWOOO)
AMAZING! IT'S SO BRIGHT, CHII-CHAN!
BA CLEAND
IT'S NIGHT-TIME NOW...

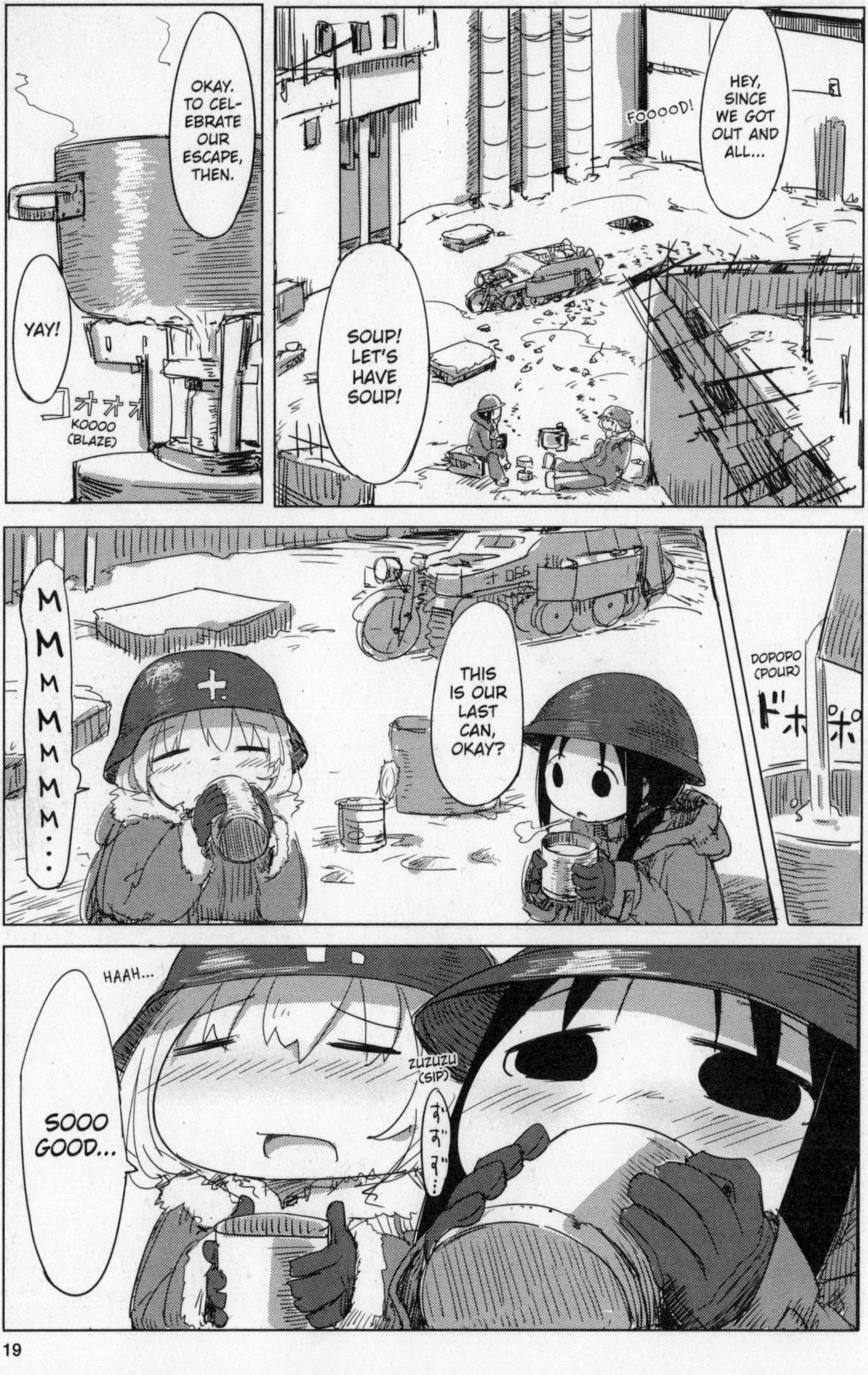
HEY, SINCE WE GOT OUT AND ALL...
FOOOOD!
SOUP! LET'S HAVE SOUP!
OKAY. TO CEL-EBRATE OUR ESCAPE, THEN.
YAY!
コオオオ
KOOOO (BLAZE)
DOPOPO (POUR)
ドポポ
THIS IS OUR LAST CAN, OKAY?
MMMMMMM...
HAAH...
ZUZUZU (SIP)
ずずず...
SOOO GOOD...

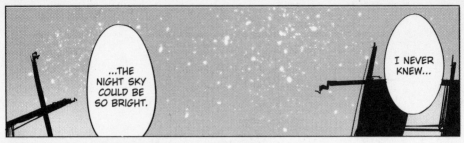

...THE NIGHT SKY COULD BE SO BRIGHT.

I NEVER KNEW...

IT'S BECAUSE WE WERE IN THAT DARK HOLE FOR SO LONG. WE'RE SENSITIVE TO THE LIGHT NOW.

WHAT'LL HAPPEN WHEN THE SUN COMES UP, THEN?

AAAAAH...

MMAAAAAH...

SHUT UP.

WE'LL BURN TO DEATH.

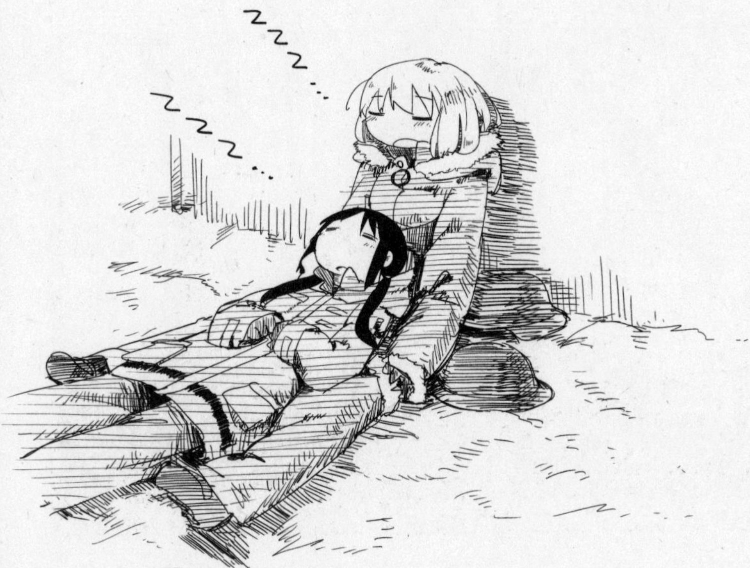
zzz...
zzz...

GIRLS' LAST TOUR

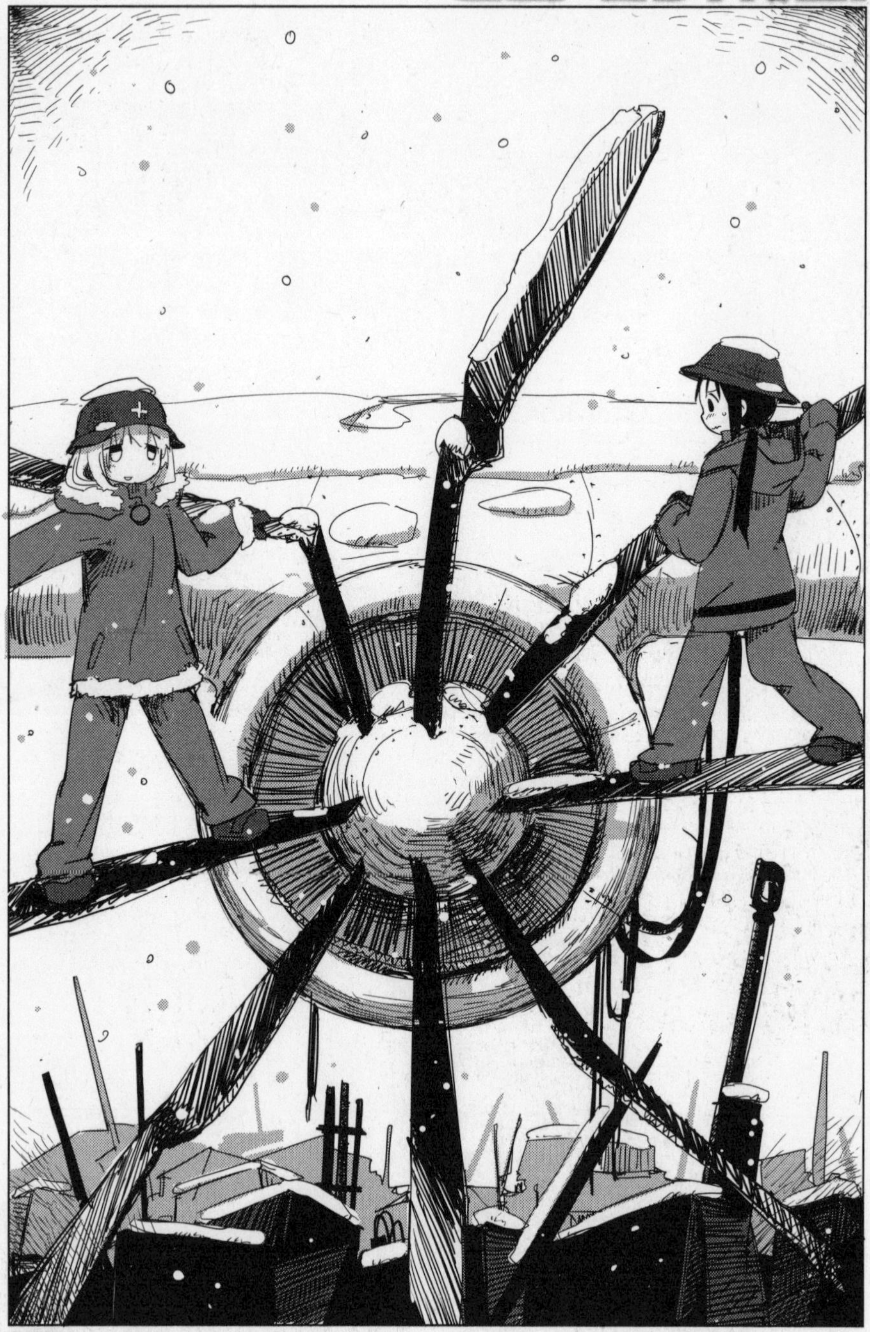

02

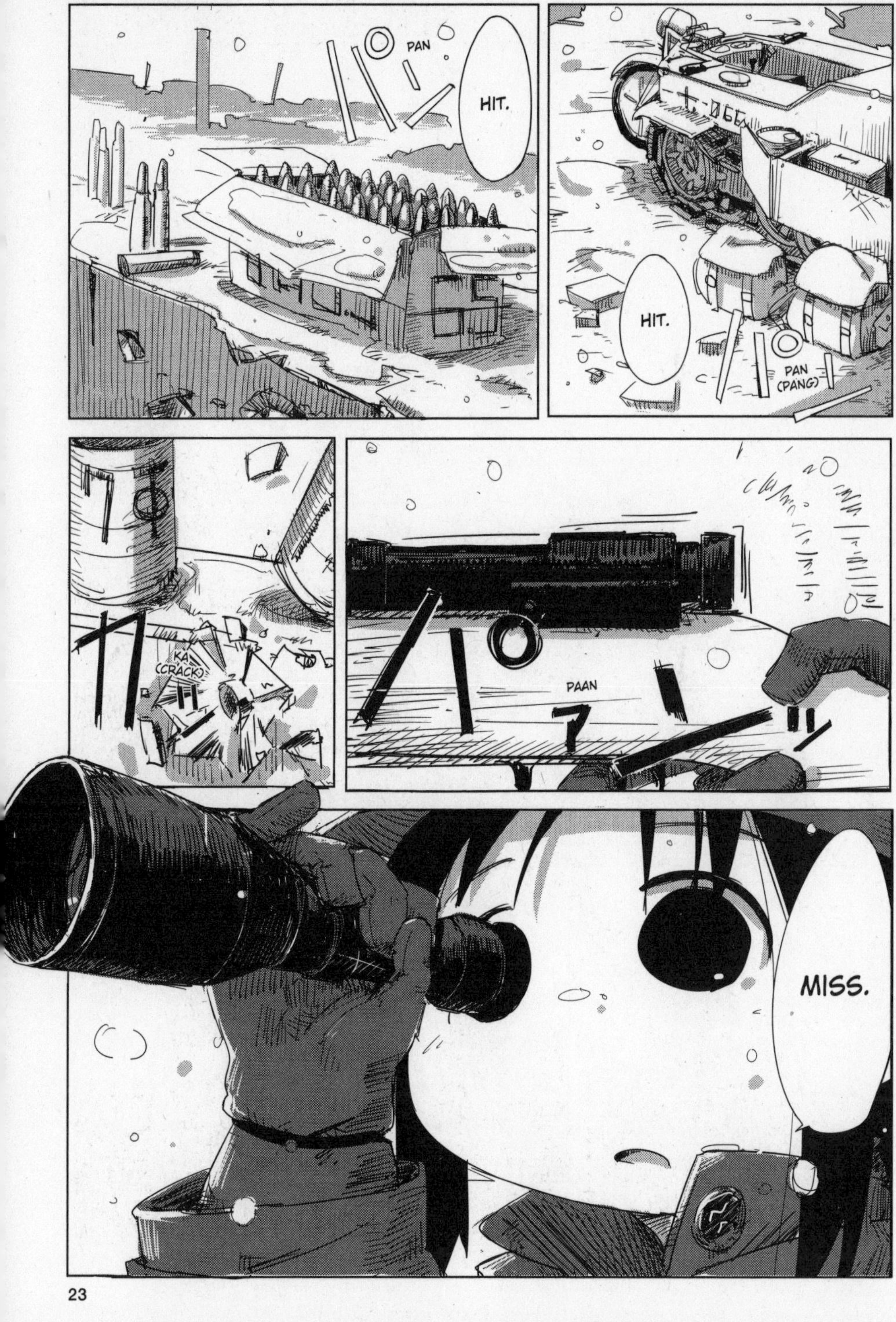
HIT.
PAN (PANG)
PAN
HIT.
PAAN
KA (CRACK)
MISS.

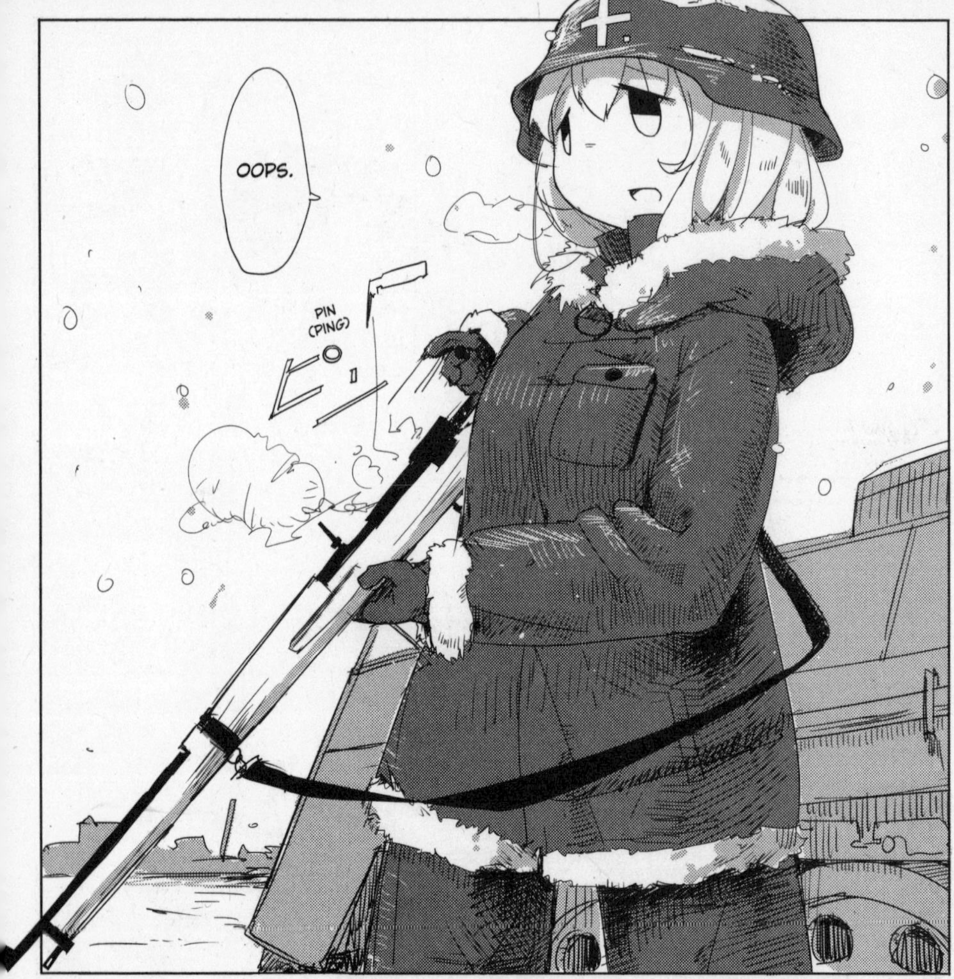
OOPS.
PIN
(PING)

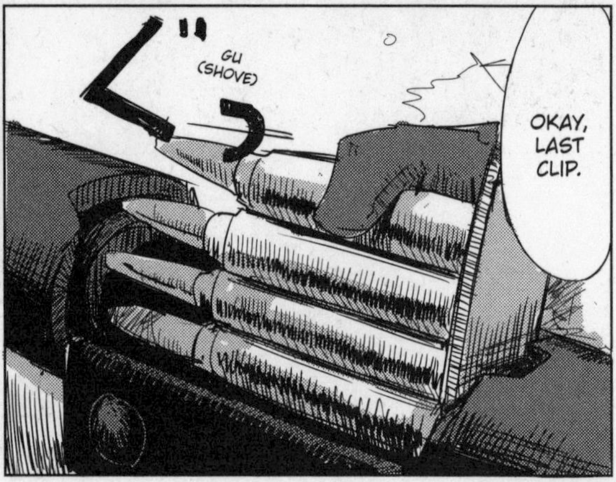
GU
(SHOVE)
OKAY, LAST CLIP.

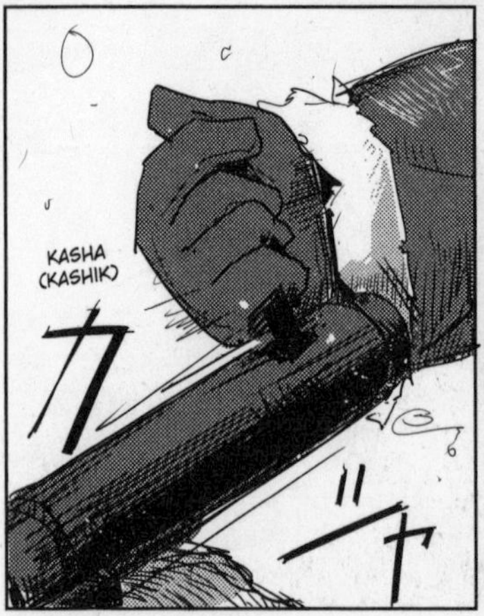
KASHA
(KASHIK)

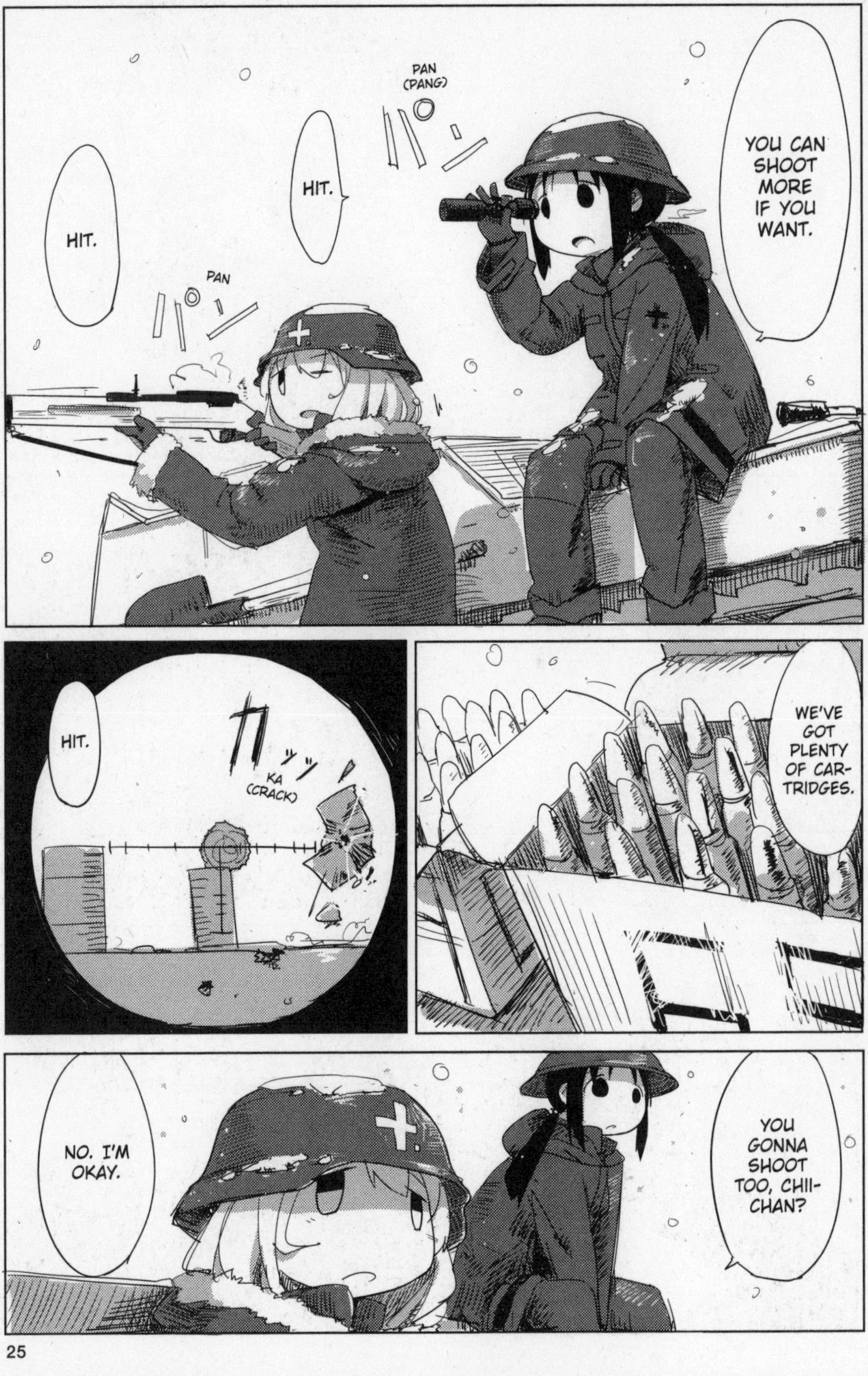
YOU CAN SHOOT MORE IF YOU WANT.
PAN (PANG)
HIT.
HIT.
PAN
WE'VE GOT PLENTY OF CAR-TRIDGES.
カッ
KA (CRACK)
HIT.
YOU GONNA SHOOT TOO, CHII-CHAN?
NO. I'M OKAY.

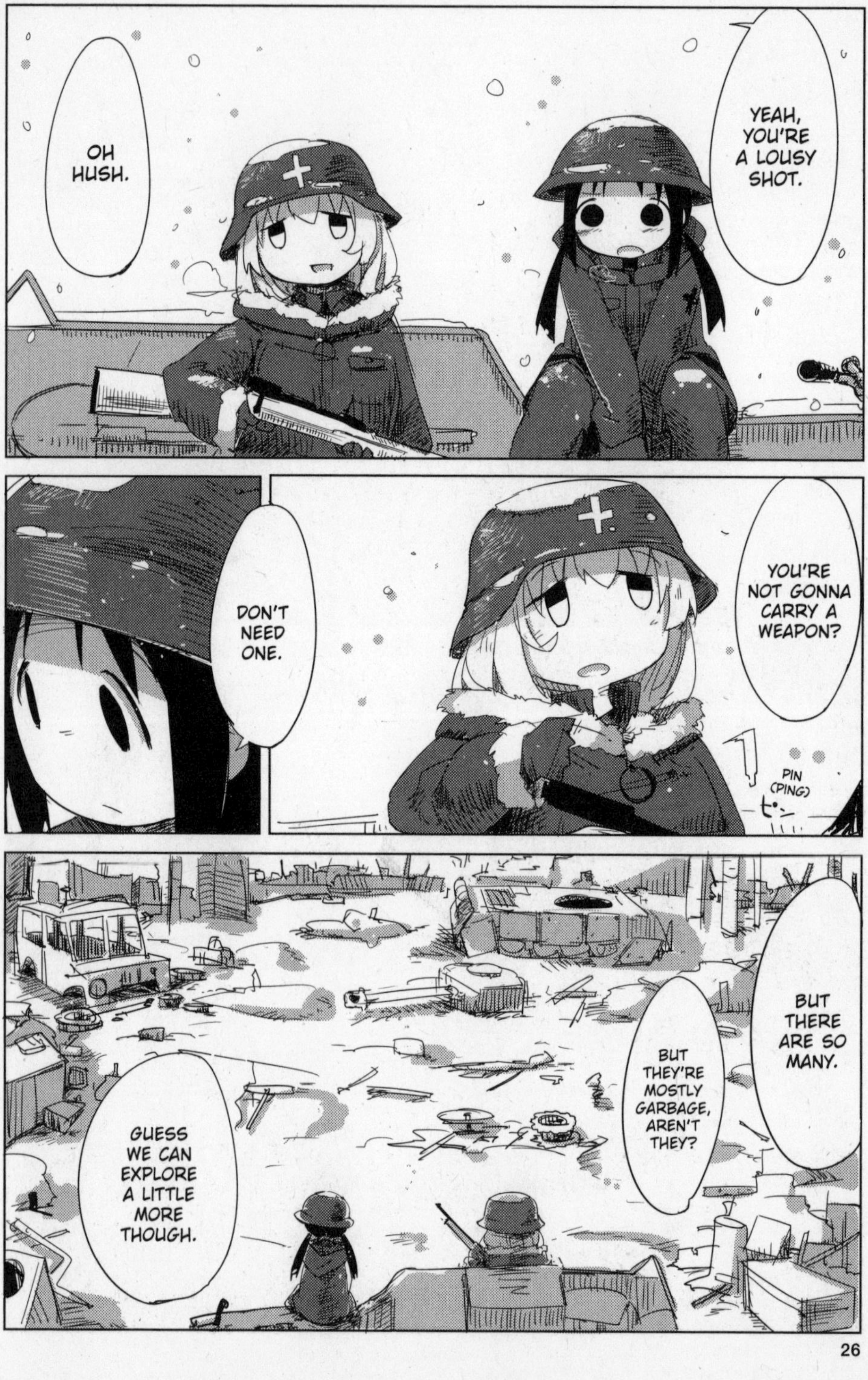
YEAH, YOU'RE A LOUSY SHOT.
OH HUSH.
YOU'RE NOT GONNA CARRY A WEAPON?
PIN (PING)
DON'T NEED ONE.
BUT THERE ARE SO MANY.
BUT THEY'RE MOSTLY GARBAGE, AREN'T THEY?
GUESS WE CAN EXPLORE A LITTLE MORE THOUGH.

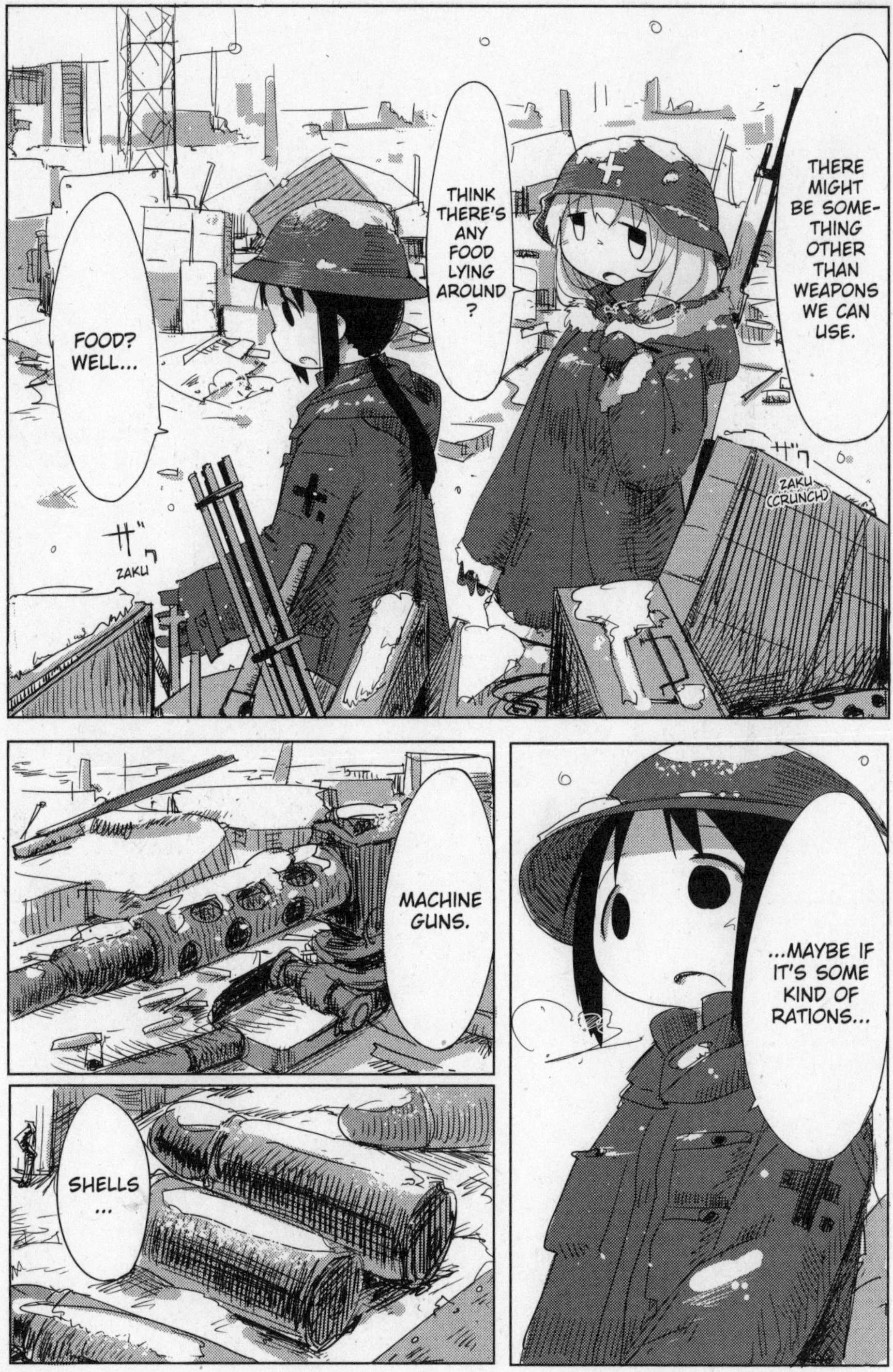
THERE MIGHT BE SOME-THING OTHER THAN WEAPONS WE CAN USE.
ザク
ZAKU (CRUNCH)
THINK THERE'S ANY FOOD LYING AROUND?
FOOD? WELL...
ザク
ZAKU
...MAYBE IF IT'S SOME KIND OF RATIONS...
MACHINE GUNS.
SHELLS ...

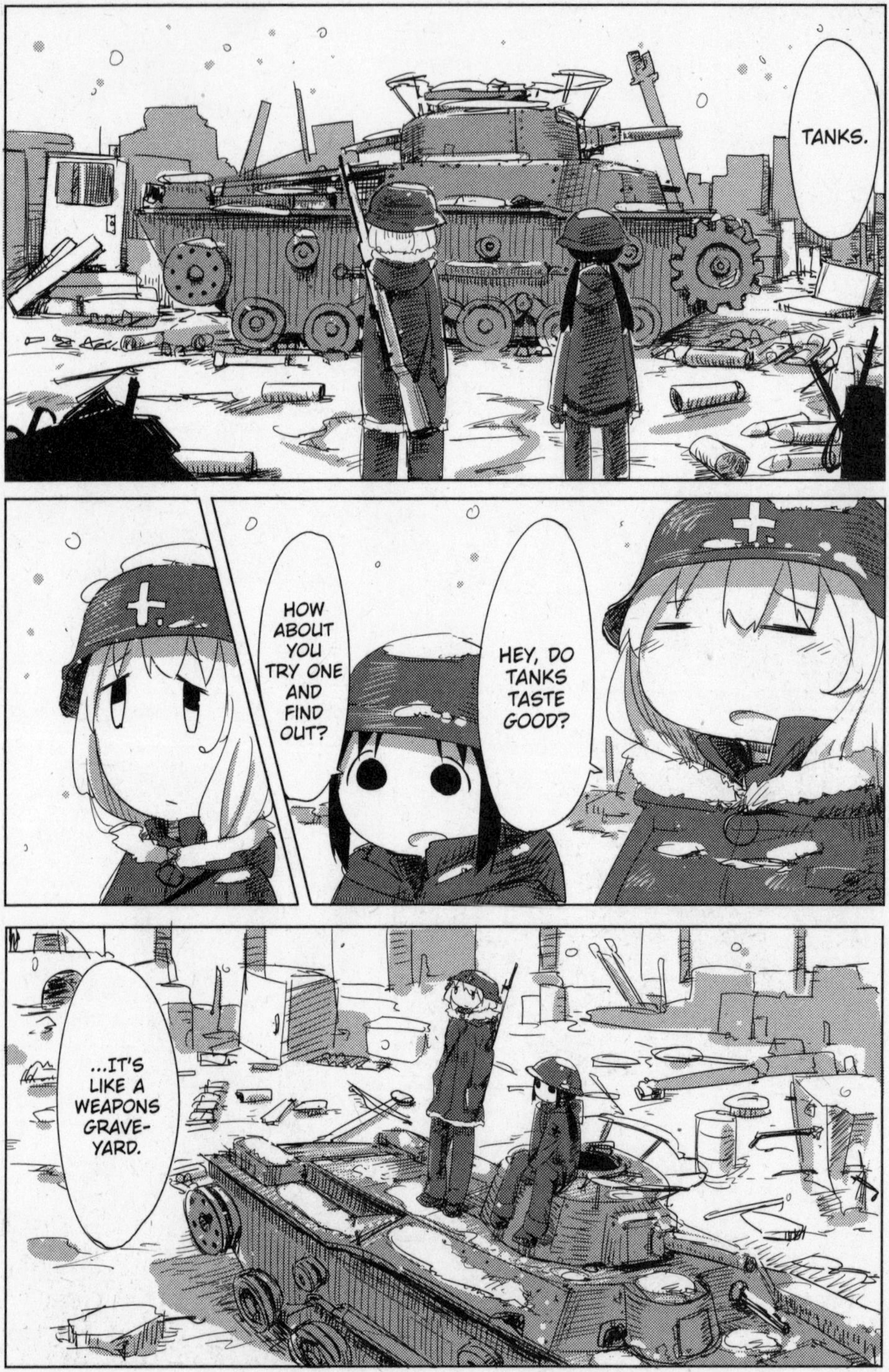
TANKS.
HEY, DO TANKS TASTE GOOD?
HOW ABOUT YOU TRY ONE AND FIND OUT?
...IT'S LIKE A WEAPONS GRAVE-YARD.

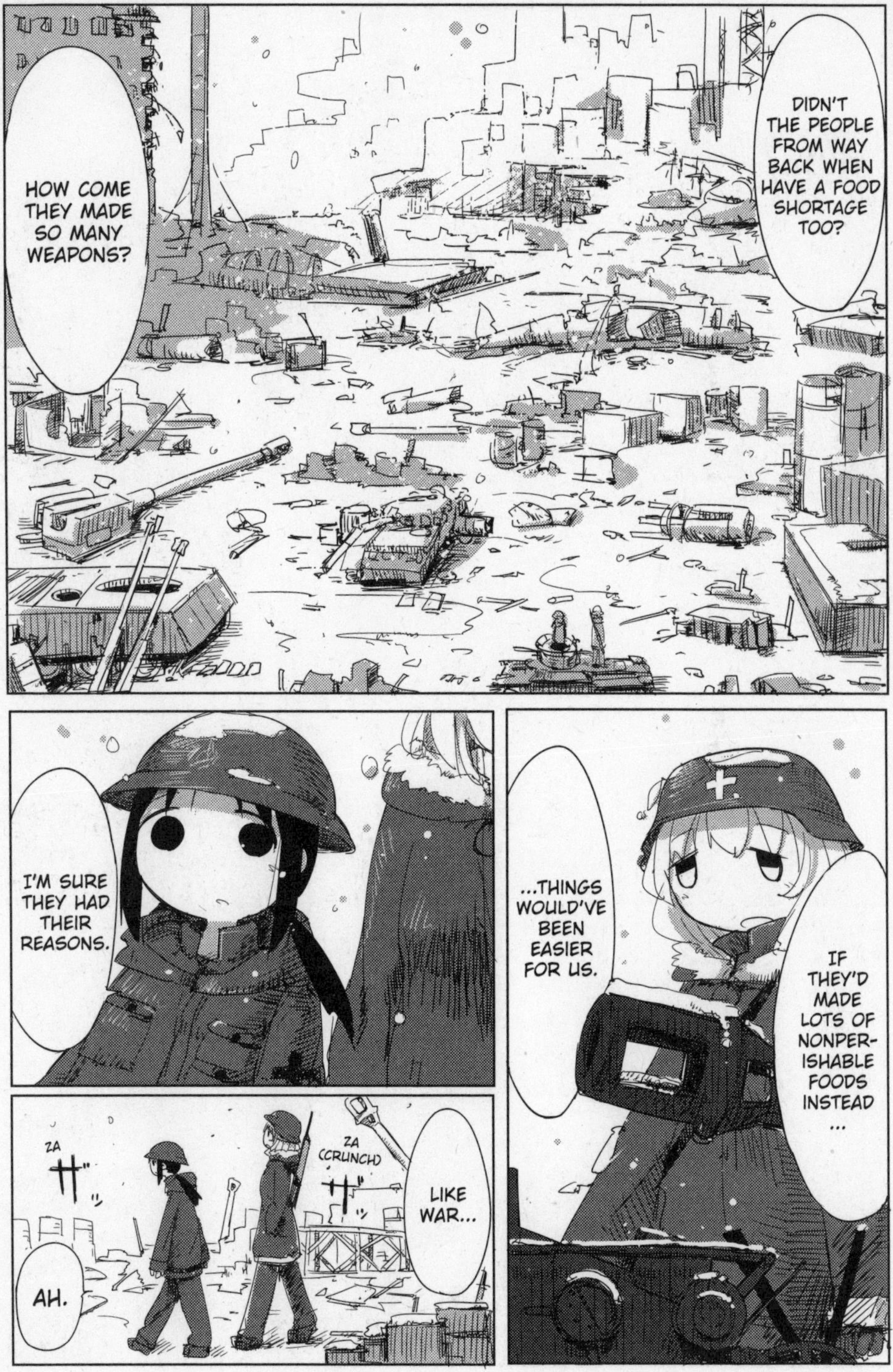
DIDN'T THE PEOPLE FROM WAY BACK WHEN HAVE A FOOD SHORTAGE TOO?
HOW COME THEY MADE SO MANY WEAPONS?
IF THEY'D MADE LOTS OF NONPER-ISHABLE FOODS INSTEAD ...
...THINGS WOULD'VE BEEN EASIER FOR US.
I'M SURE THEY HAD THEIR REASONS.
ZA (CRUNCH)
ザッ
LIKE WAR...
ZA
ザッ
AH.

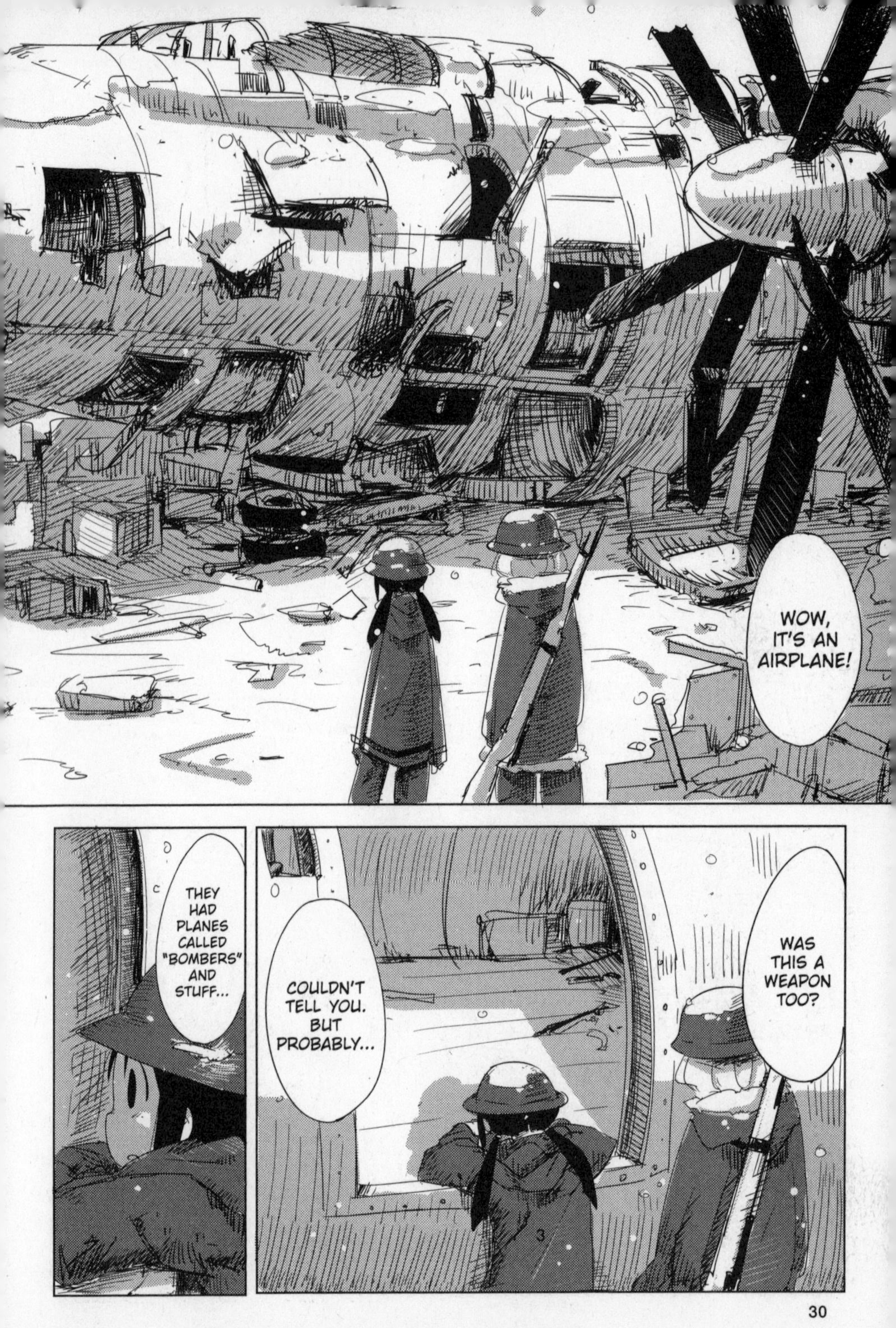
WOW, IT'S AN AIRPLANE!
WAS THIS A WEAPON TOO?
COULDN'T TELL YOU. BUT PROBABLY...
THEY HAD PLANES CALLED "BOMBERS" AND STUFF...

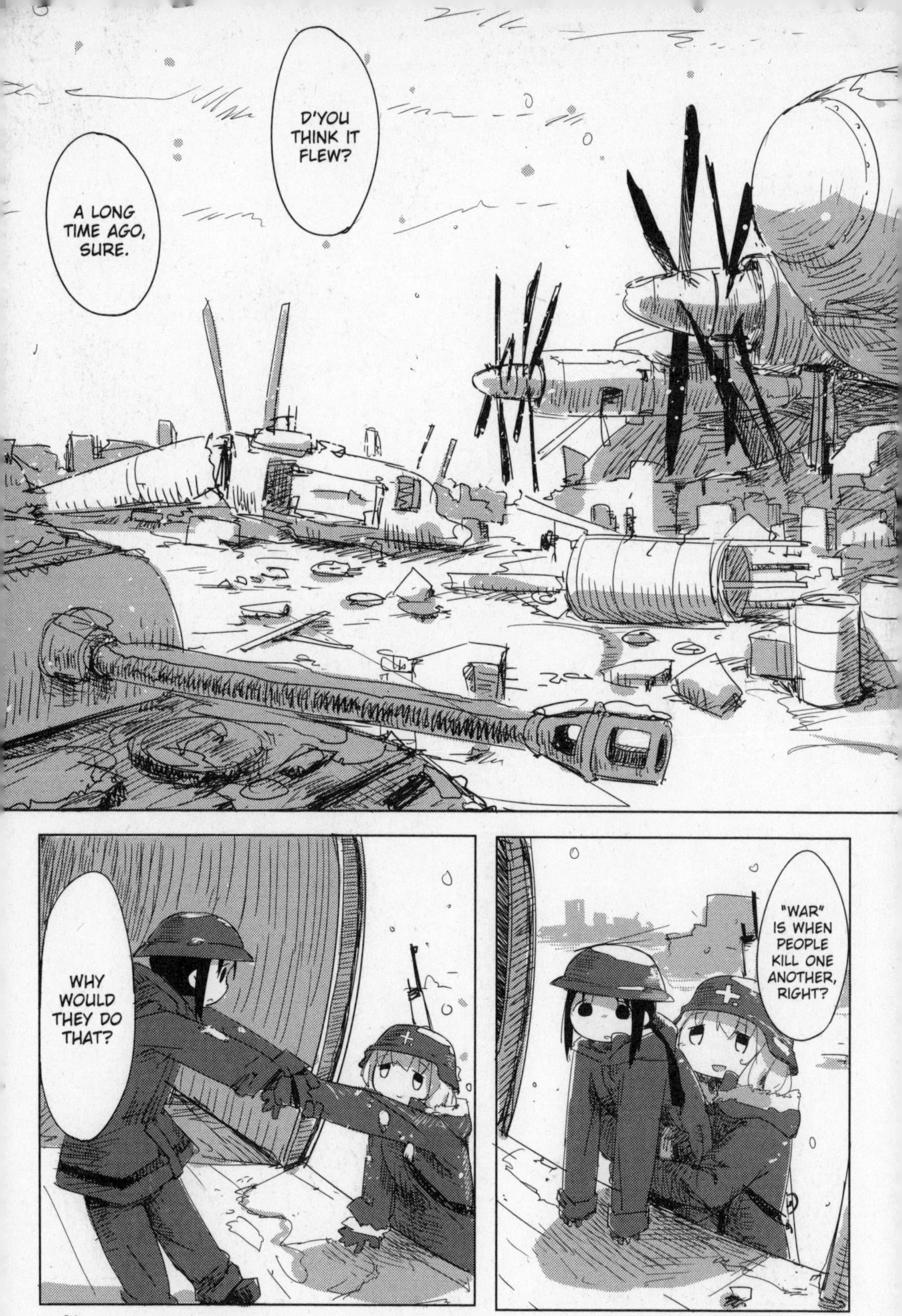
D'YOU THINK IT FLEW?
A LONG TIME AGO, SURE.
"WAR" IS WHEN PEOPLE KILL ONE ANOTHER, RIGHT?
WHY WOULD THEY DO THAT?

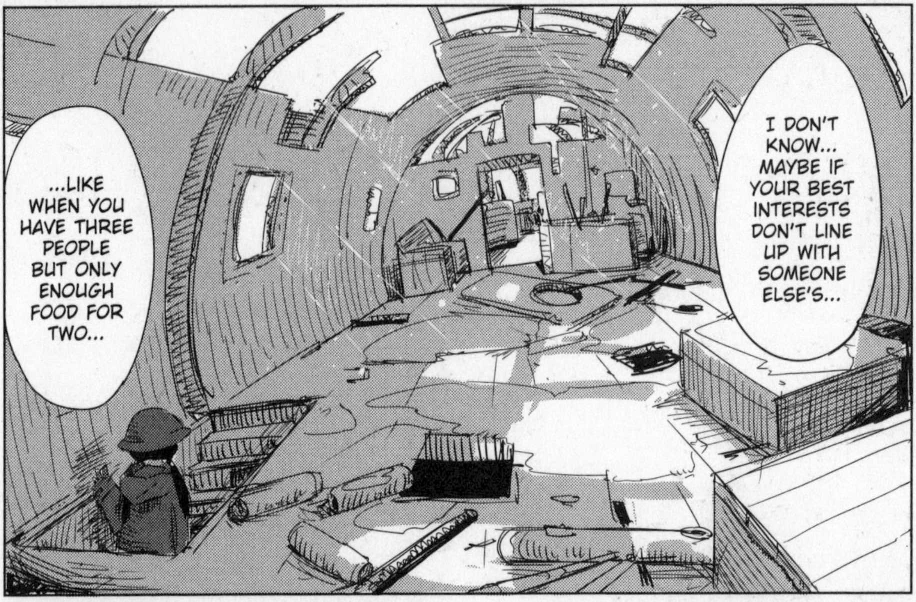
I DON'T KNOW... MAYBE IF YOUR BEST INTERESTS DON'T LINE UP WITH SOMEONE ELSE'S...
...LIKE WHEN YOU HAVE THREE PEOPLE BUT ONLY ENOUGH FOOD FOR TWO...
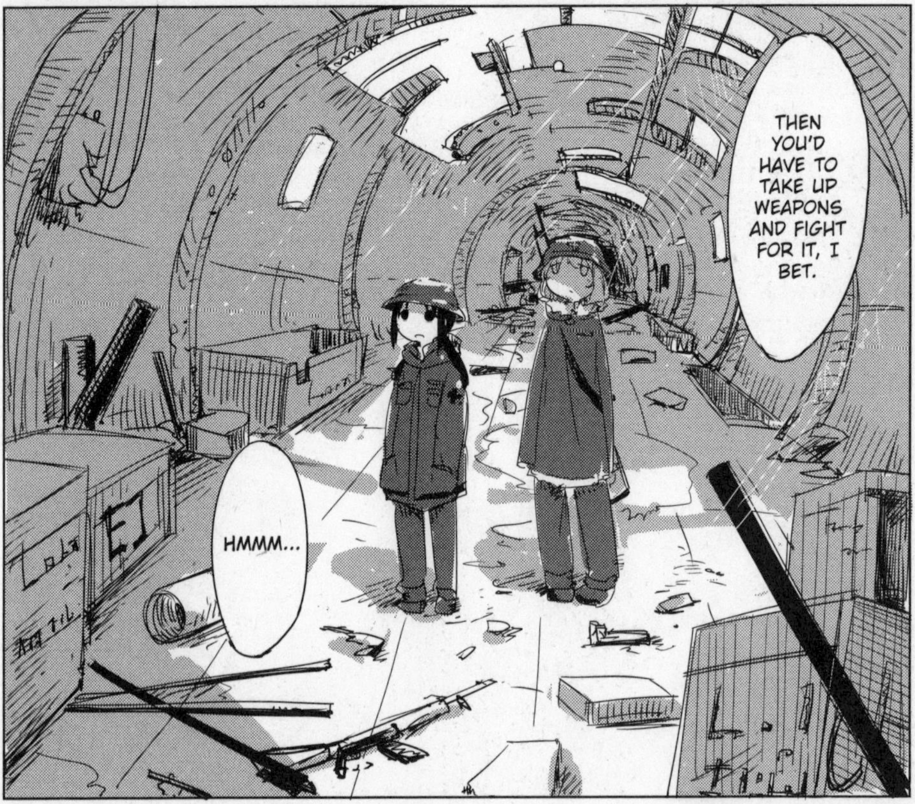
THEN YOU'D HAVE TO TAKE UP WEAPONS AND FIGHT FOR IT, I BET.
HMMM...

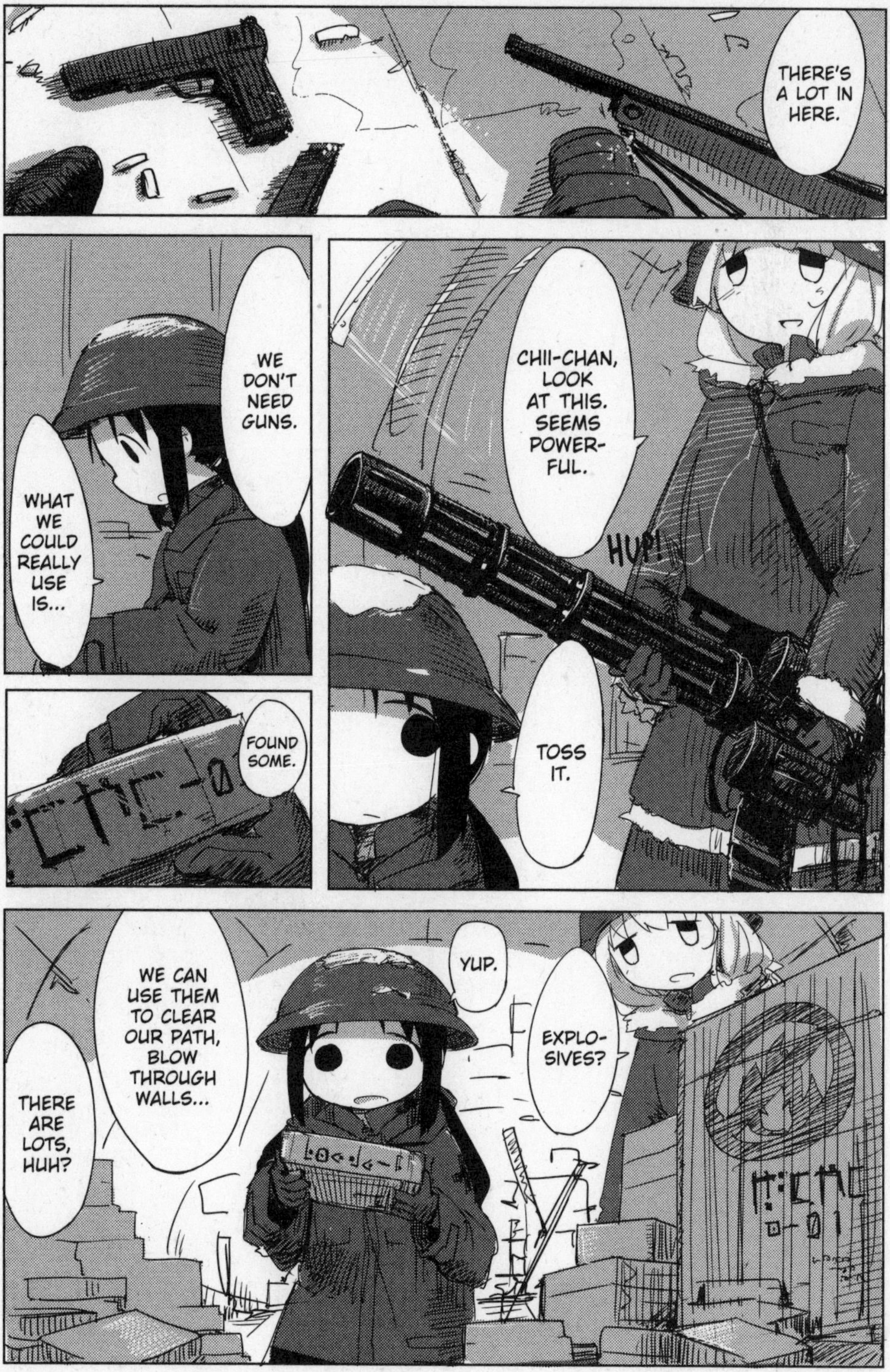
THERE'S A LOT IN HERE.
CHII-CHAN, LOOK AT THIS. SEEMS POWER-FUL.
HUP!
TOSS IT.
WE DON'T NEED GUNS.
WHAT WE COULD REALLY USE IS...
FOUND SOME.
YUP.
EXPLO-SIVES?
WE CAN USE THEM TO CLEAR OUR PATH, BLOW THROUGH WALLS...
THERE ARE LOTS, HUH?

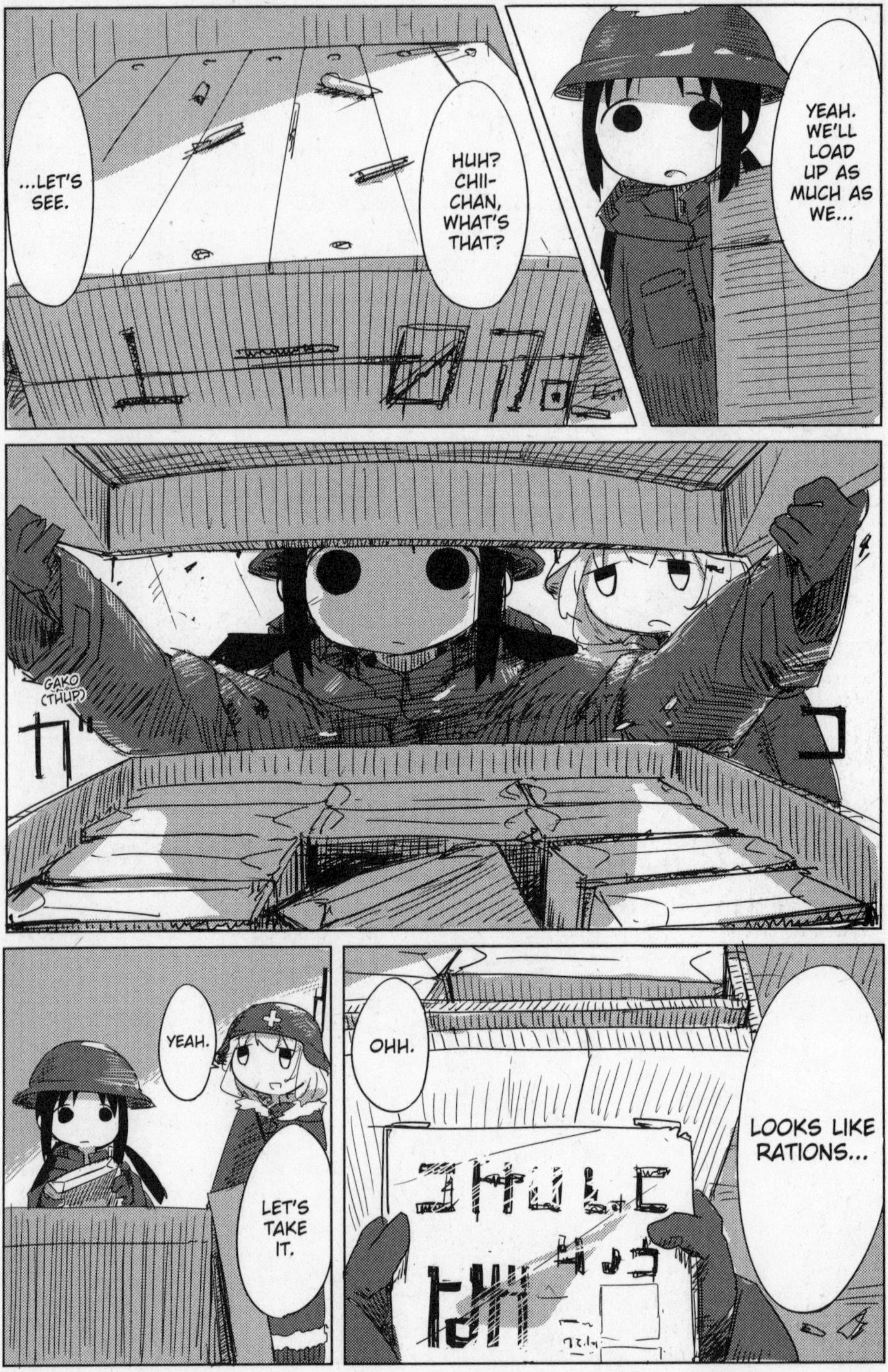
YEAH. WE'LL LOAD UP AS MUCH AS WE...
HUH? CHII-CHAN, WHAT'S THAT?
...LET'S SEE.
GAKO (THUP)
LOOKS LIKE RATIONS...
OHH.
YEAH.
LET'S TAKE IT.

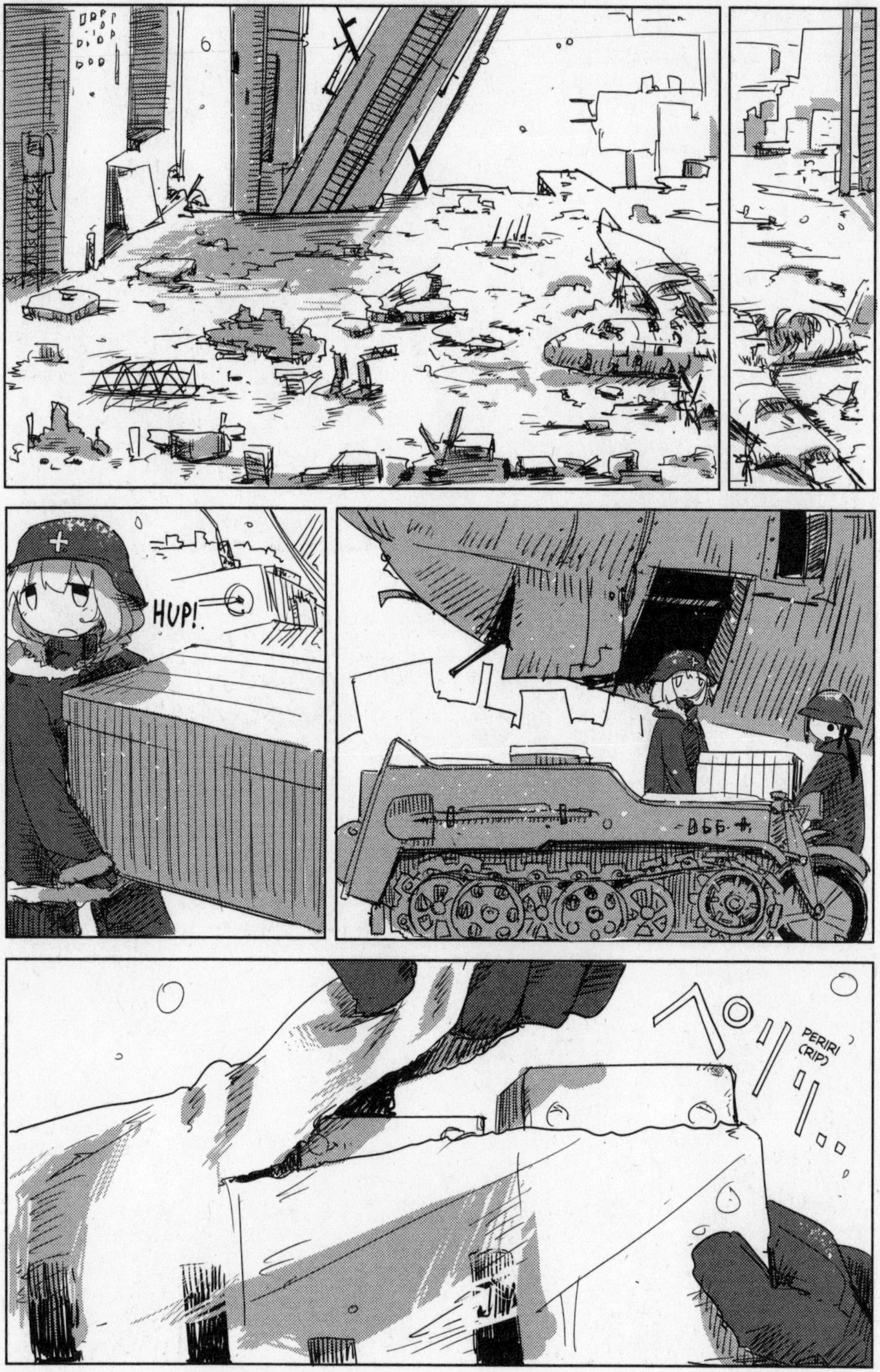
HUP!
PERIRI (RIP)

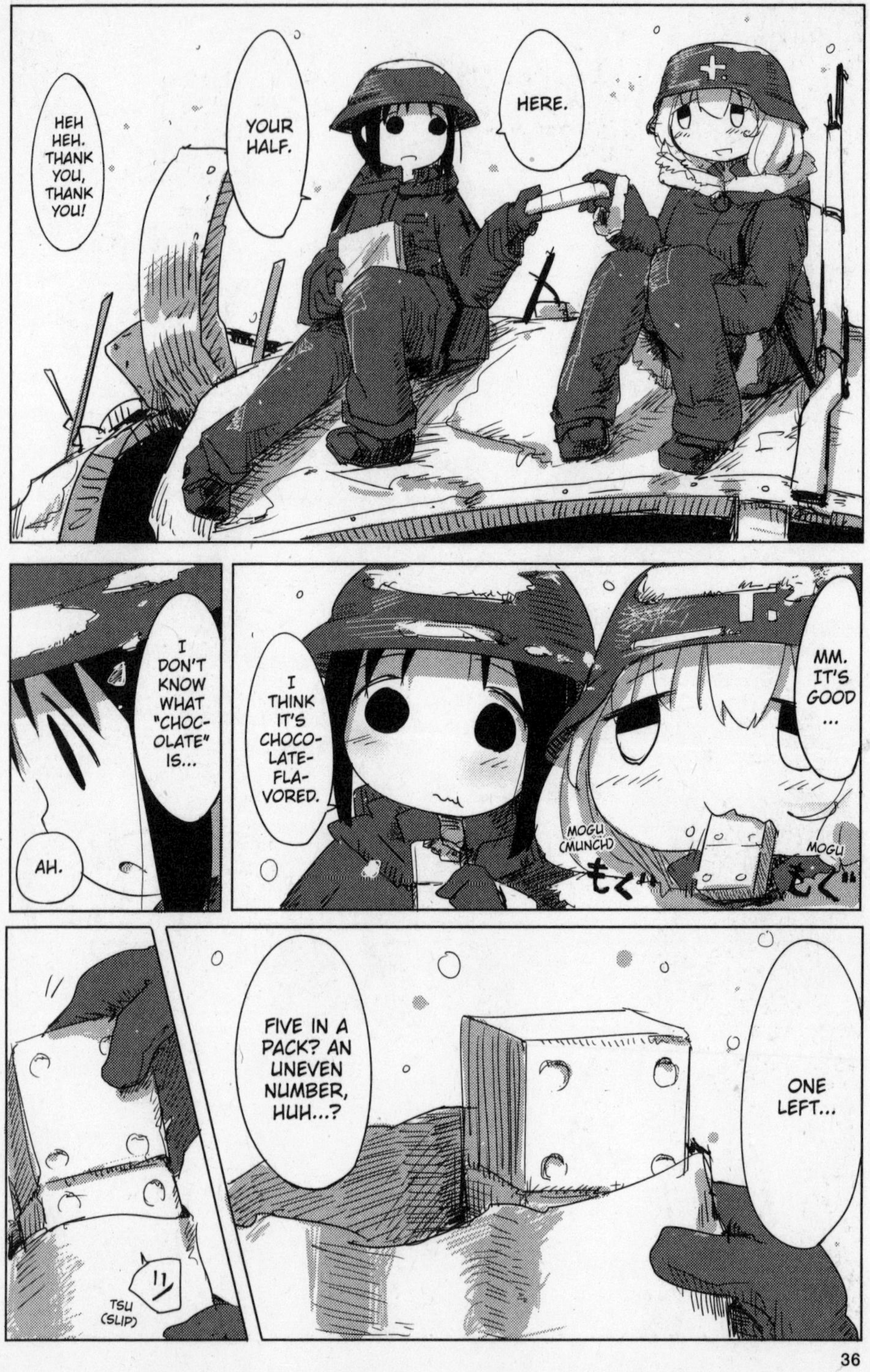
HERE.
YOUR HALF.
HEH HEH. THANK YOU, THANK YOU!
MM. IT'S GOOD ...
MOGU
もぐ
MOGU (MUNCH)
もぐ
I THINK IT'S CHOCOLATE-FLAVORED.
I DON'T KNOW WHAT "CHOCOLATE" IS...
AH.
ONE LEFT...
FIVE IN A PACK? AN UNEVEN NUMBER, HUH...?
TSU (SLIP)

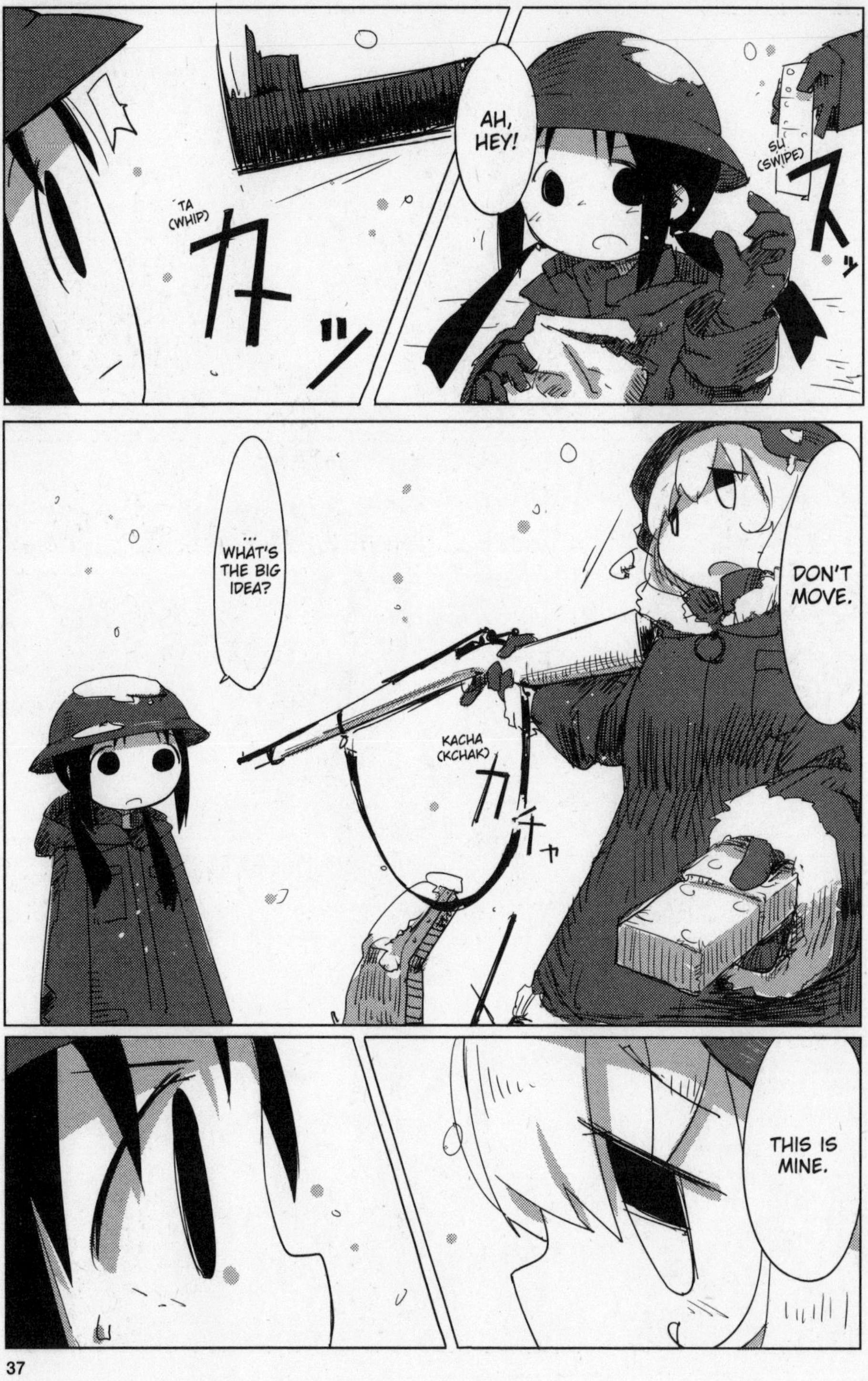
AH, HEY!
SU (SWIPE)
TA (WHIP)
DON'T MOVE.
KACHA (KCHAK)
... WHAT'S THE BIG IDEA?
THIS IS MINE.

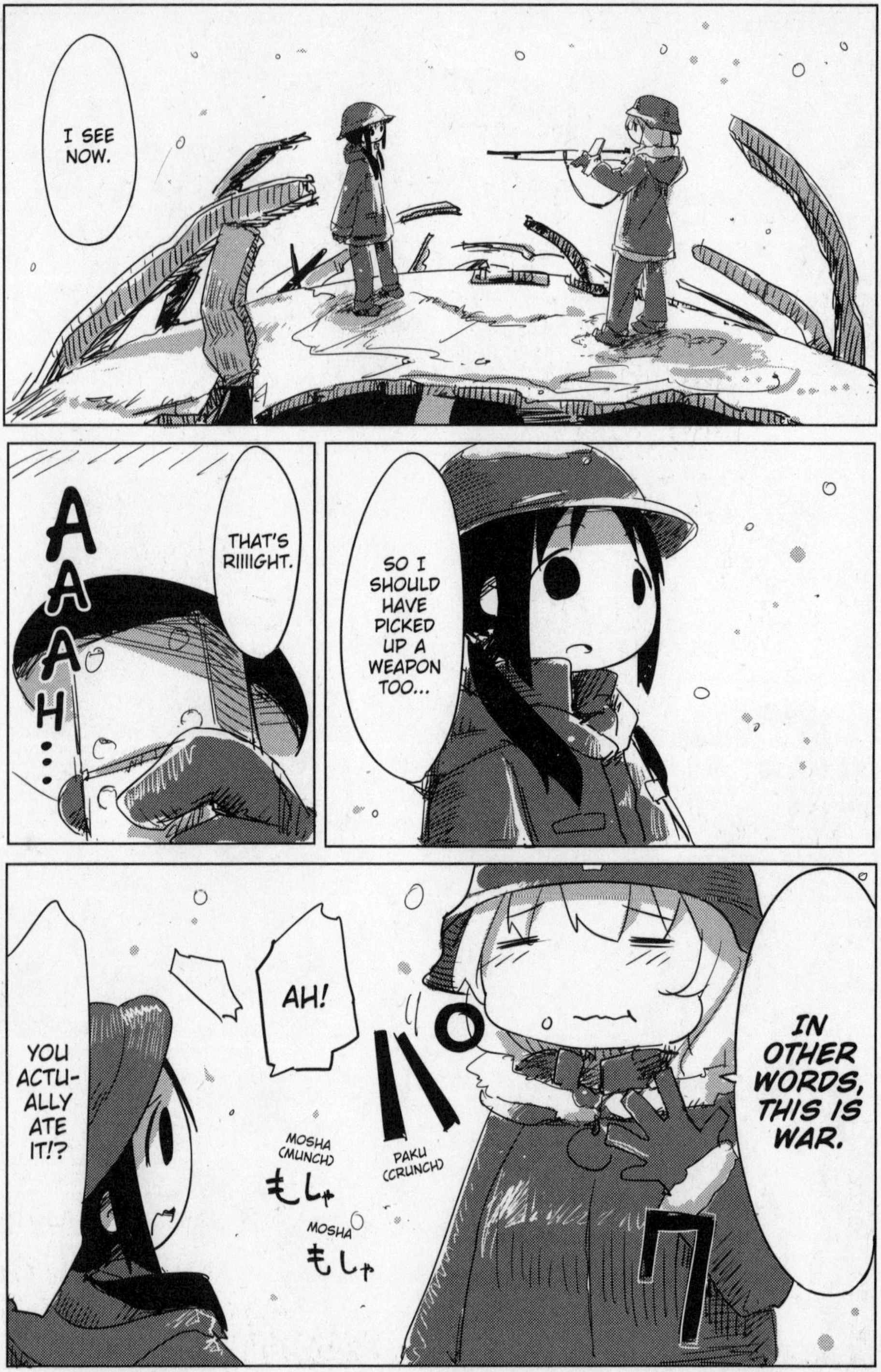
I SEE NOW.
SO I SHOULD HAVE PICKED UP A WEAPON TOO...
THAT'S RIIIIGHT.
AAAAH...
IN OTHER WORDS, THIS IS WAR.
パク
PAKU (CRUNCH)
AH!
MOSHA (MUNCH)
もしゃ
MOSHA
もしゃ
YOU ACTUALLY ATE IT!?

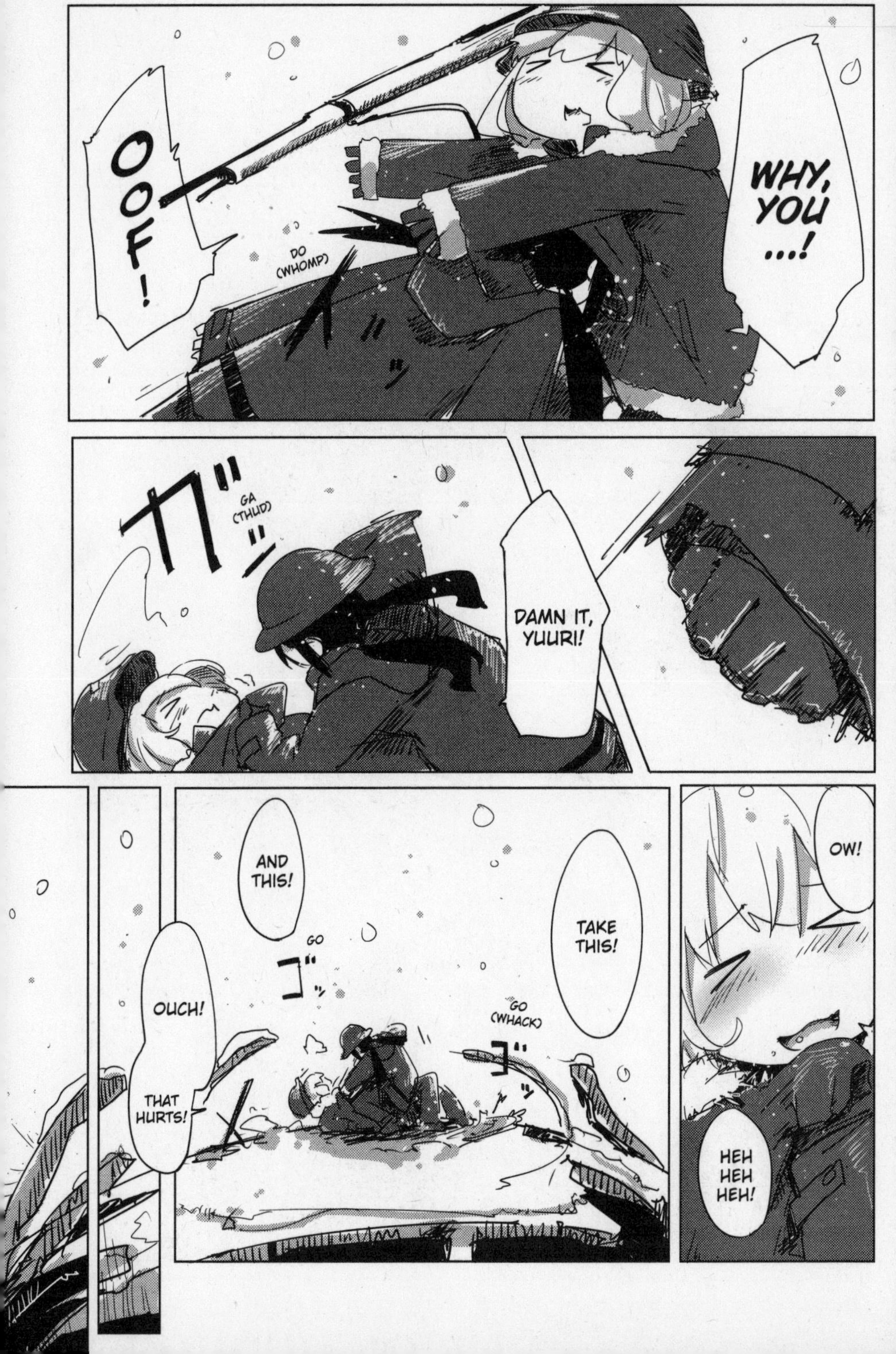
WHY, YOU...!
DO (WHOMP)
OOF!
DAMN IT, YUURI!
GA (THUD)
OW!
HEH HEH HEH!
TAKE THIS!
GO (WHACK)
AND THIS!
GO
OUCH!
THAT HURTS!

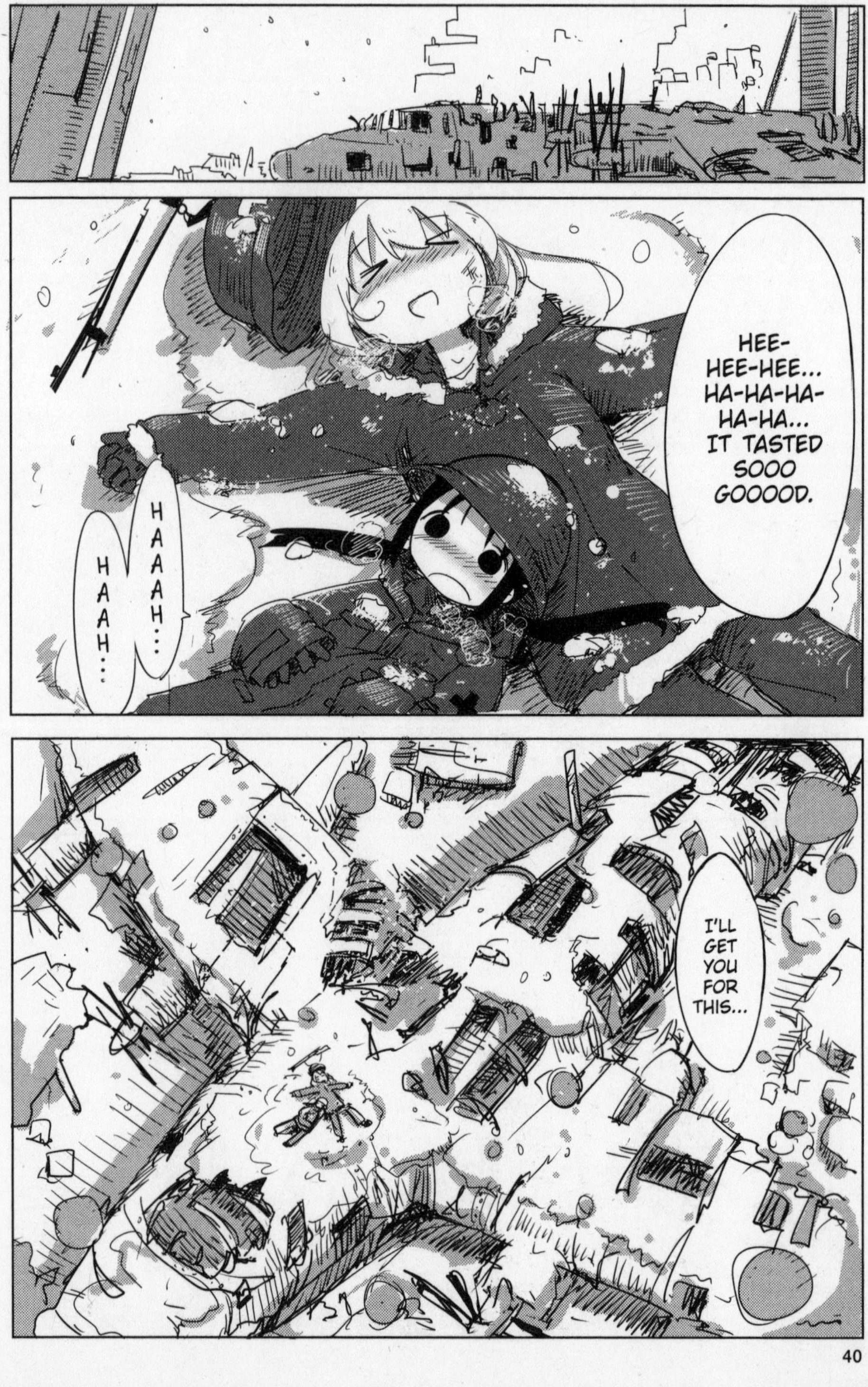
HEE-HEE-HEE... HA-HA-HA-HA-HA... IT TASTED SOOO GOOOOD.
HAAAH...
HAAAH...
I'LL GET YOU FOR THIS...

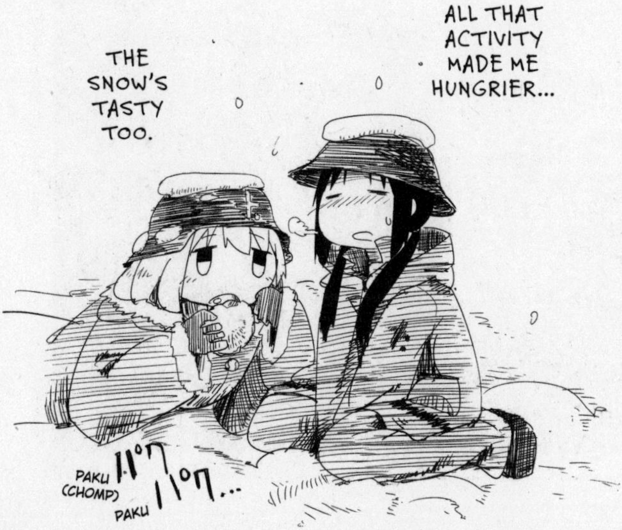
ALL THAT ACTIVITY MADE ME HUNGRIER...
THE SNOW'S TASTY TOO.
PAKU (CHOMP)
PAKU

GIRLS' LAST TOUR

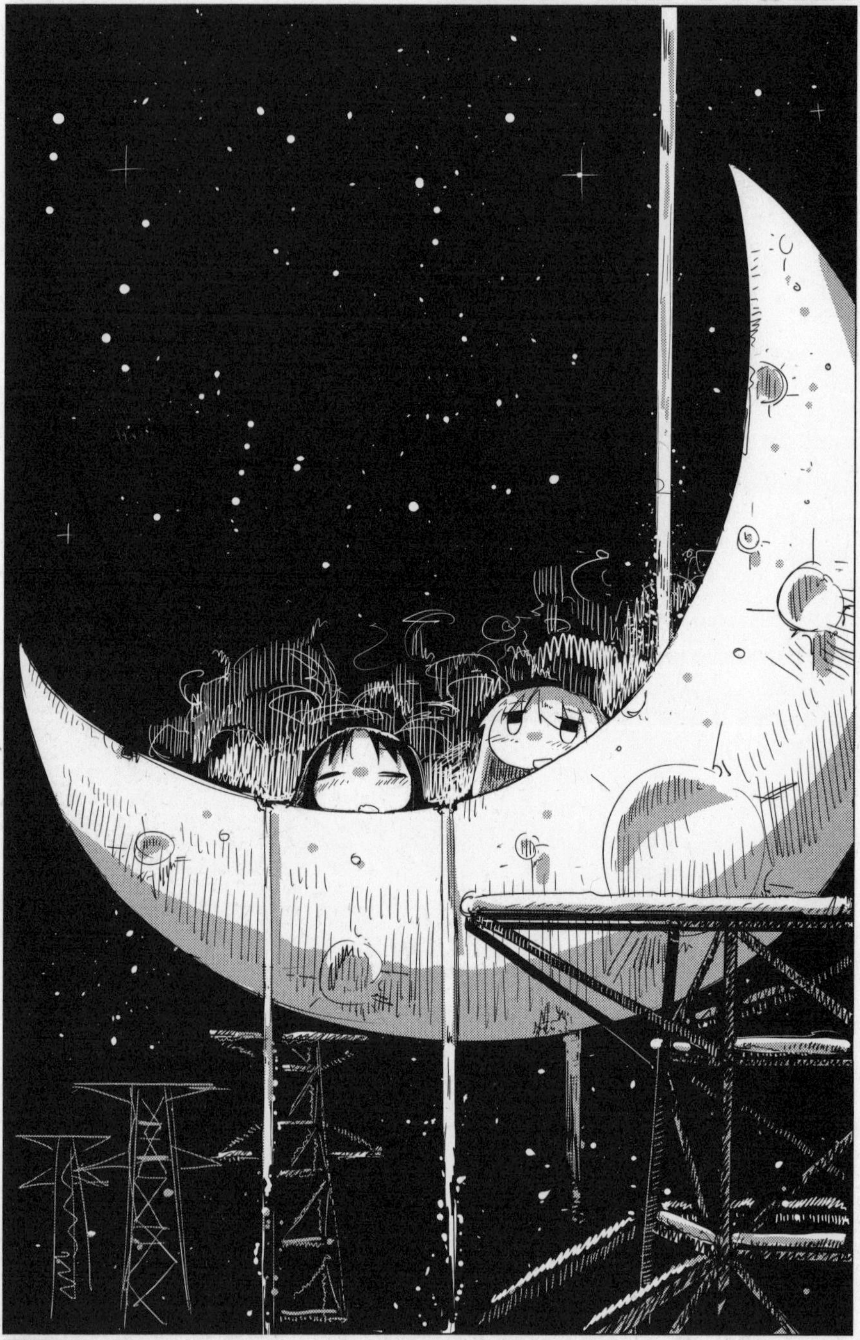

03

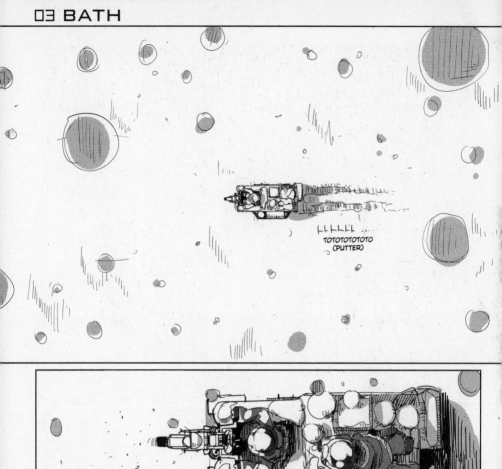

TOTOTOTOTOTO
(PUTTER)

TOTOTOTOTOTOTO

TO
(THMP)

UH-
HUH?

GYU
(SMOOSH)

GYU

HEY,
YUU?

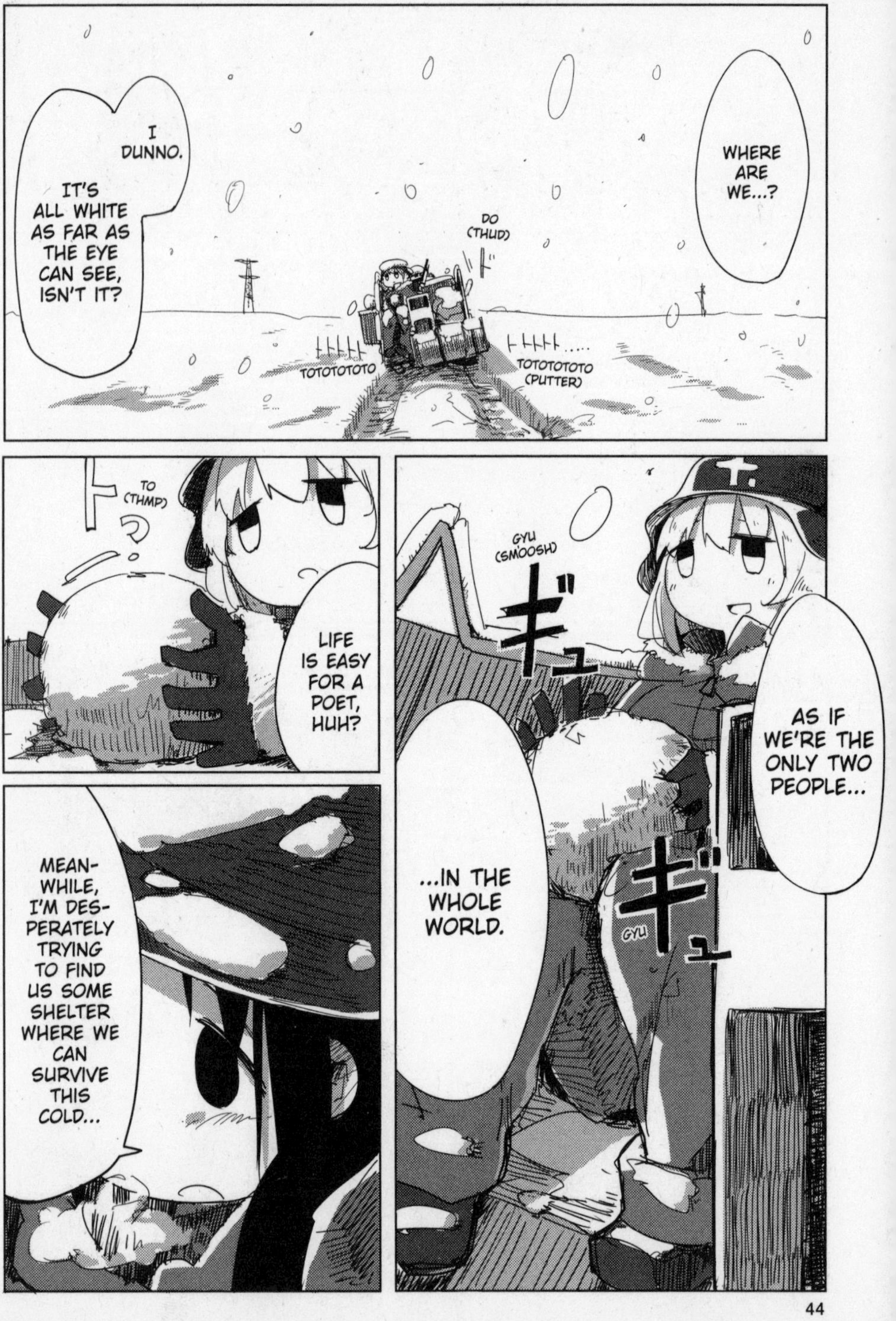
WHERE ARE WE...?
DO (THUD)
TOTOTOTOTO (PUTTER)
TOTOTOTOTO
I DUNNO.
IT'S ALL WHITE AS FAR AS THE EYE CAN SEE, ISN'T IT?
GYU (SMOOSH)
AS IF WE'RE THE ONLY TWO PEOPLE...
...IN THE WHOLE WORLD.
GYU
TO (THMP)
LIFE IS EASY FOR A POET, HUH?
MEAN-WHILE, I'M DES-PERATELY TRYING TO FIND US SOME SHELTER WHERE WE CAN SURVIVE THIS COLD...

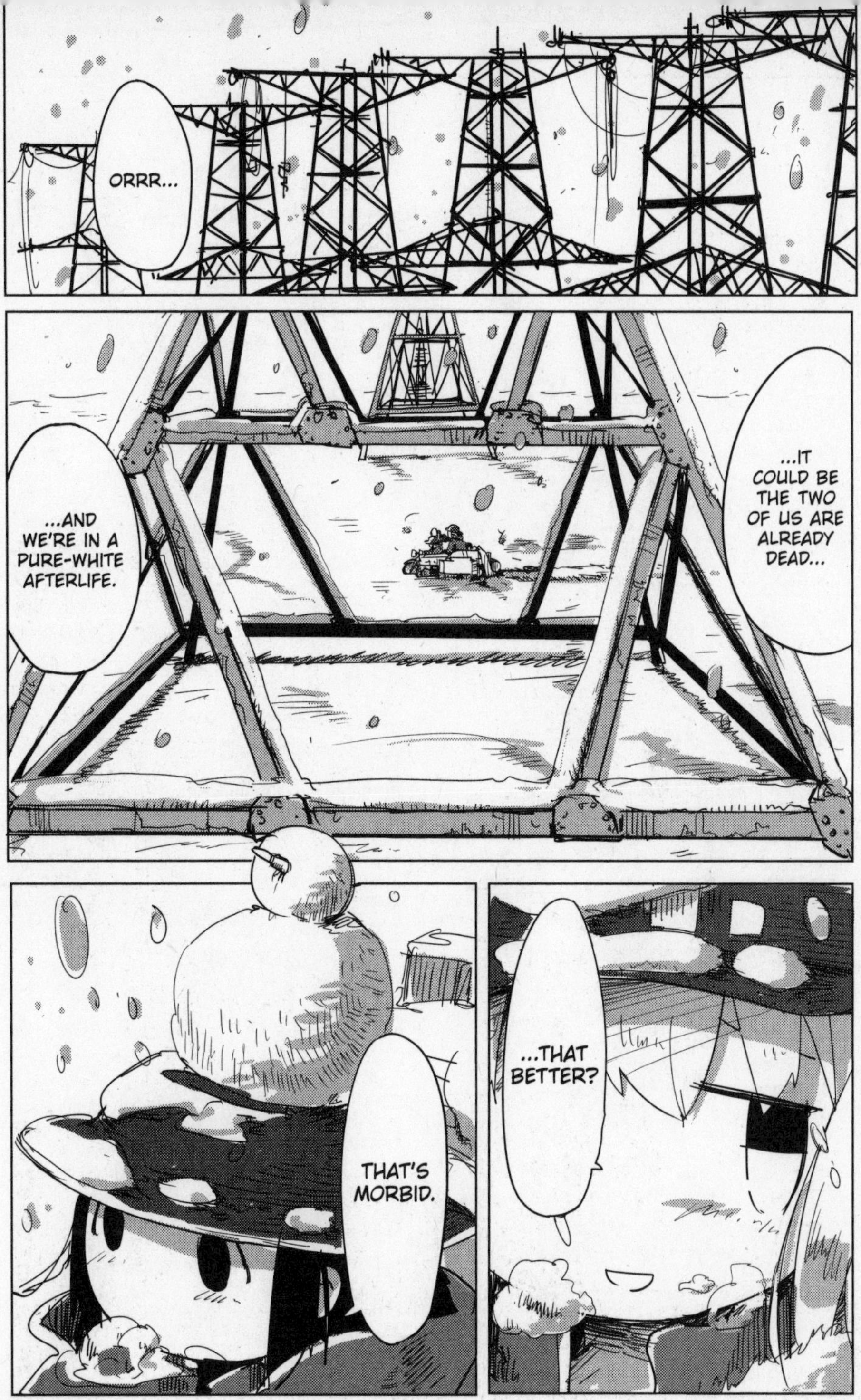
ORRR...
...IT COULD BE THE TWO OF US ARE ALREADY DEAD...
...AND WE'RE IN A PURE-WHITE AFTERLIFE.
...THAT BETTER?
THAT'S MORBID.

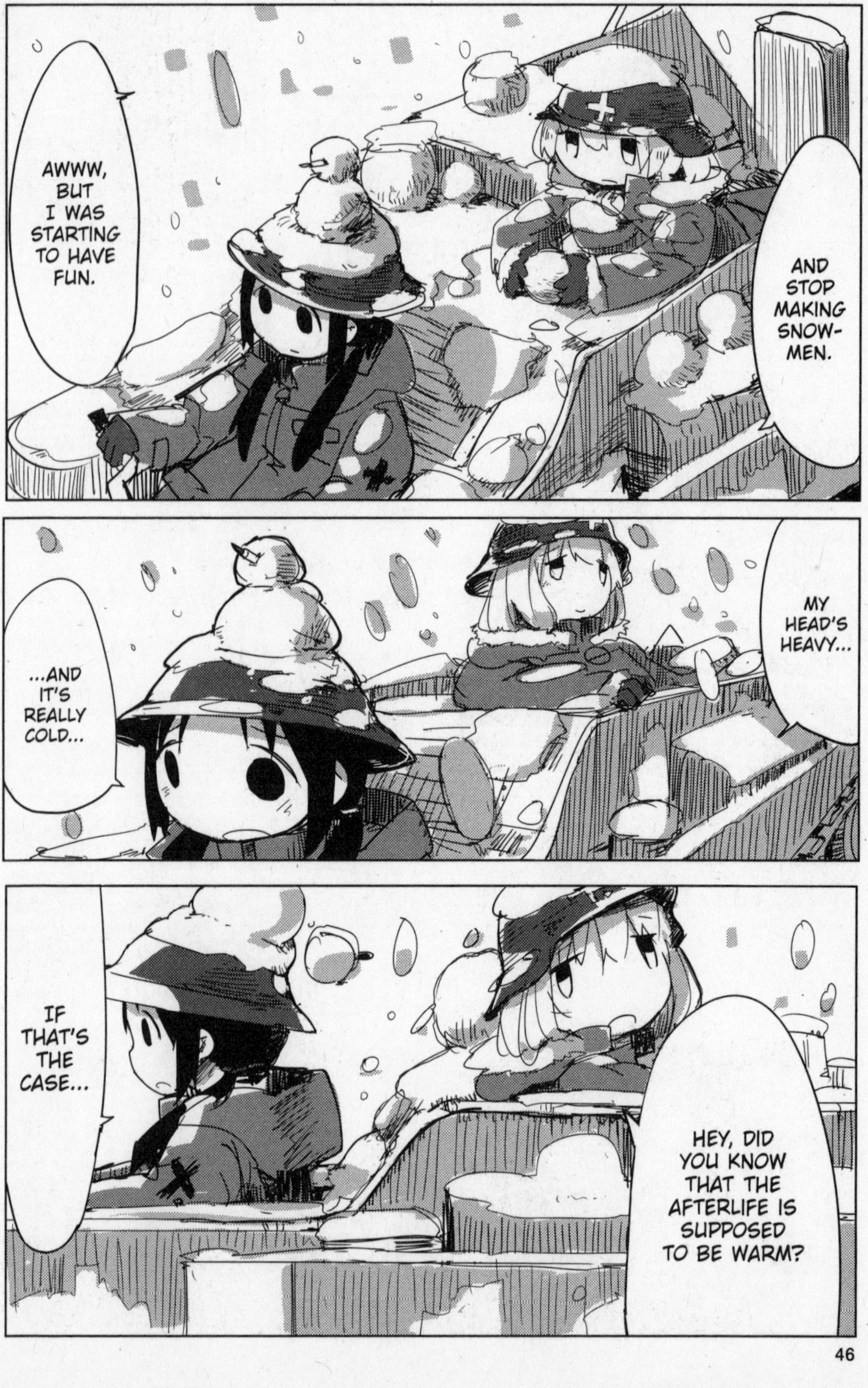
AND STOP MAKING SNOW-MEN.
AWWW, BUT I WAS STARTING TO HAVE FUN.
MY HEAD'S HEAVY...
...AND IT'S REALLY COLD...
IF THAT'S THE CASE...
HEY, DID YOU KNOW THAT THE AFTERLIFE IS SUPPOSED TO BE WARM?

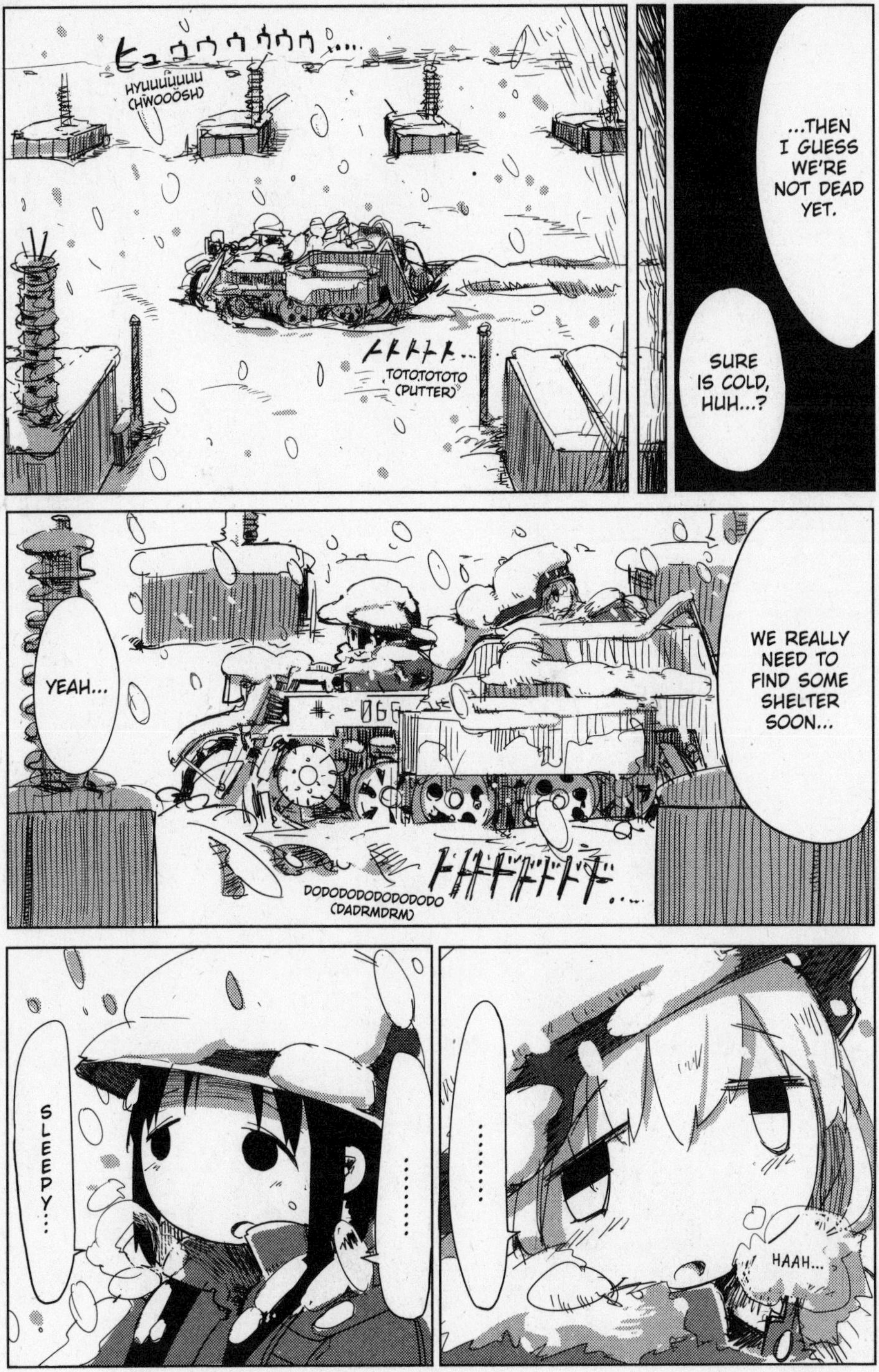

...THEN I GUESS WE'RE NOT DEAD YET.
SURE IS COLD, HUH...?
ヒュウウウウウウ....
HYUUUUUUUU (HWOOOSH)
トトトトト...
TOTOTOTOTO (PUTTER)
WE REALLY NEED TO FIND SOME SHELTER SOON...
YEAH...
ドドドドドドドド...
DODODODODODODODO (DADRMDRM)
......
HAAH...
......
SLEEPY...

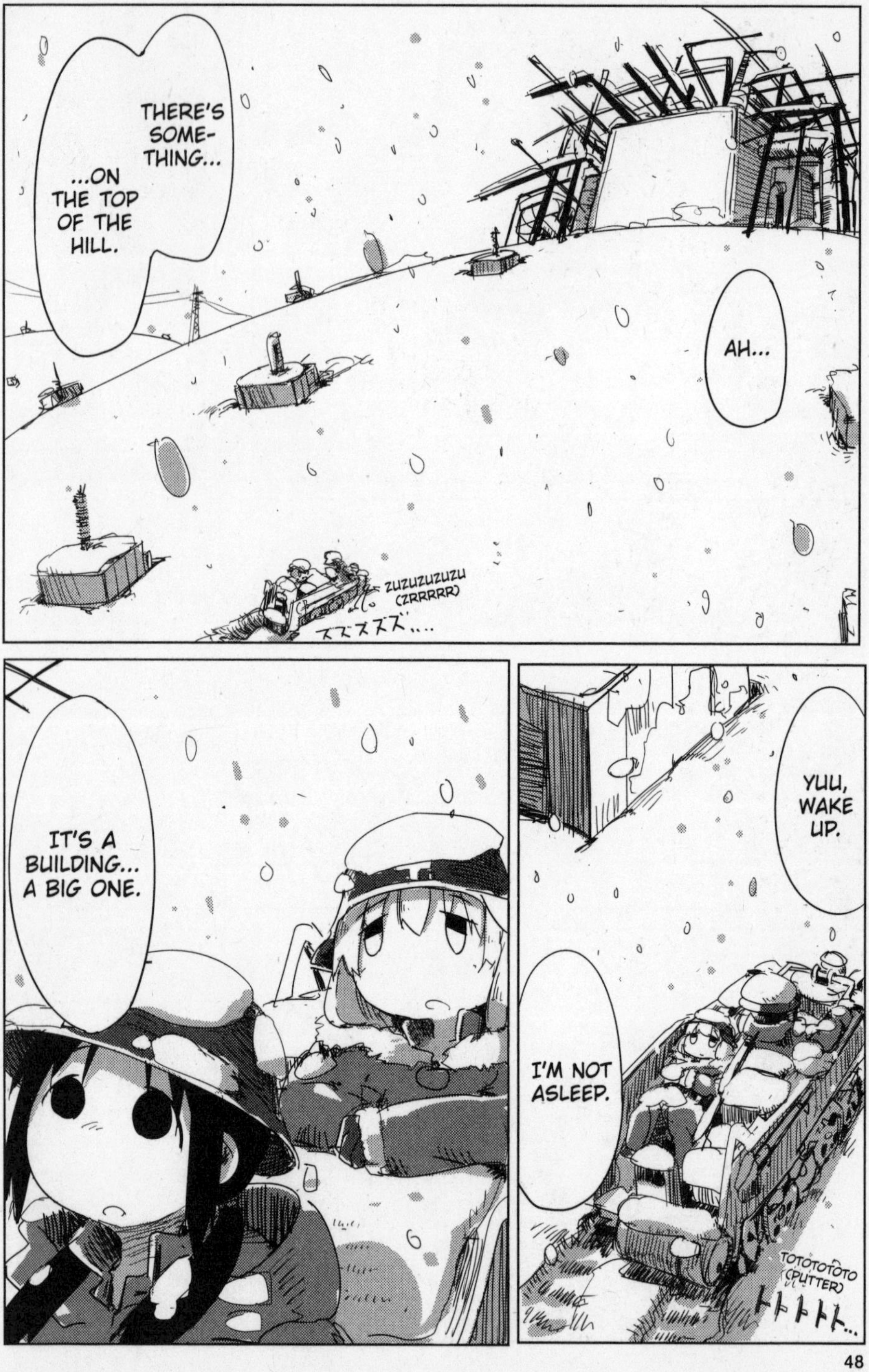
THERE'S SOMETHING... ...ON THE TOP OF THE HILL.
AH...
ZUZUZUZUZU (ZRRRRR)
ズズズズ...
YUU, WAKE UP.
I'M NOT ASLEEP.
TOTOTOTOTO (PUTTER)
トトトト...
IT'S A BUILDING... A BIG ONE.

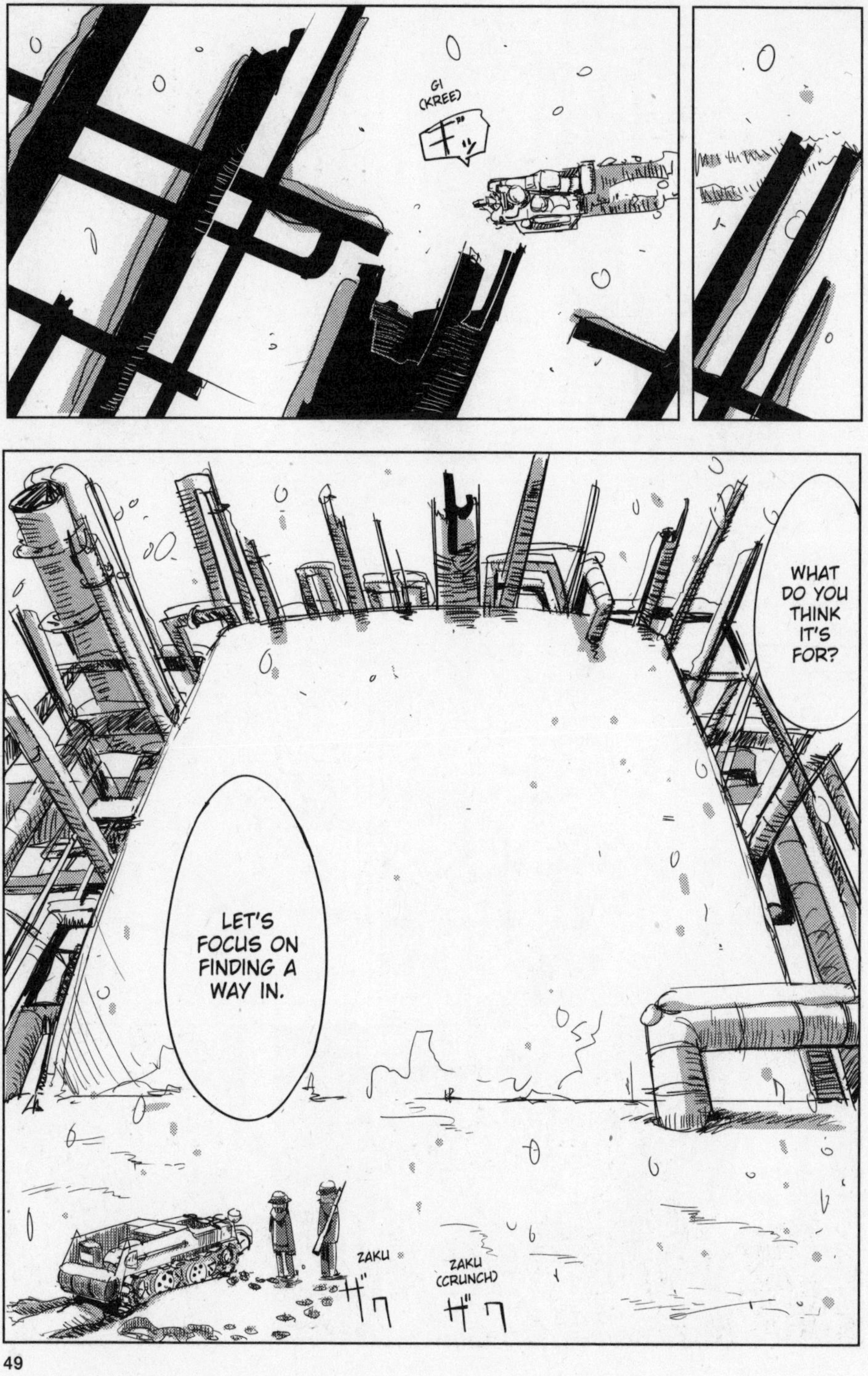
GI (KREE)
ギッ
WHAT DO YOU THINK IT'S FOR?
LET'S FOCUS ON FINDING A WAY IN.
ZAKU (CRUNCH)
ザク
ZAKU
ザク

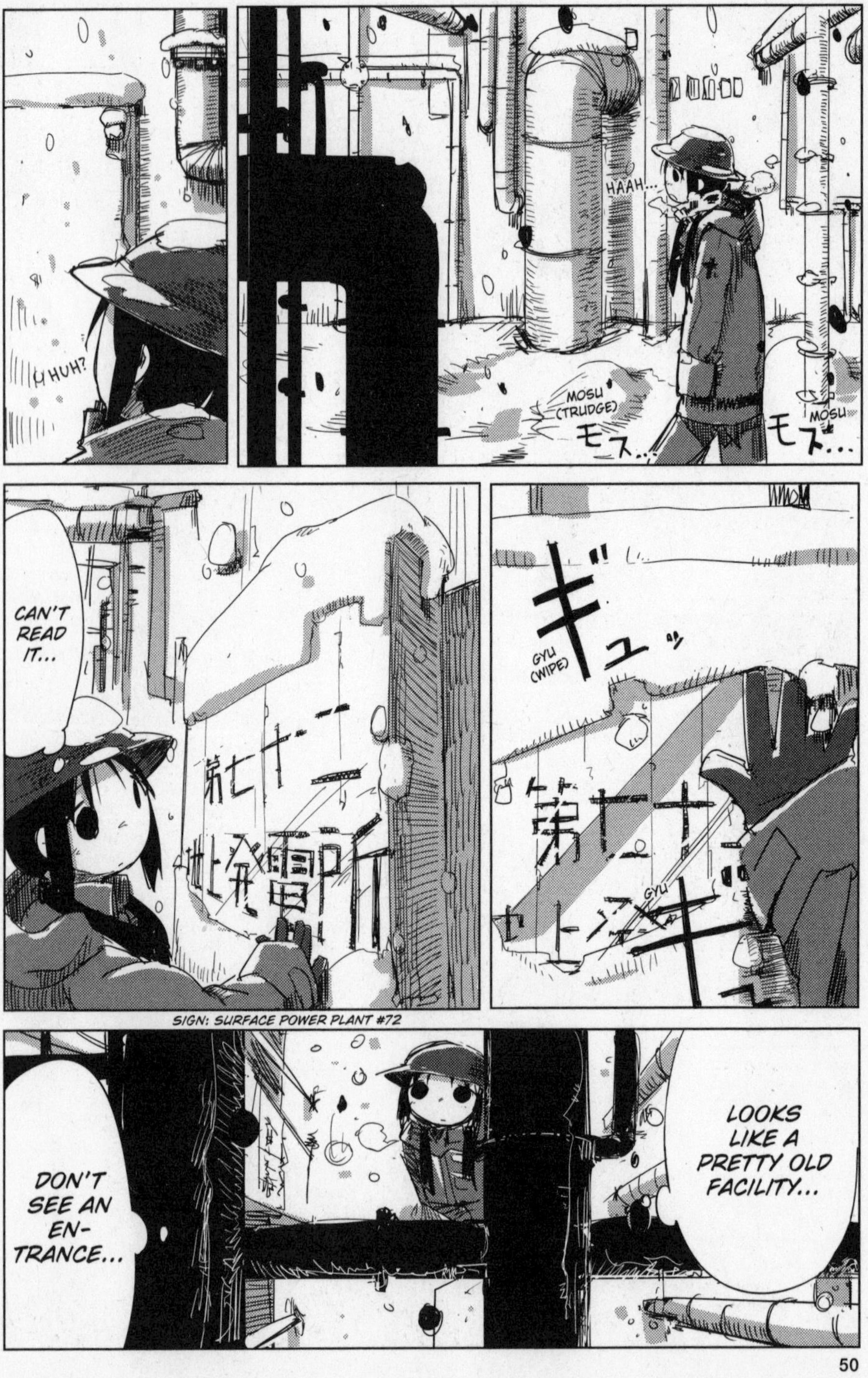
HAAH...
MOSU
モス...
MOSU (TRUDGE)
モス...
HUH?
GYU (WIPE)
ギュッ
GYU
ギュ
CAN'T READ IT...
SIGN: SURFACE POWER PLANT #72
LOOKS LIKE A PRETTY OLD FACILITY...
DON'T SEE AN EN- TRANCE...

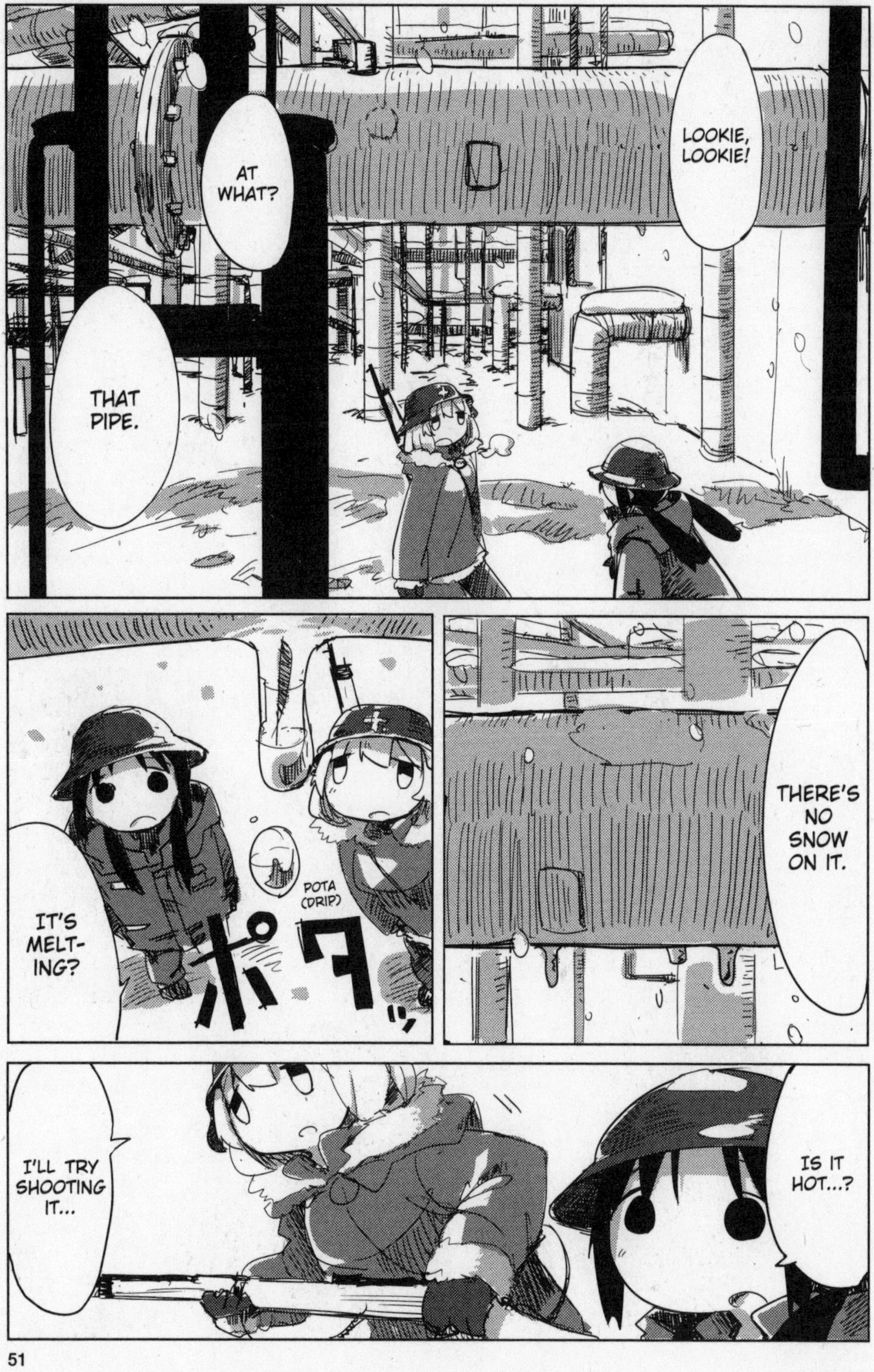
LOOKIE, LOOKIE!
AT WHAT?
THAT PIPE.
THERE'S NO SNOW ON IT.
POTA (DRIP)
ポタッ
IT'S MELT-ING?
IS IT HOT...?
I'LL TRY SHOOTING IT...

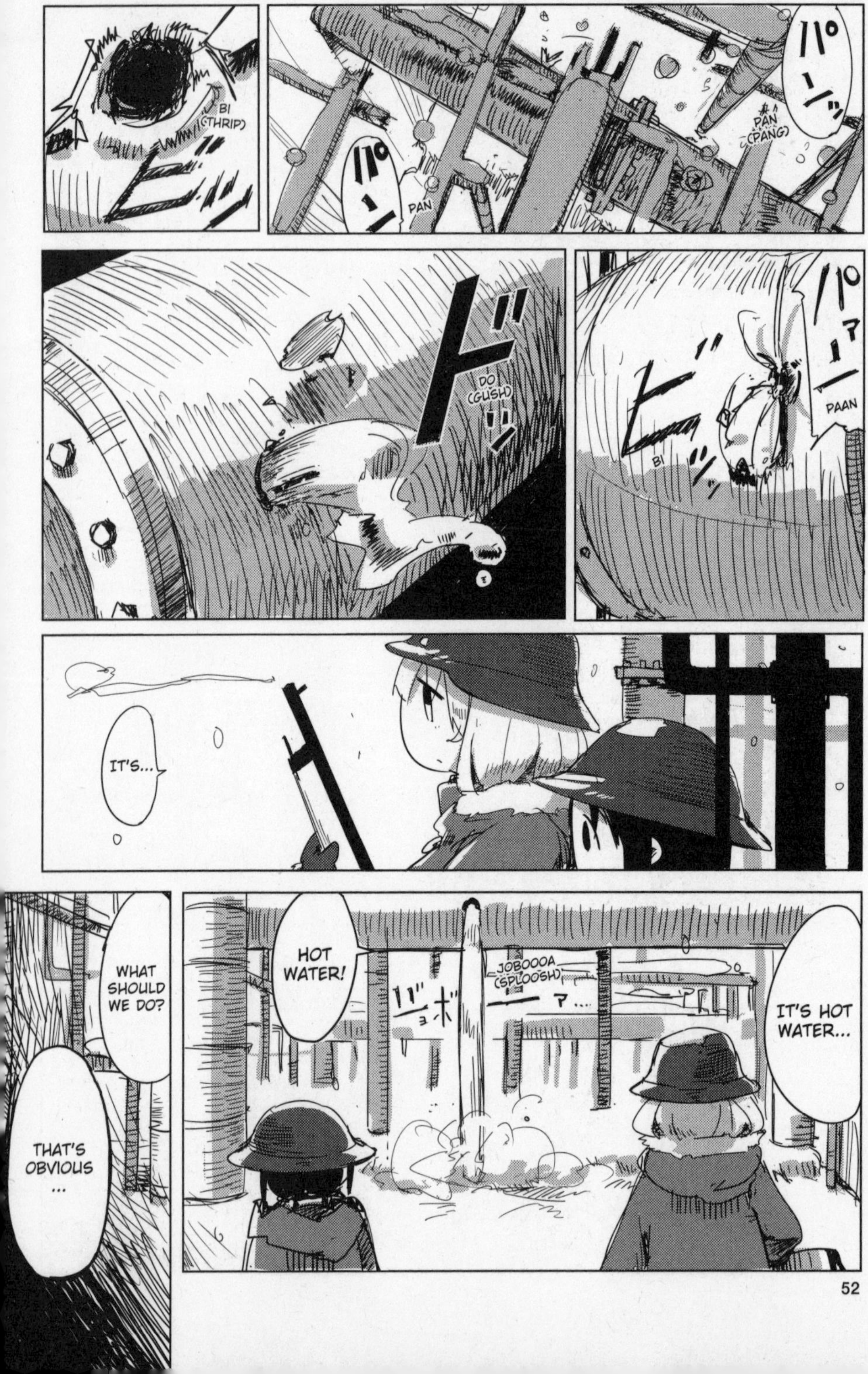
PAN (PANG)
PAN
BI (THRIP)
PAAN
BI
DO (GUSH)
IT'S...
HOT WATER!
JOBOOOA (SPLOOSH)
IT'S HOT WATER...
WHAT SHOULD WE DO?
THAT'S OBVIOUS ...

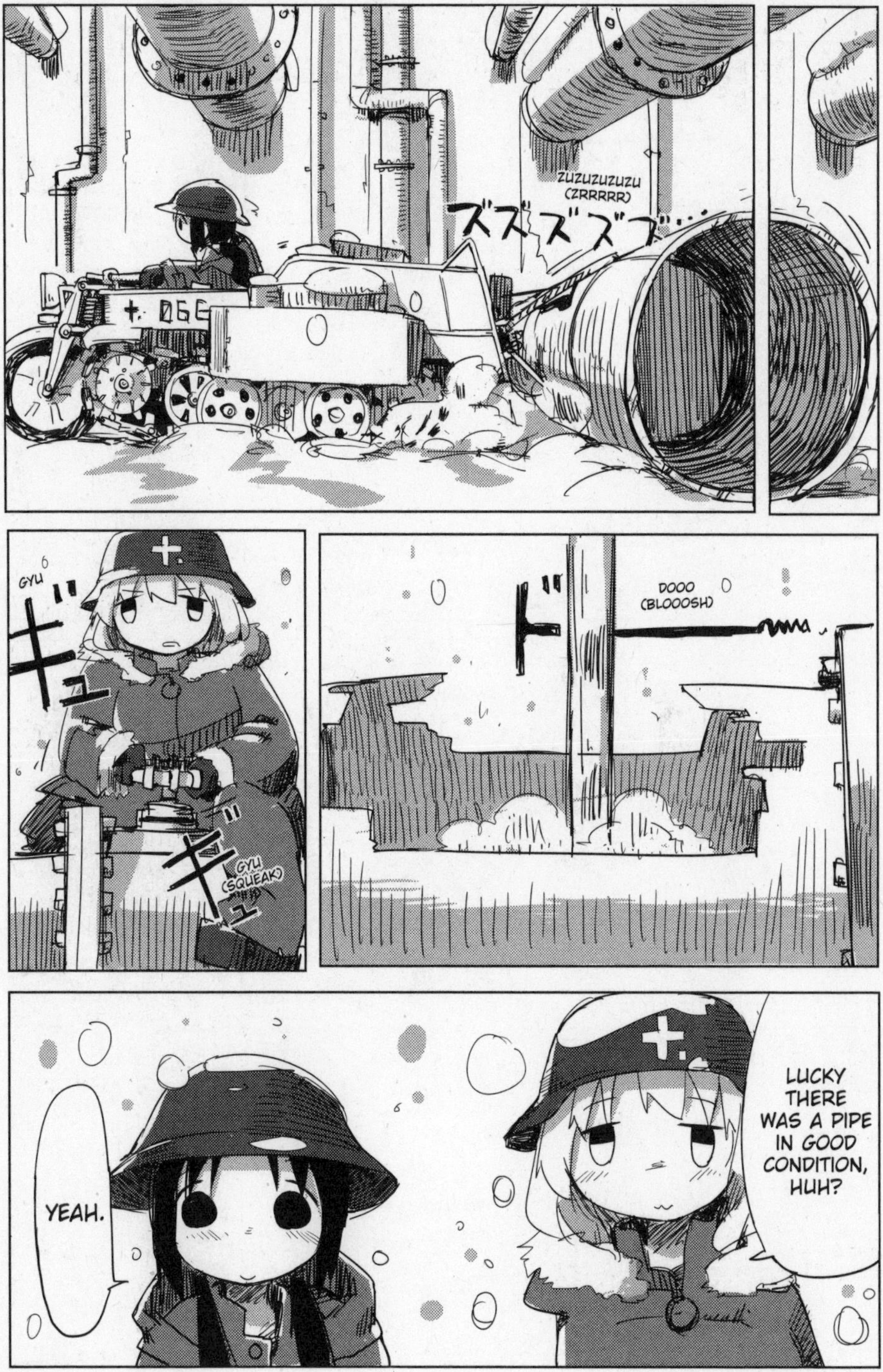
ズズズズズ…
ZUZUZUZUZU (ZRRRRR)
ド
DOOO (BLOOOSH)
ギュ
GYU
ギュ
GYU (SQUEAK)
LUCKY THERE WAS A PIPE IN GOOD CONDITION, HUH?
YEAH.

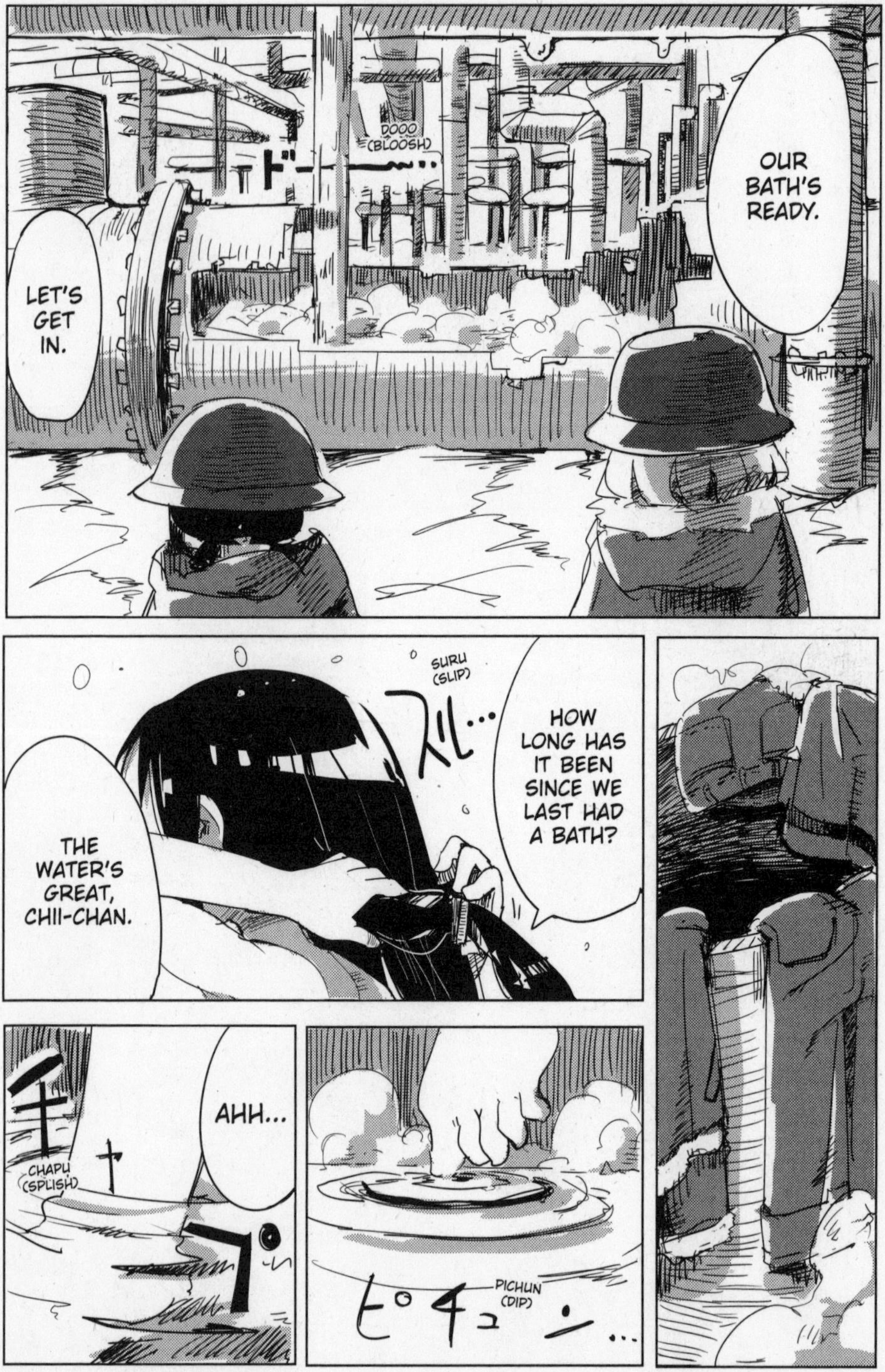
OUR BATH'S READY.
DOOO (BLOOSH)
LET'S GET IN.
SURU (SLIP)
HOW LONG HAS IT BEEN SINCE WE LAST HAD A BATH?
THE WATER'S GREAT, CHII-CHAN.
PICHUN (DIP)
AHH...
CHAPU (SPLISH)

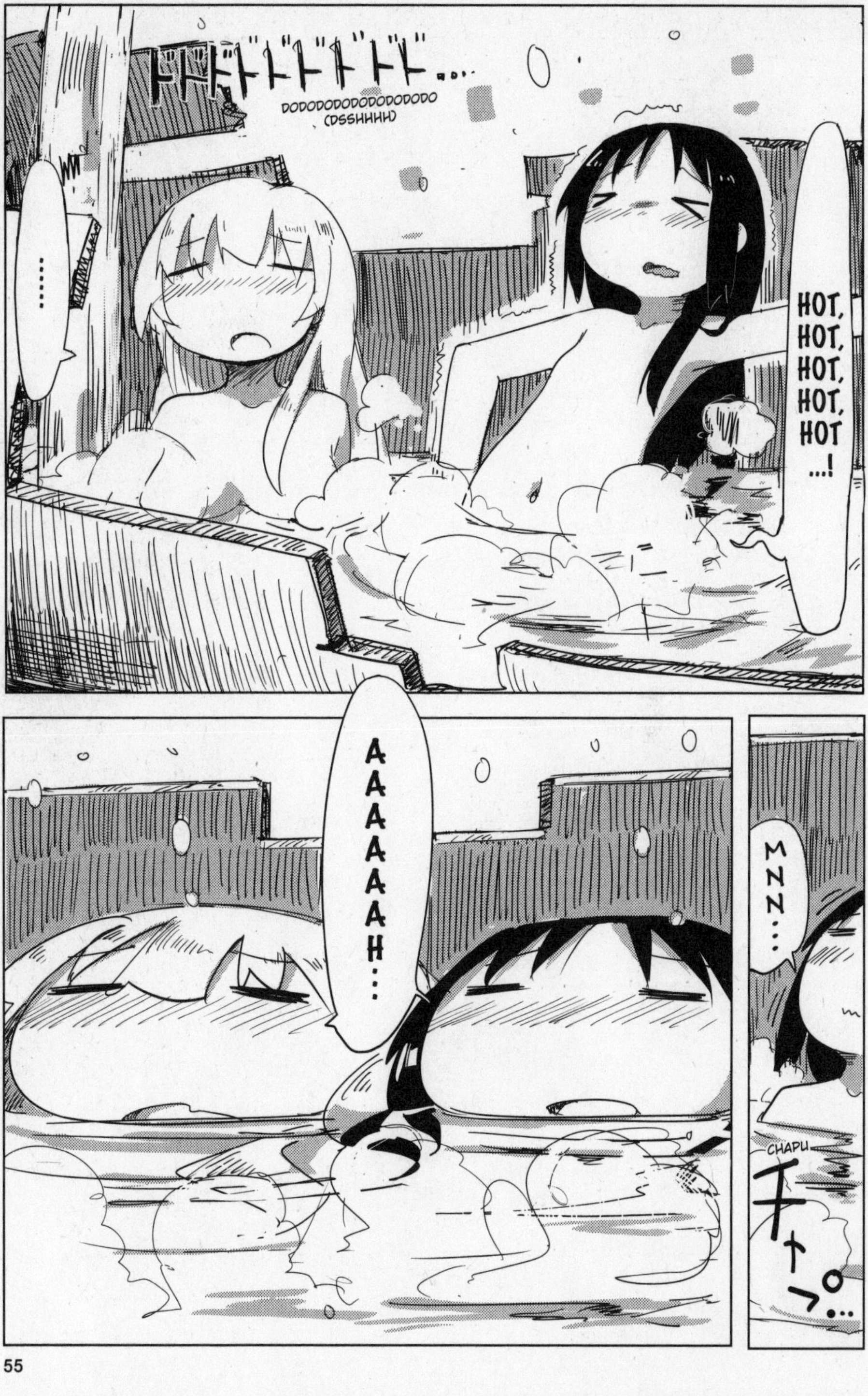
HOT, HOT, HOT, HOT, HOT ...!
ドドドドドドドド...
DODODODODODODODODO
(DSSHHHH)
......
MNN...
CHAPU
チャプ...
AAAAAAH...

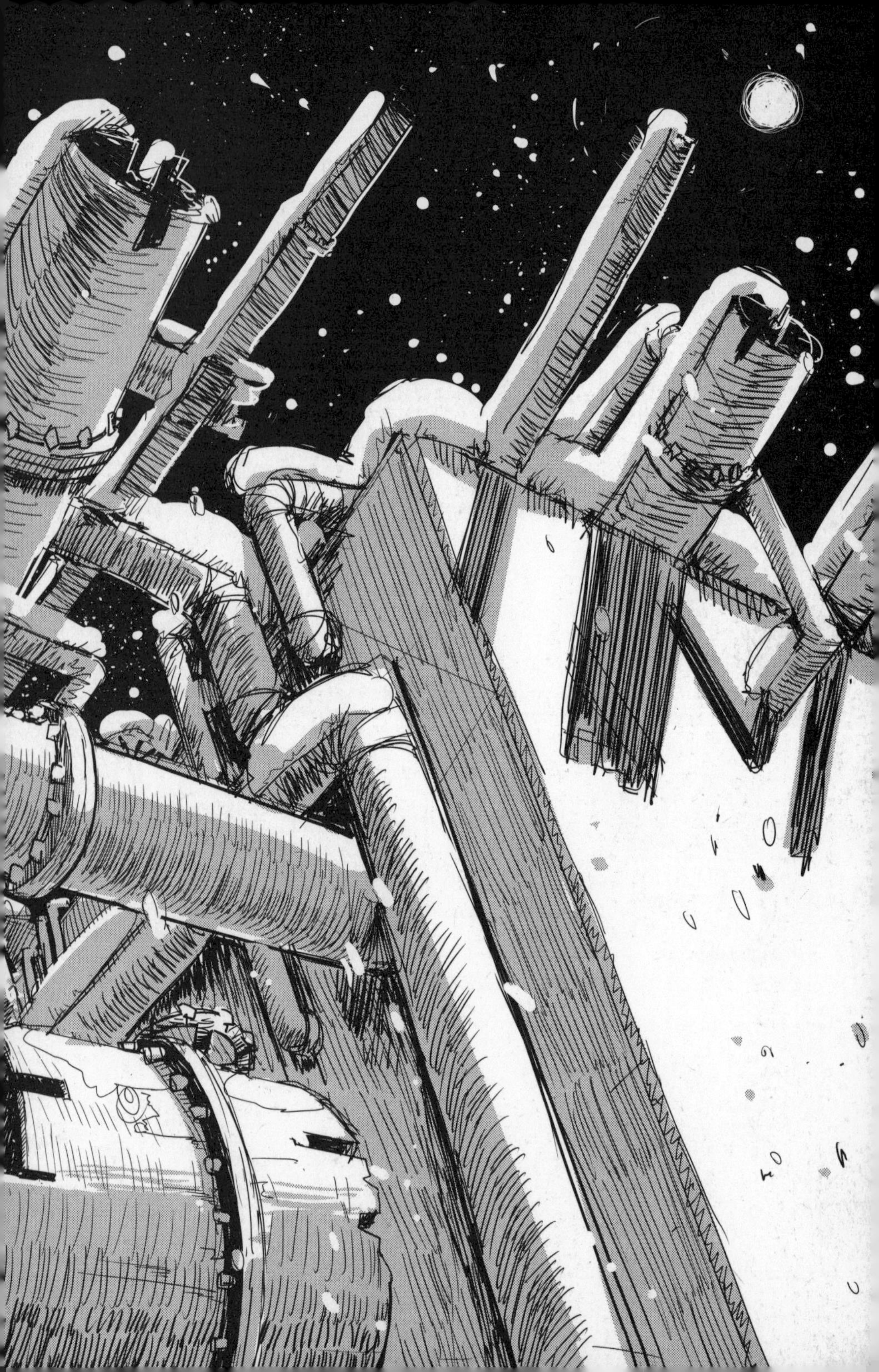

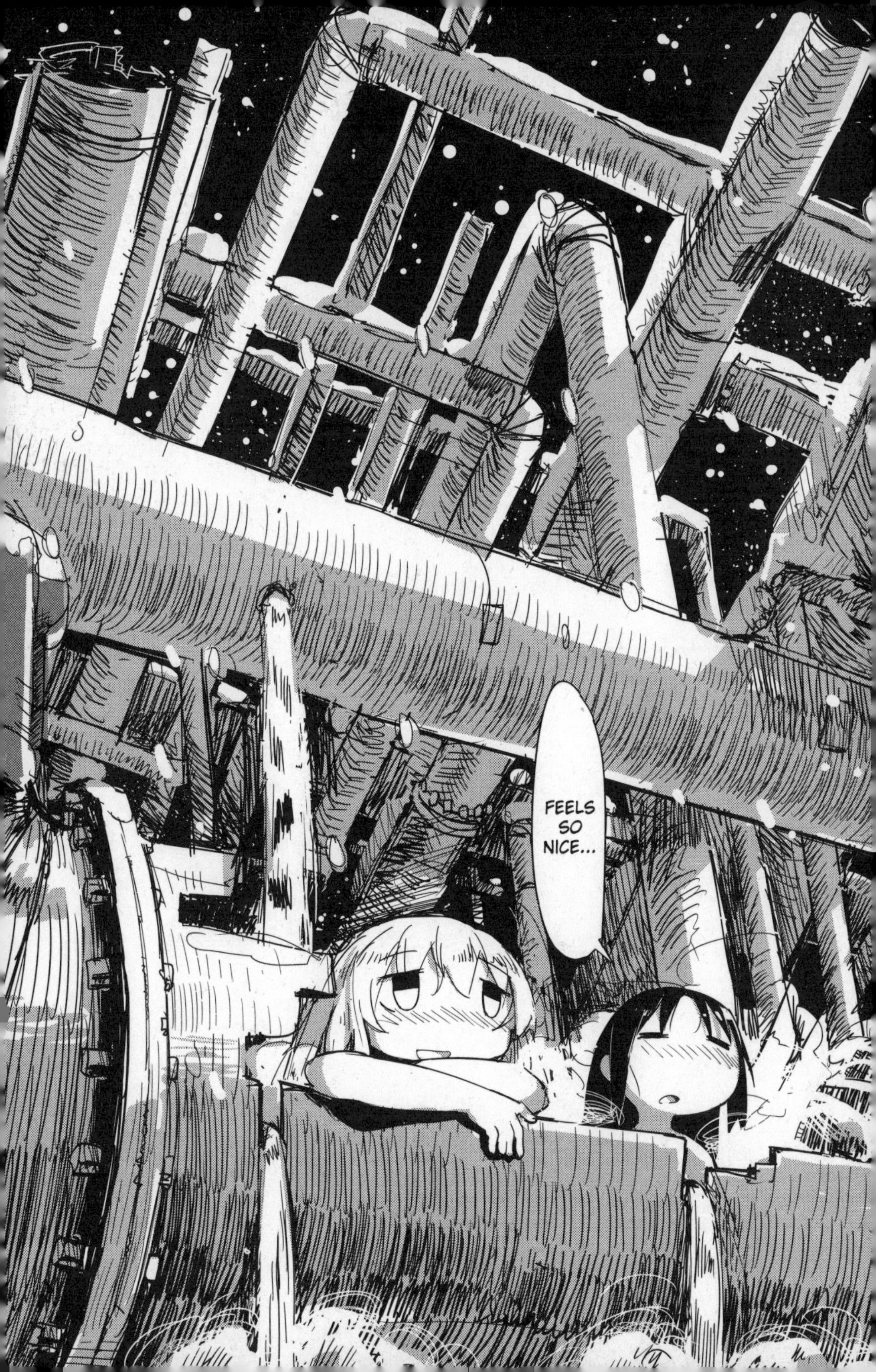
FEELS SO NICE...

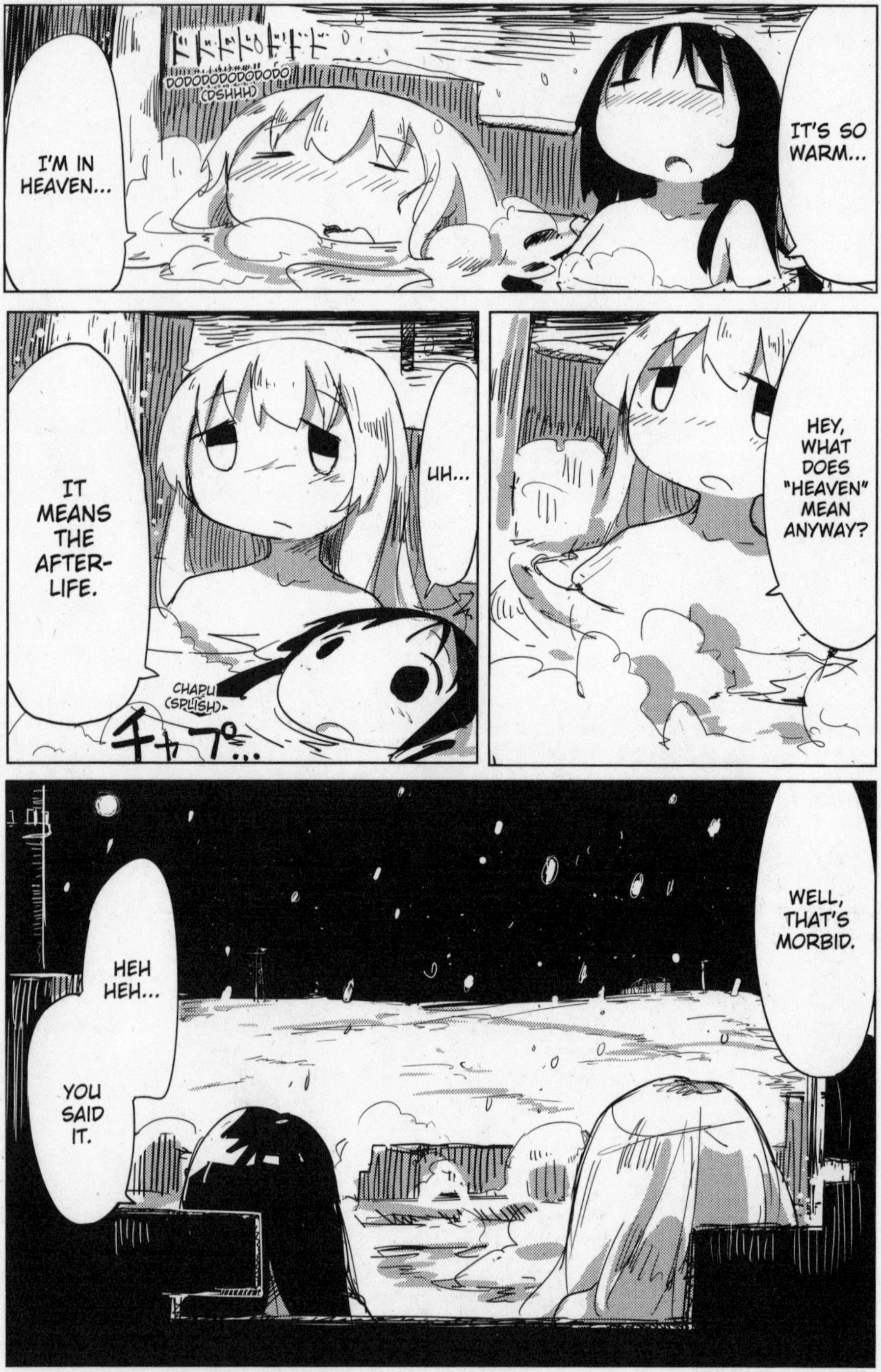
IT'S SO WARM...
ドドドドドドドド…
DODODODODODODO (DSHHH)
I'M IN HEAVEN...
HEY, WHAT DOES "HEAVEN" MEAN ANYWAY?
UH...
IT MEANS THE AFTER-LIFE.
CHAPU (SPLISH)
チャプ…
WELL, THAT'S MORBID.
HEH HEH...
YOU SAID IT.

AHHH... ALL LOOSENED UP...
ブクブクブク....
BUKU BUKU BUKU
(BRBL)

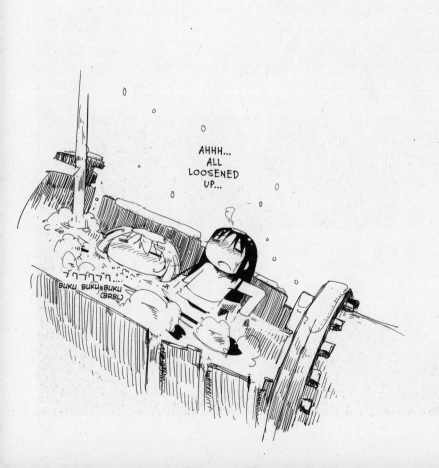

GIRLS' LAST TOUR

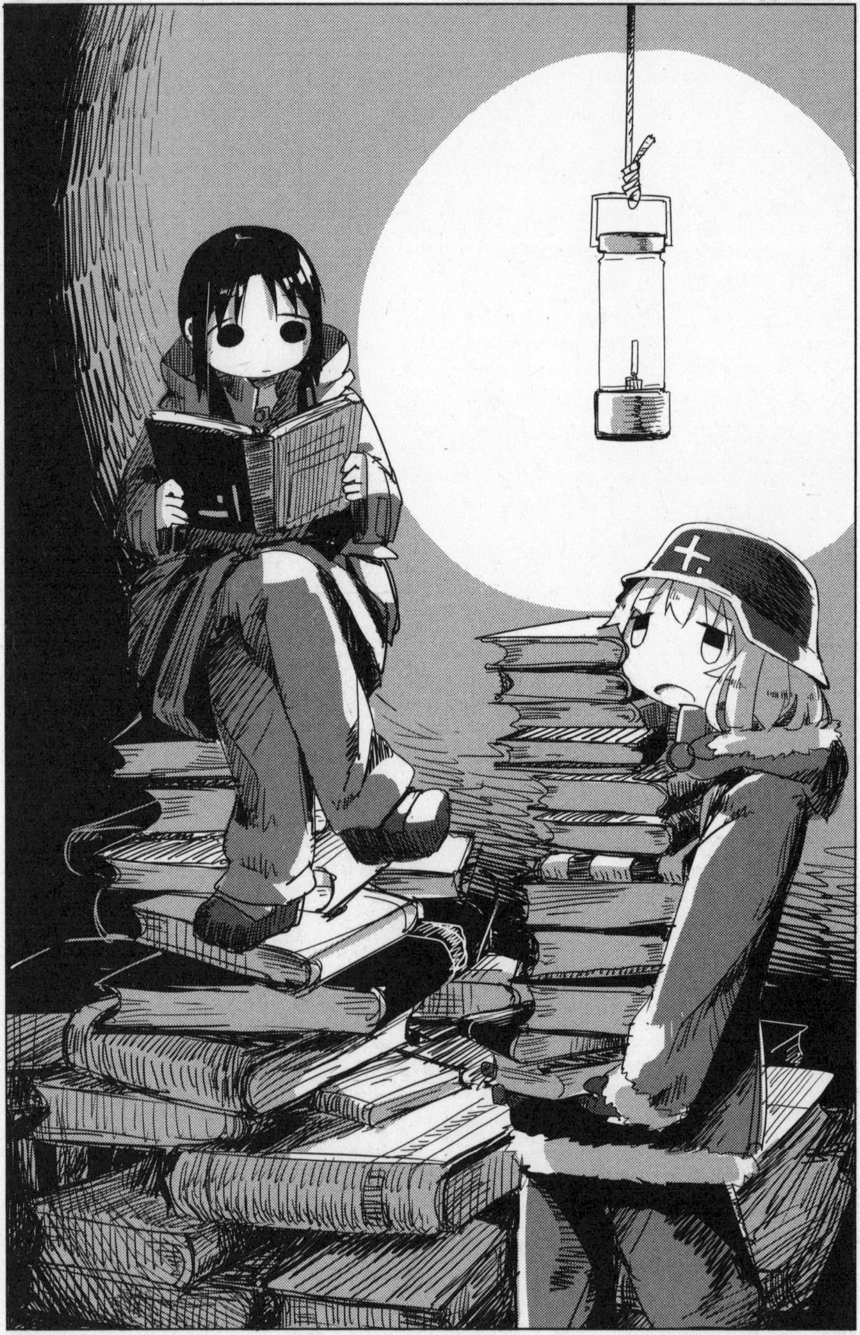

04

04 JOURNAL

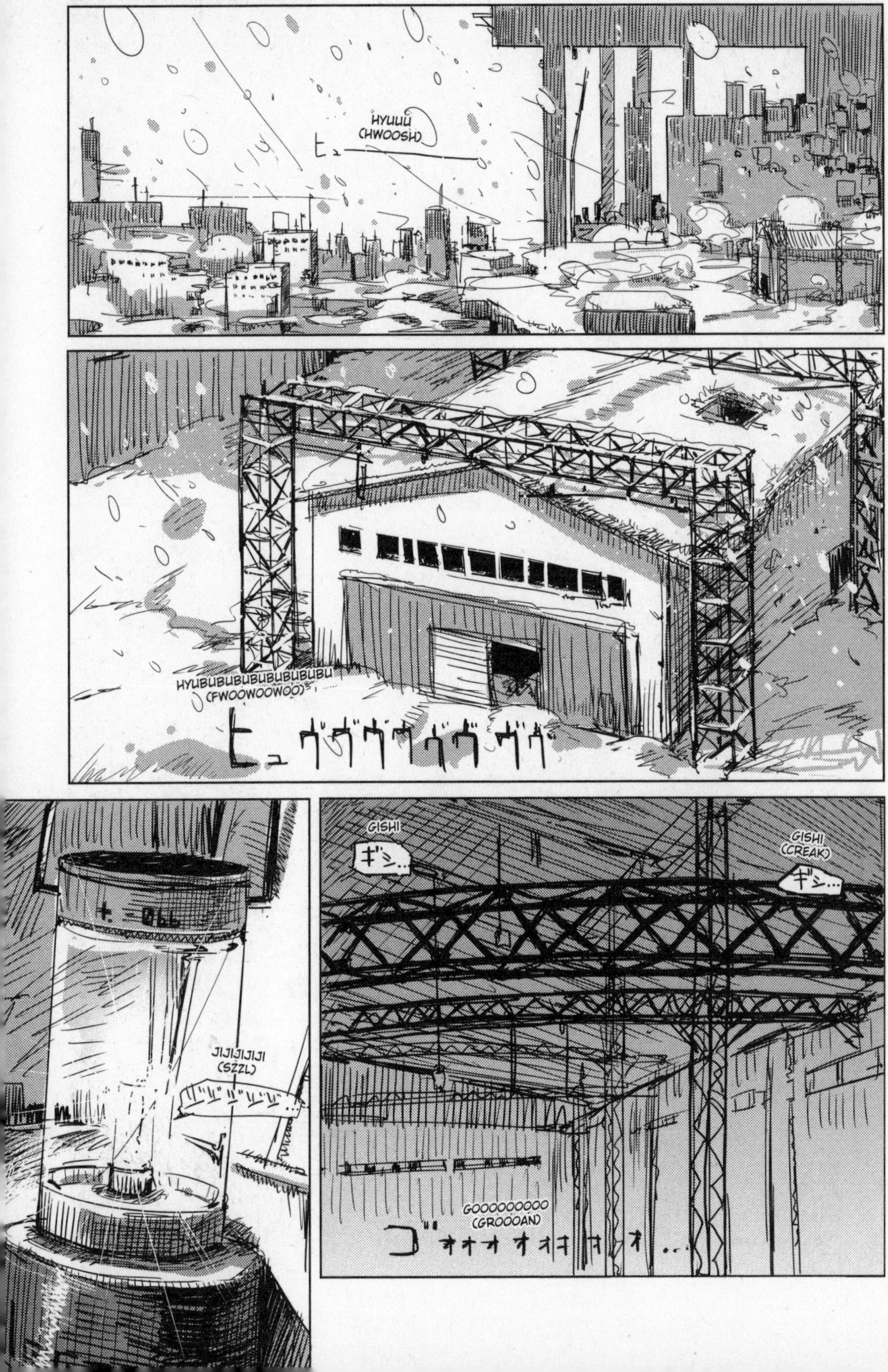
HYUUU (HWOOSH)
ヒュ
HYUBUBUBUBUBUBUBUBU (FWOOWOOWOO)
GISHI (CREAK)
ギシ…
GISHI
ギシ…
GOOOOOOOOO (GROOOAN)
JIJIJIJIJI (SZZL)

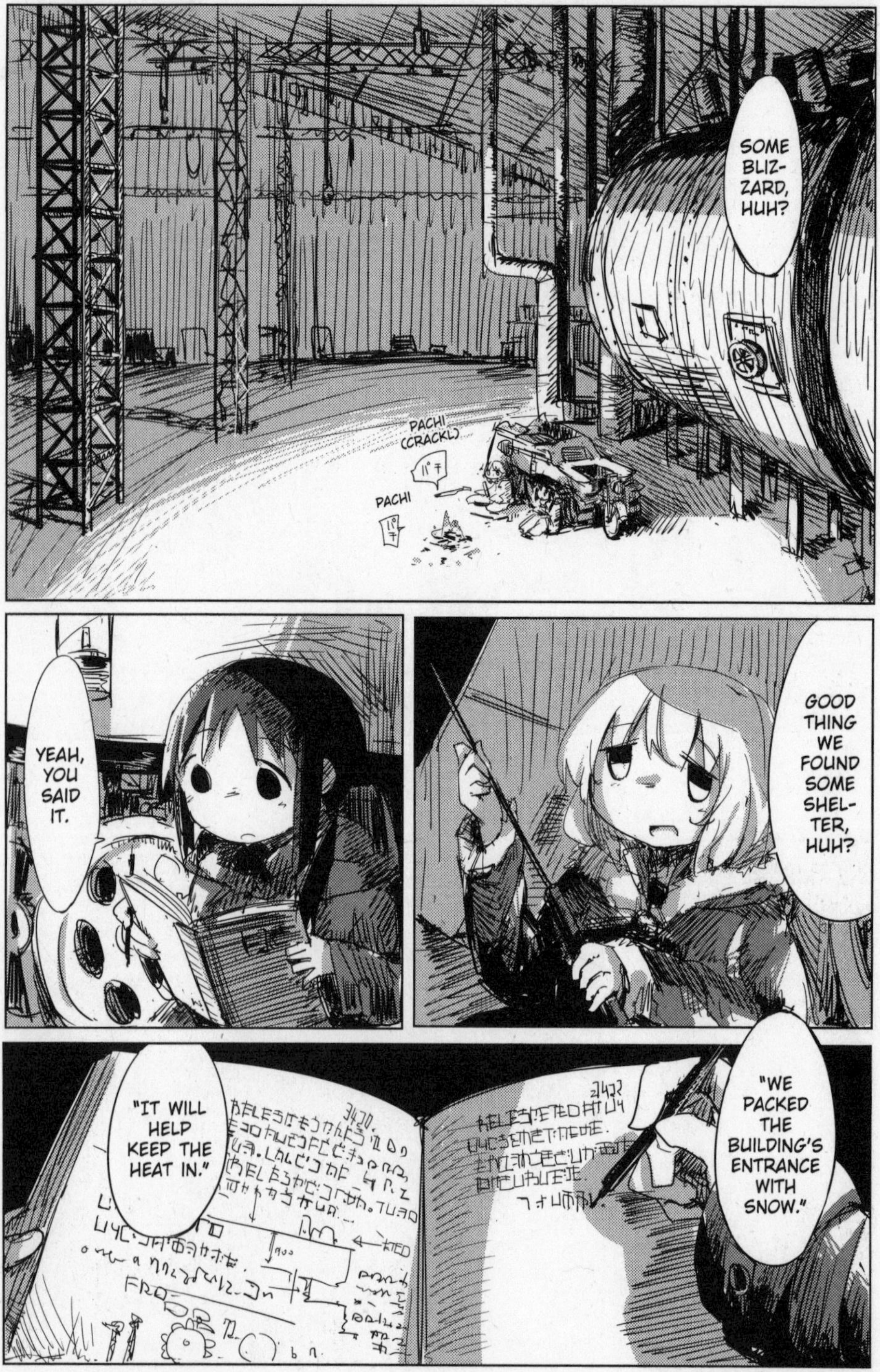
SOME BLIZ-ZARD, HUH?
PACHI (CRACKL)
パチ
PACHI
パチ
GOOD THING WE FOUND SOME SHEL-TER, HUH?
YEAH, YOU SAID IT.
"WE PACKED THE BUILDING'S ENTRANCE WITH SNOW."
"IT WILL HELP KEEP THE HEAT IN."

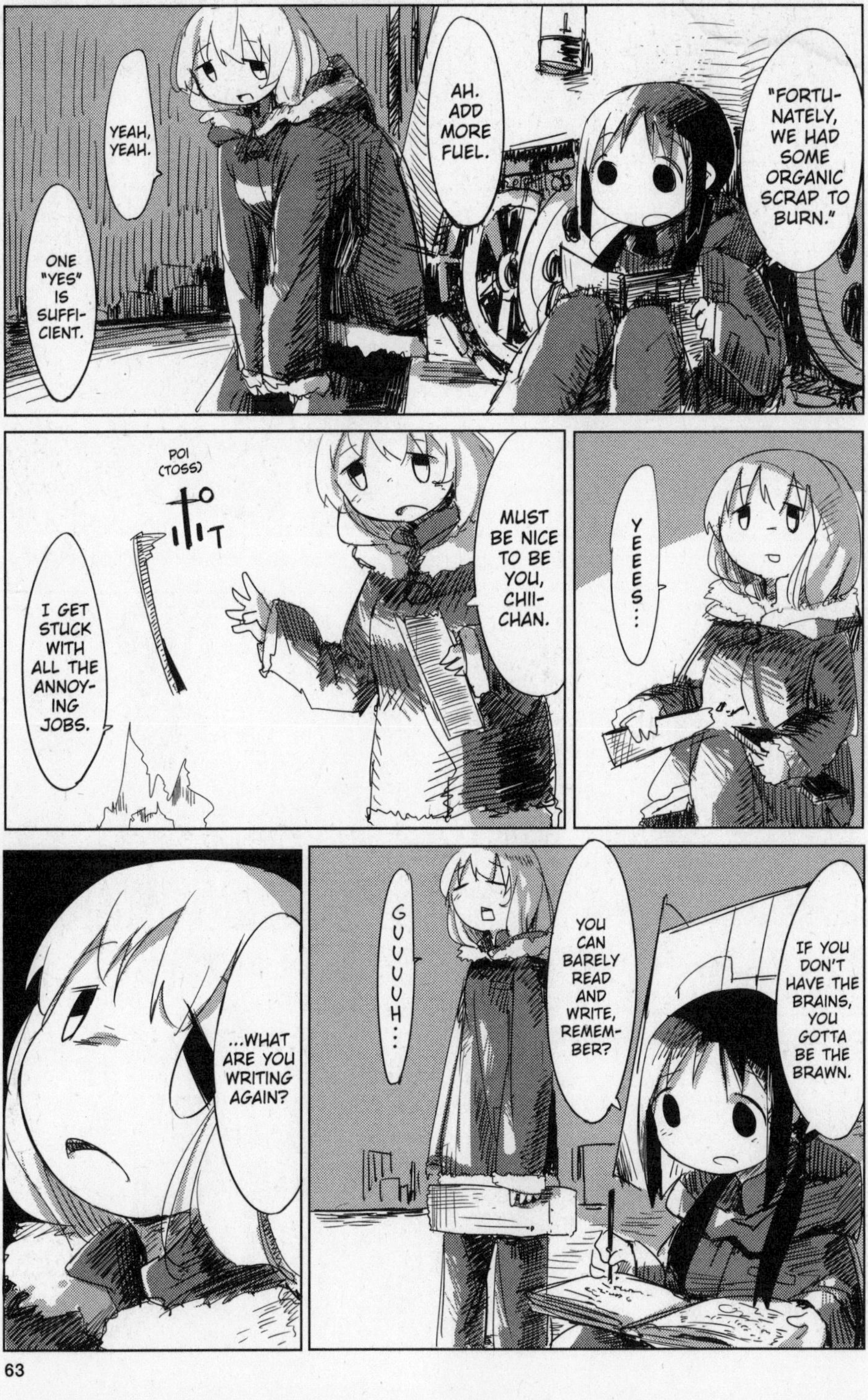
"FORTUNATELY, WE HAD SOME ORGANIC SCRAP TO BURN."
AH. ADD MORE FUEL.
YEAH, YEAH.
ONE "YES" IS SUFFICIENT.
YEEES...
MUST BE NICE TO BE YOU, CHII-CHAN.
POI (TOSS)
I GET STUCK WITH ALL THE ANNOYING JOBS.
IF YOU DON'T HAVE THE BRAINS, YOU GOTTA BE THE BRAWN.
YOU CAN BARELY READ AND WRITE, REMEMBER?
GUUUUH...
...WHAT ARE YOU WRITING AGAIN?

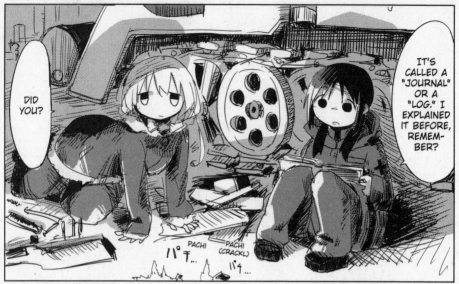

IT'S CALLED A "JOURNAL" OR A "LOG." I EXPLAINED IT BEFORE, REMEMBER?
DID YOU?
PACHI (CRACKL)
パチ...
PACHI
パチ...
IT'S PEOPLE LIKE YOU...
...WHO NEED RECORDS LIKE THIS THE MOST.
MEMORIES FADE.
THAT'S WHY WE RECORD THEM.

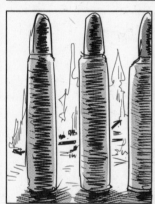

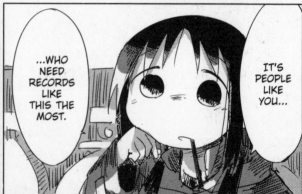

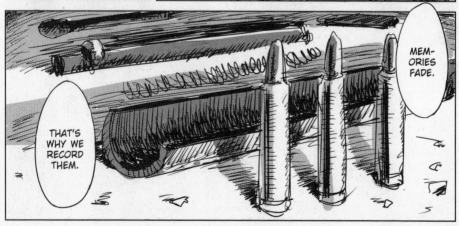

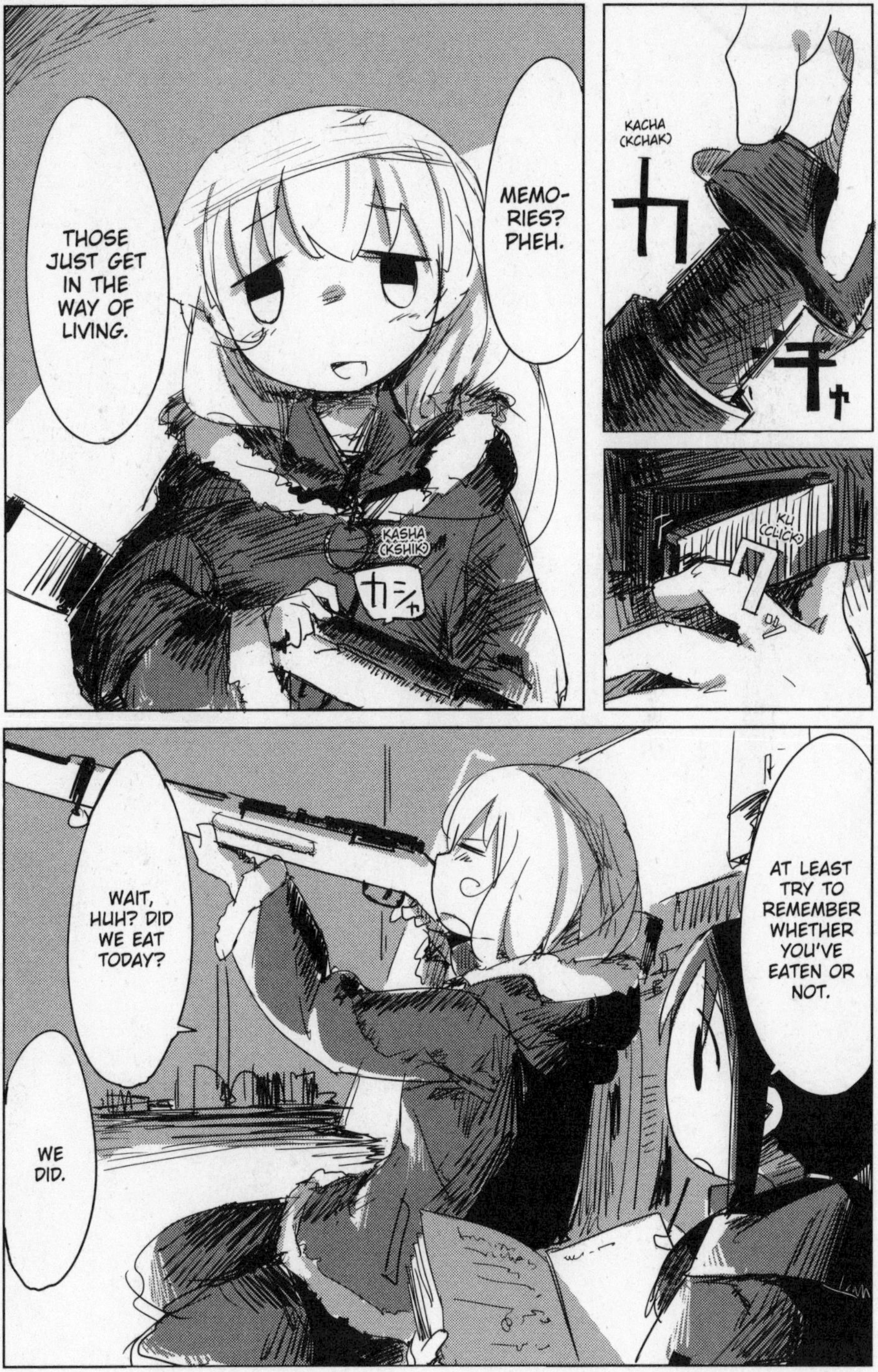
KACHA (KCHAK)
KU (CLICK)
MEMORIES? PHEH.
THOSE JUST GET IN THE WAY OF LIVING.
KASHA (KSHIK)
AT LEAST TRY TO REMEMBER WHETHER YOU'VE EATEN OR NOT.
WAIT, HUH? DID WE EAT TODAY?
WE DID.

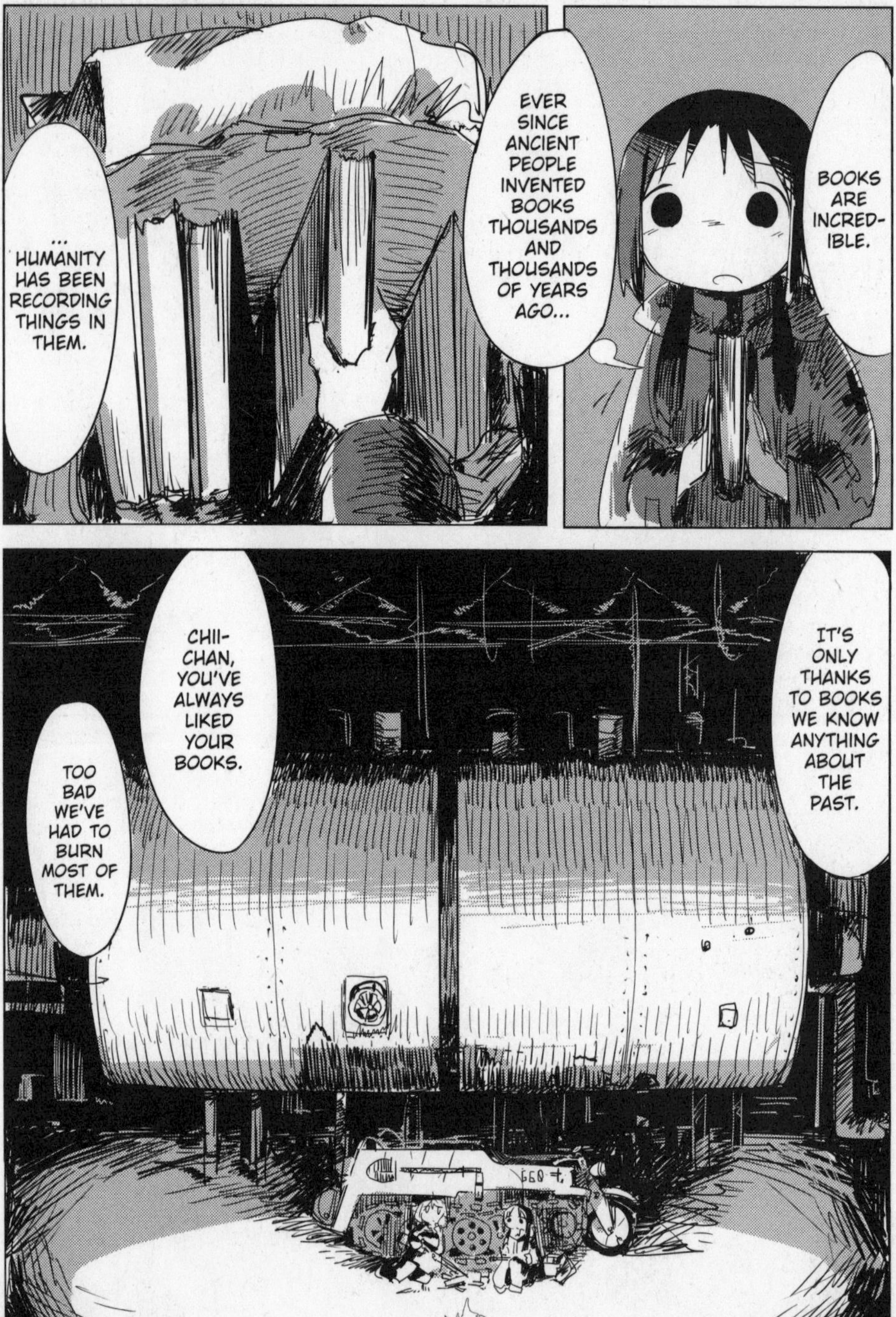
BOOKS ARE INCRED-IBLE.
EVER SINCE ANCIENT PEOPLE INVENTED BOOKS THOUSANDS AND THOUSANDS OF YEARS AGO...
... HUMANITY HAS BEEN RECORDING THINGS IN THEM.
IT'S ONLY THANKS TO BOOKS WE KNOW ANYTHING ABOUT THE PAST.
CHII-CHAN, YOU'VE ALWAYS LIKED YOUR BOOKS.
TOO BAD WE'VE HAD TO BURN MOST OF THEM.

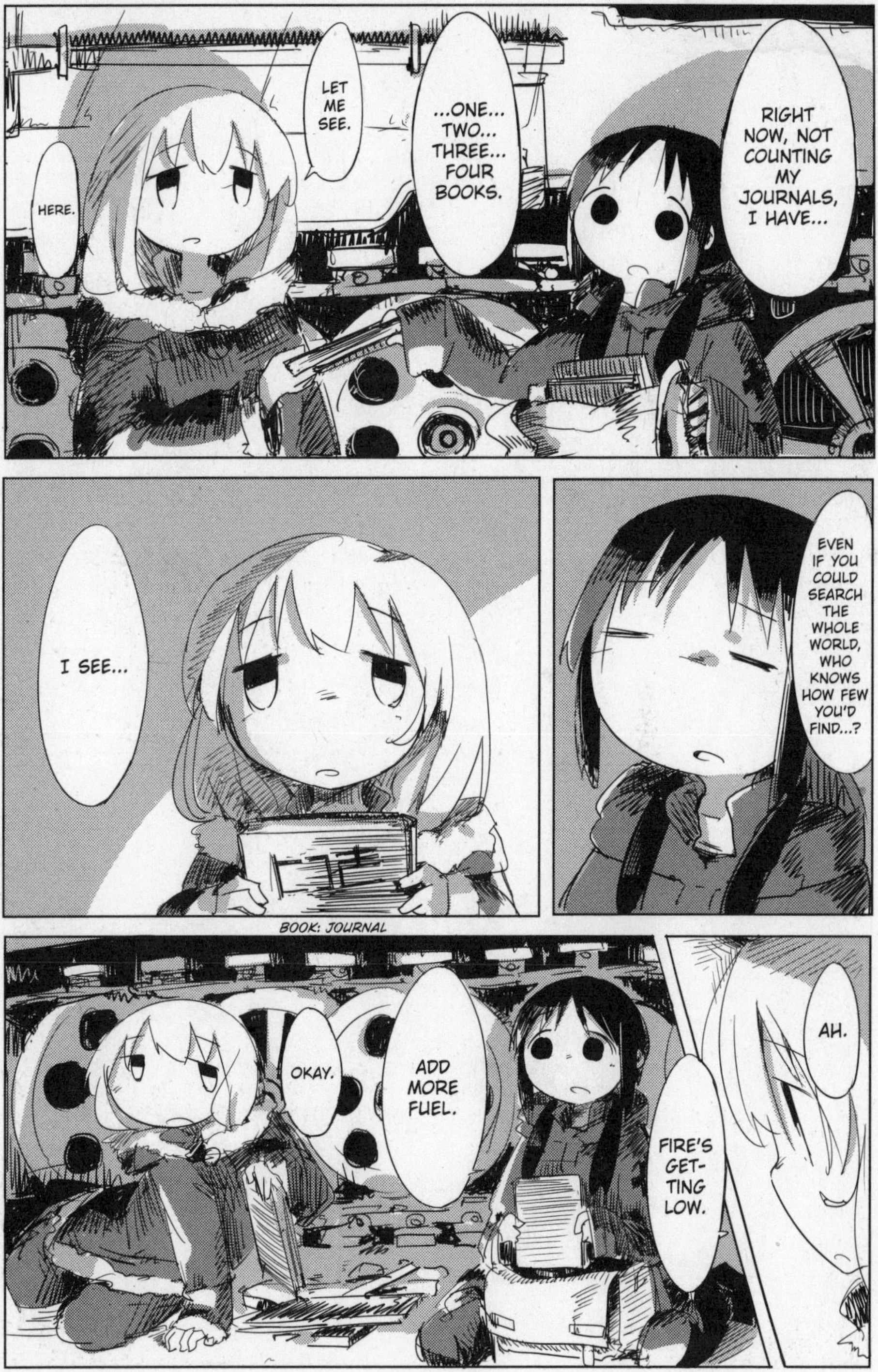
RIGHT NOW, NOT COUNTING MY JOURNALS, I HAVE...
...ONE... TWO... THREE... FOUR BOOKS.
LET ME SEE.
HERE.
EVEN IF YOU COULD SEARCH THE WHOLE WORLD, WHO KNOWS HOW FEW YOU'D FIND...?
I SEE...
BOOK: JOURNAL
AH.
FIRE'S GET-TING LOW.
ADD MORE FUEL.
OKAY.

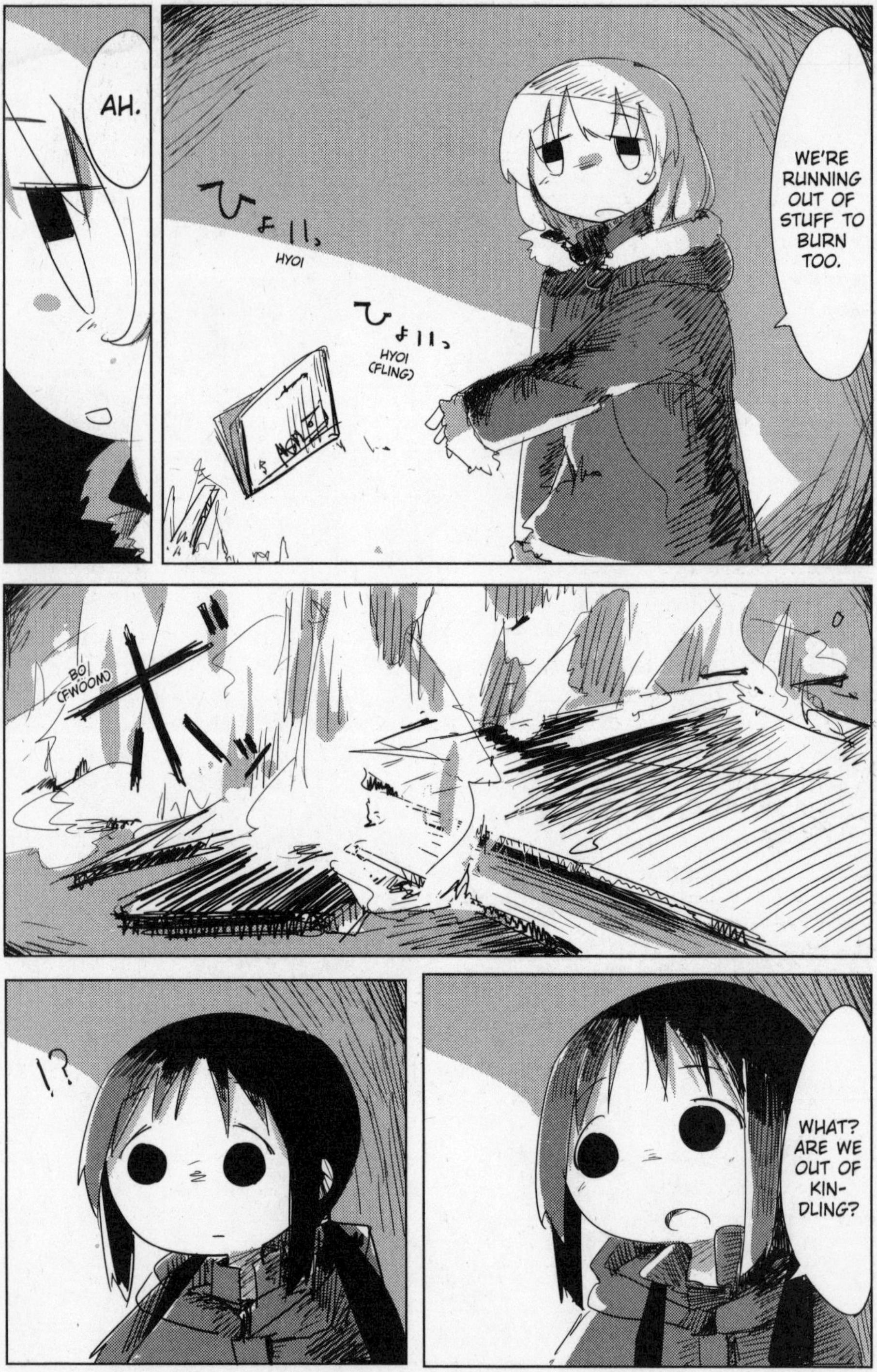
WE'RE RUNNING OUT OF STUFF TO BURN TOO.
HYOI
HYOI (FLING)
AH.
BO (FWOOM)
WHAT? ARE WE OUT OF KIN-DLING?
!?

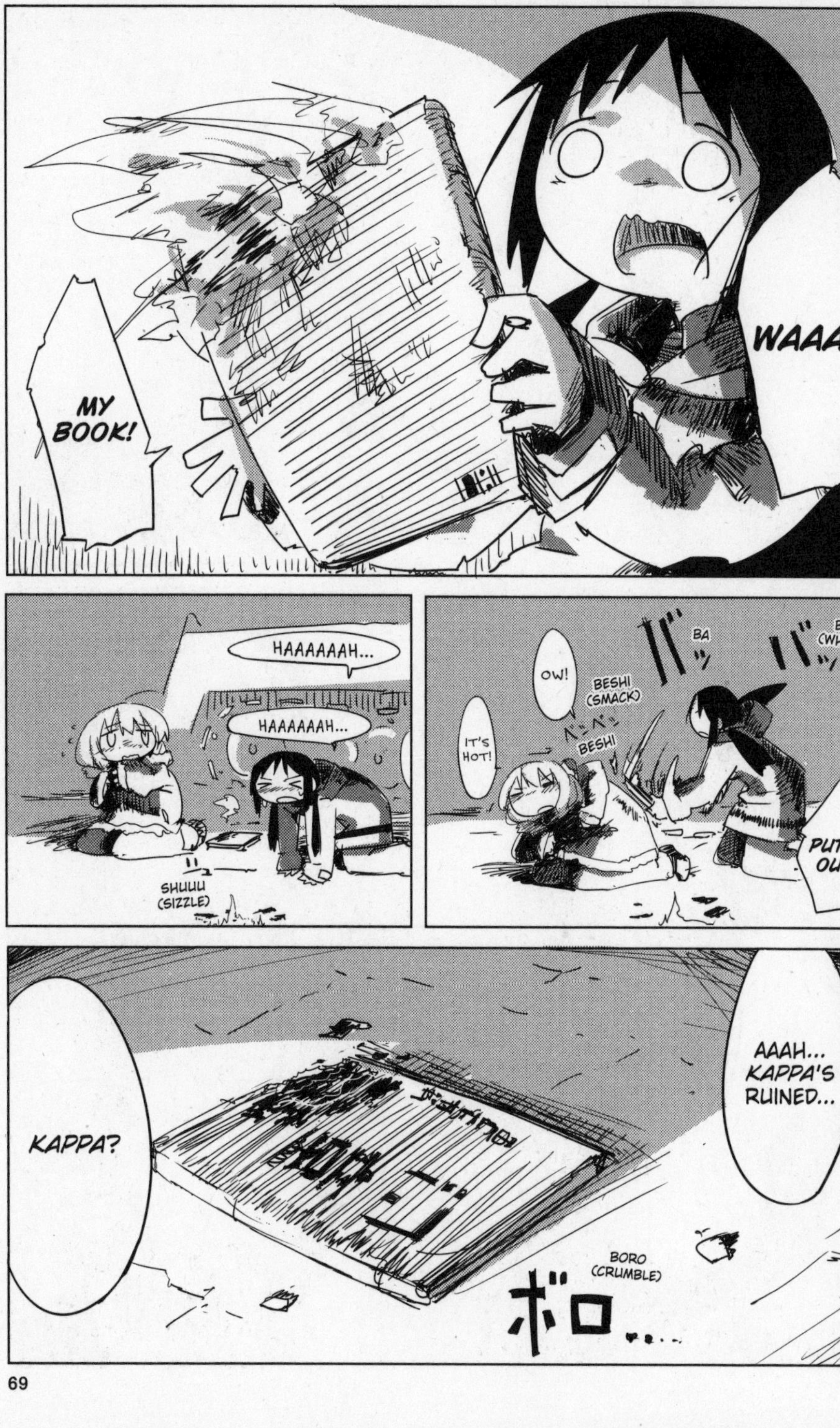
WAAAH!
MY BOOK!
BA (WHAP)
BA
OW!
BESHI (SMACK)
IT'S HOT!
BESHI
PUT IT OUT!
HAAAAAAH...
HAAAAAAH...
SHUUU (SIZZLE)
AAAH... KAPPA'S RUINED...
KAPPA?
BORO (CRUMBLE)
ボロ...

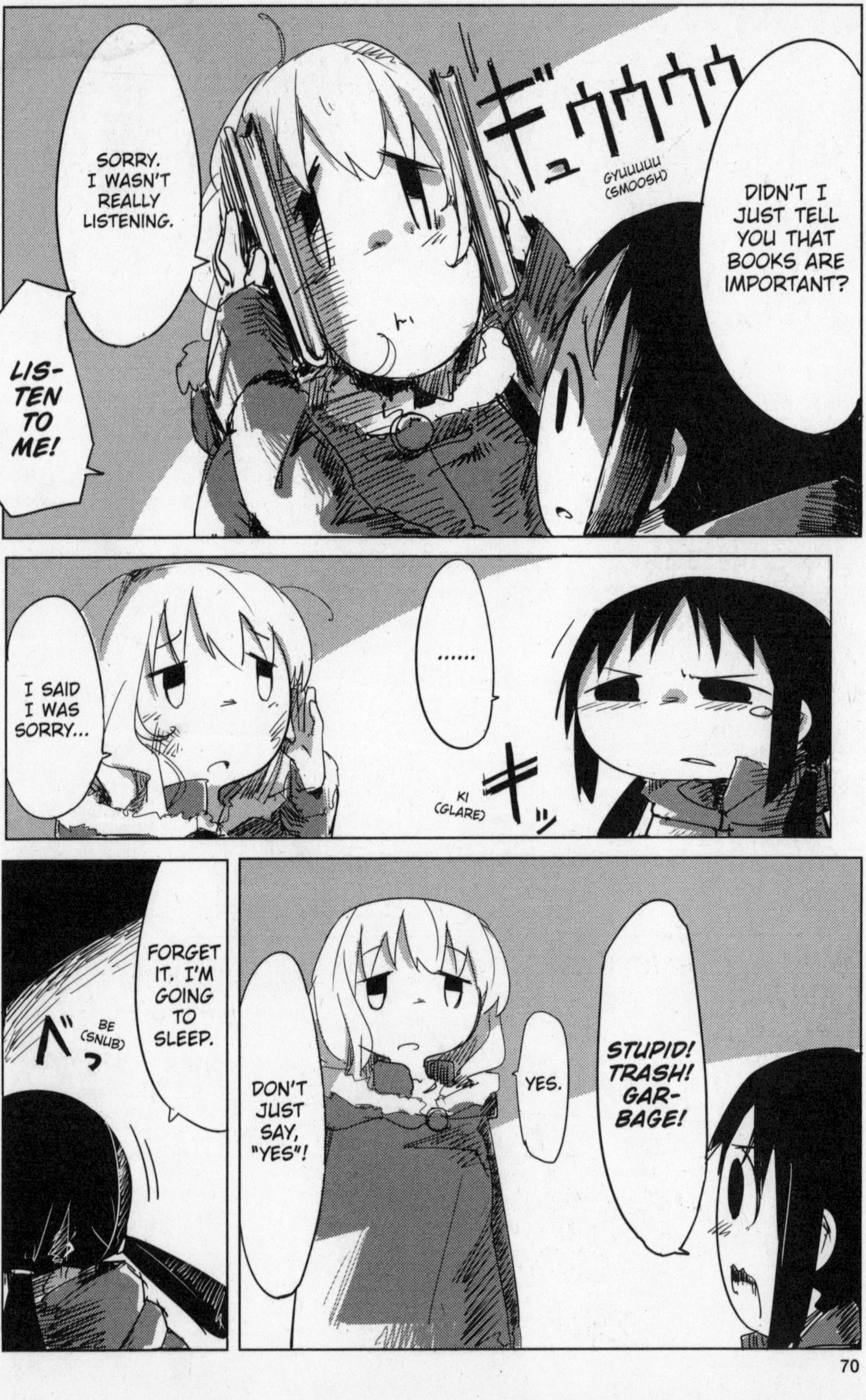
DIDN'T I JUST TELL YOU THAT BOOKS ARE IMPORTANT?
ギュウウウウ
GYUUUUU (SMOOSH)
SORRY. I WASN'T REALLY LISTENING.
LIS-TEN TO ME!
......
キッ
KI (GLARE)
I SAID I WAS SORRY...
STUPID! TRASH! GAR-BAGE!
YES.
DON'T JUST SAY, "YES"!
FORGET IT. I'M GOING TO SLEEP.
べっ
BE (SNUB)

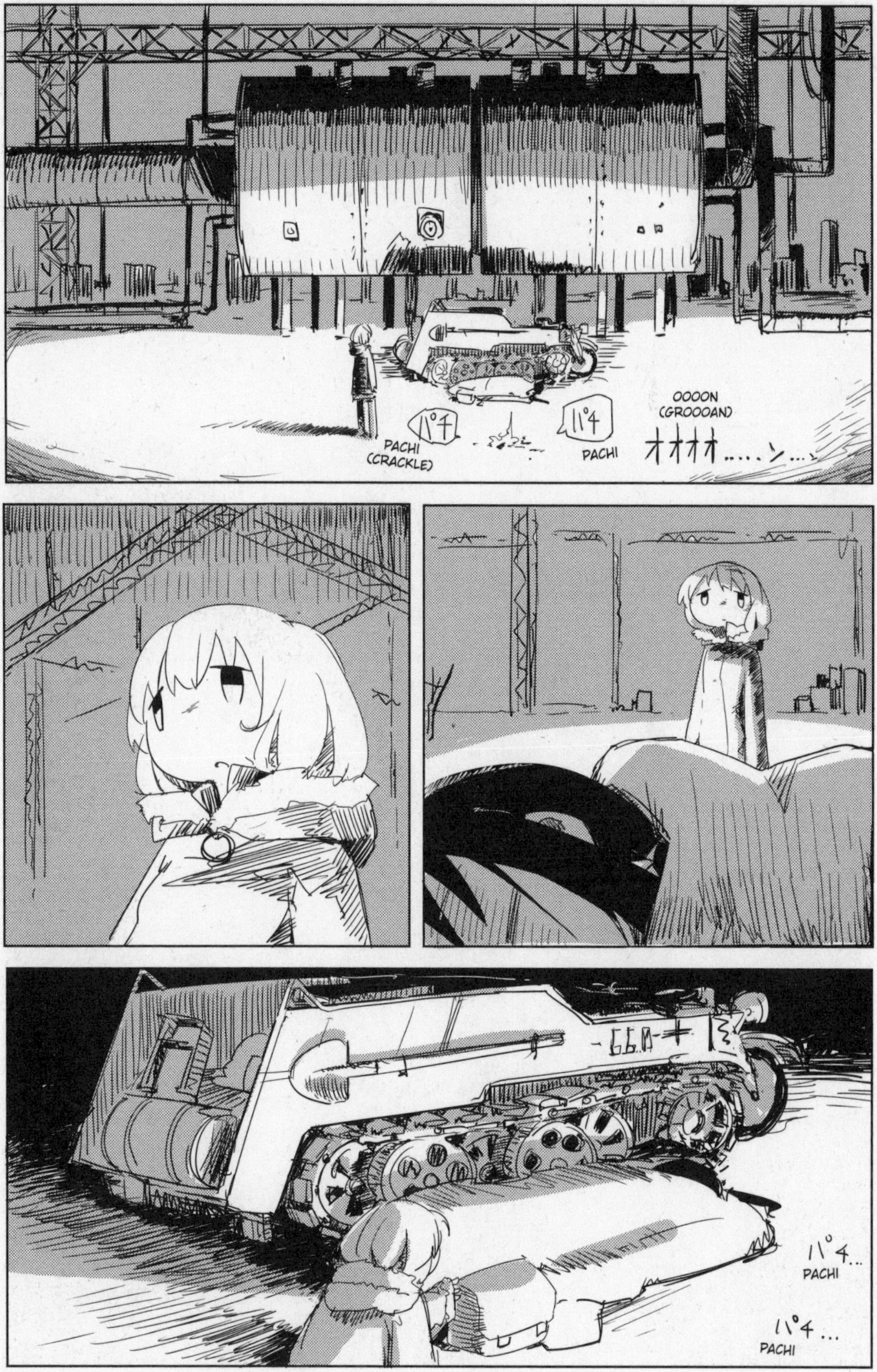

OOOON (GROOOAN)
オオオオ……ン……
パチ
PACHI
パチ
PACHI (CRACKLE)
パチ…
PACHI
パチ…
PACHI

JOURNAL: CHITO

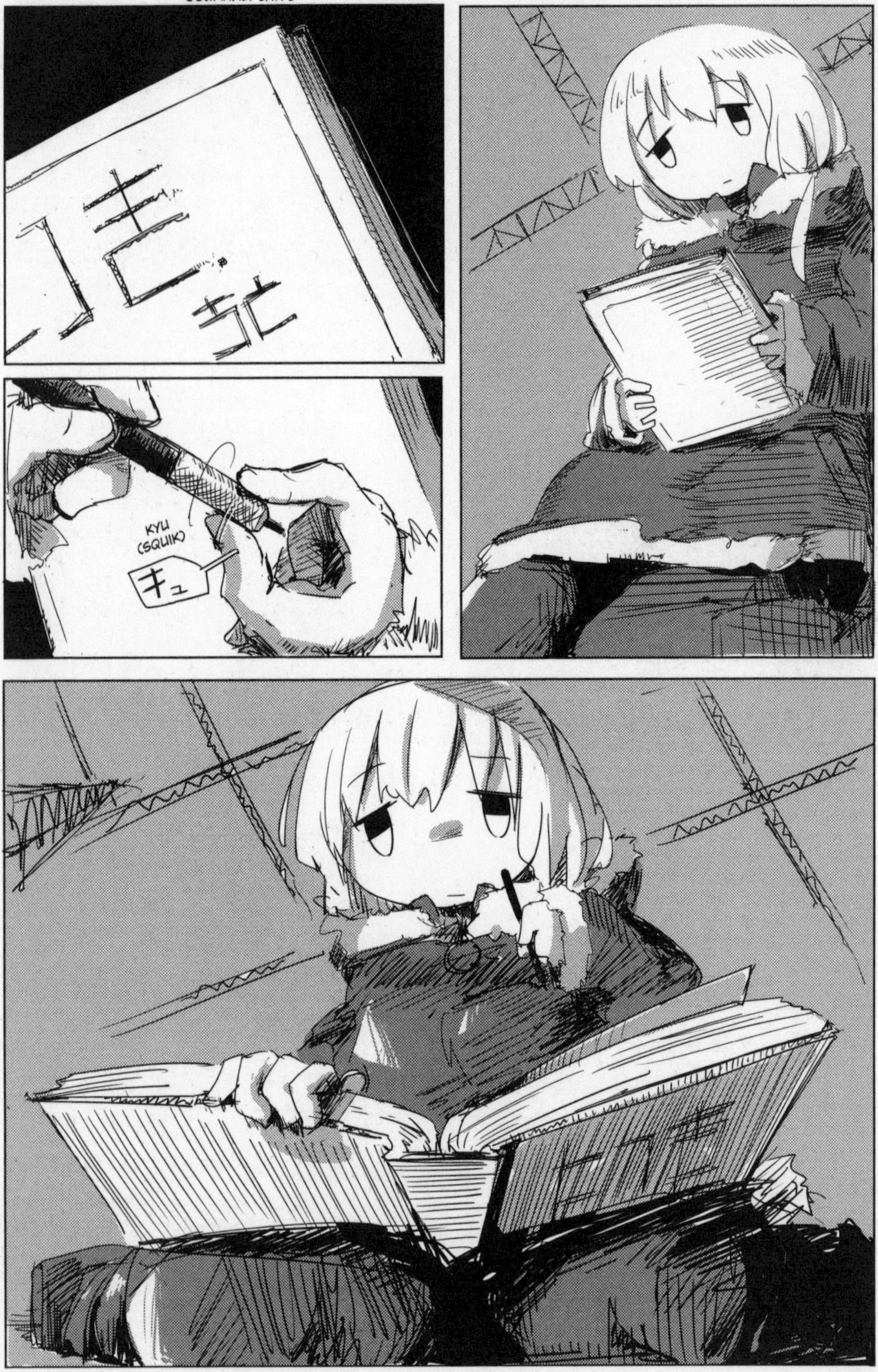
KYU (SQUIK)
キュ

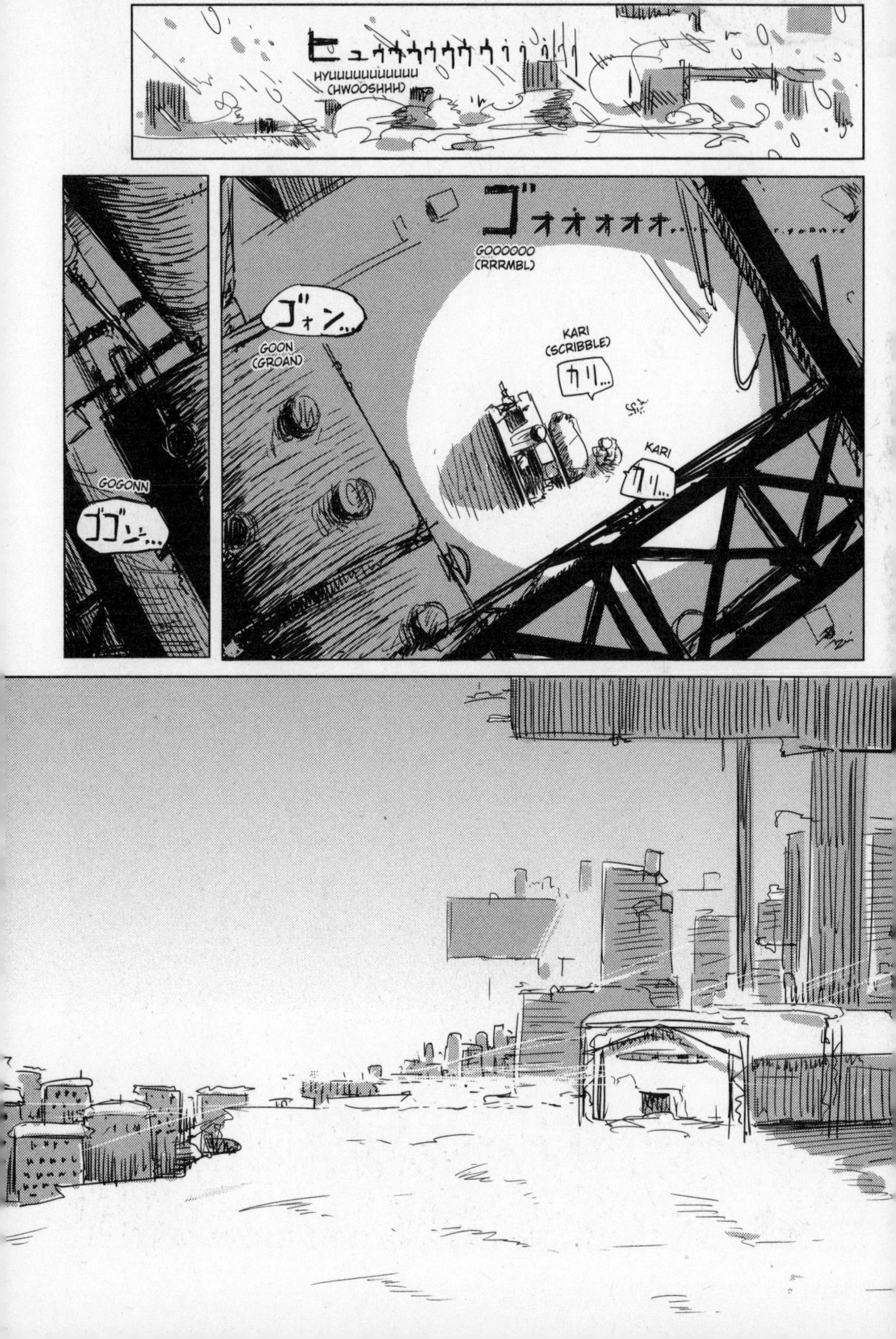
ヒュウウウウウウウウゥゥゥ
HYUUUUUUUUUUUU (HWOOSHHH)
ゴォォォォォ……
GOOOOOO (RRRMBL)
ゴォン…
GOON (GROAN)
KARI (SCRIBBLE)
カリ…
KARI
カリ…
GOGONN
ゴゴン…

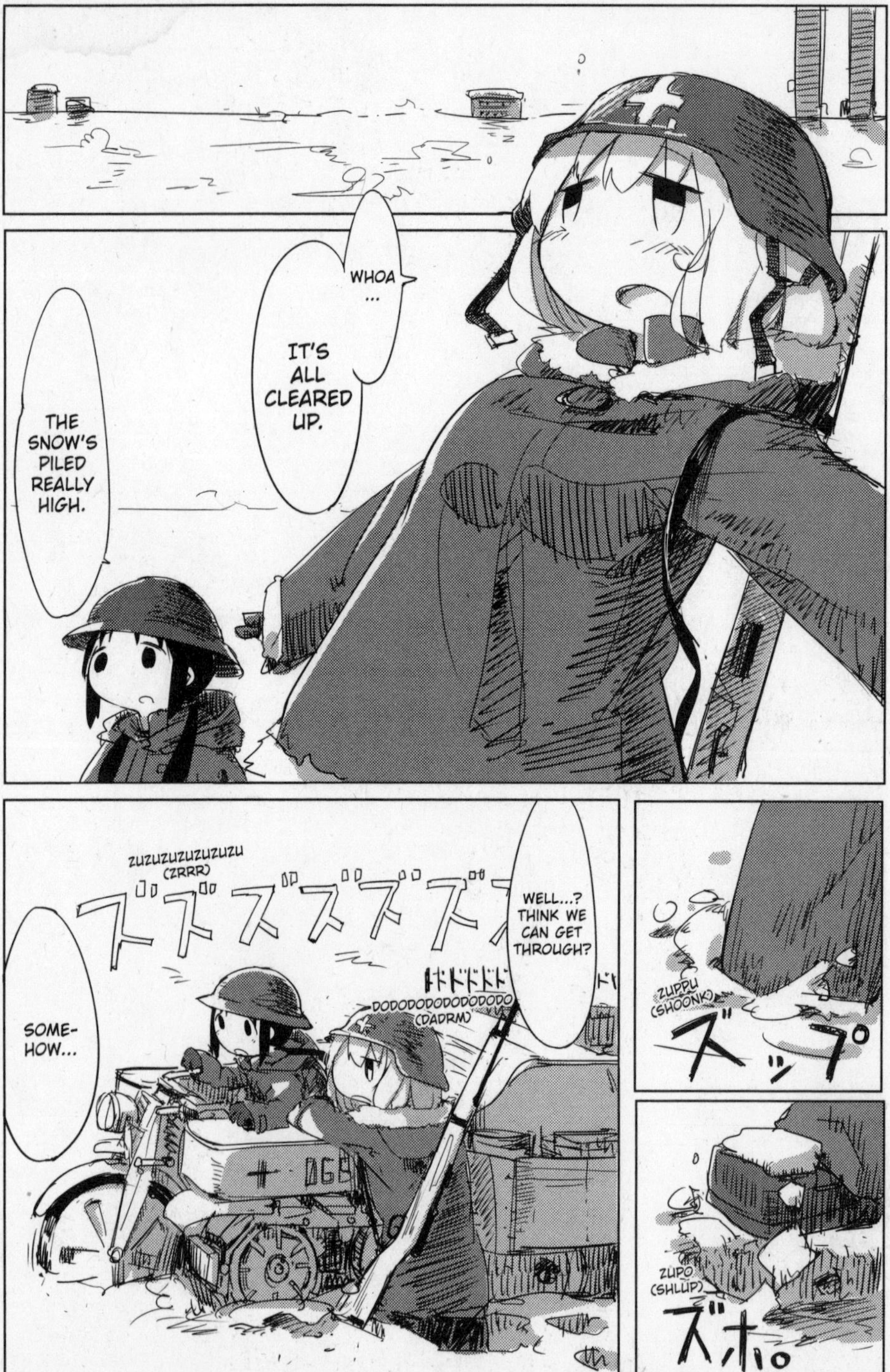
WHOA...
IT'S ALL CLEARED UP.
THE SNOW'S PILED REALLY HIGH.
ZUPPU (SHOONK)
ズップ
ZUPO (SHLUP)
ズポ
WELL...? THINK WE CAN GET THROUGH?
DODODODODODODODO (DADRM)
ZUZUZUZUZUZUZU (ZRRR)
ズズズズズズズ
SOME-HOW...

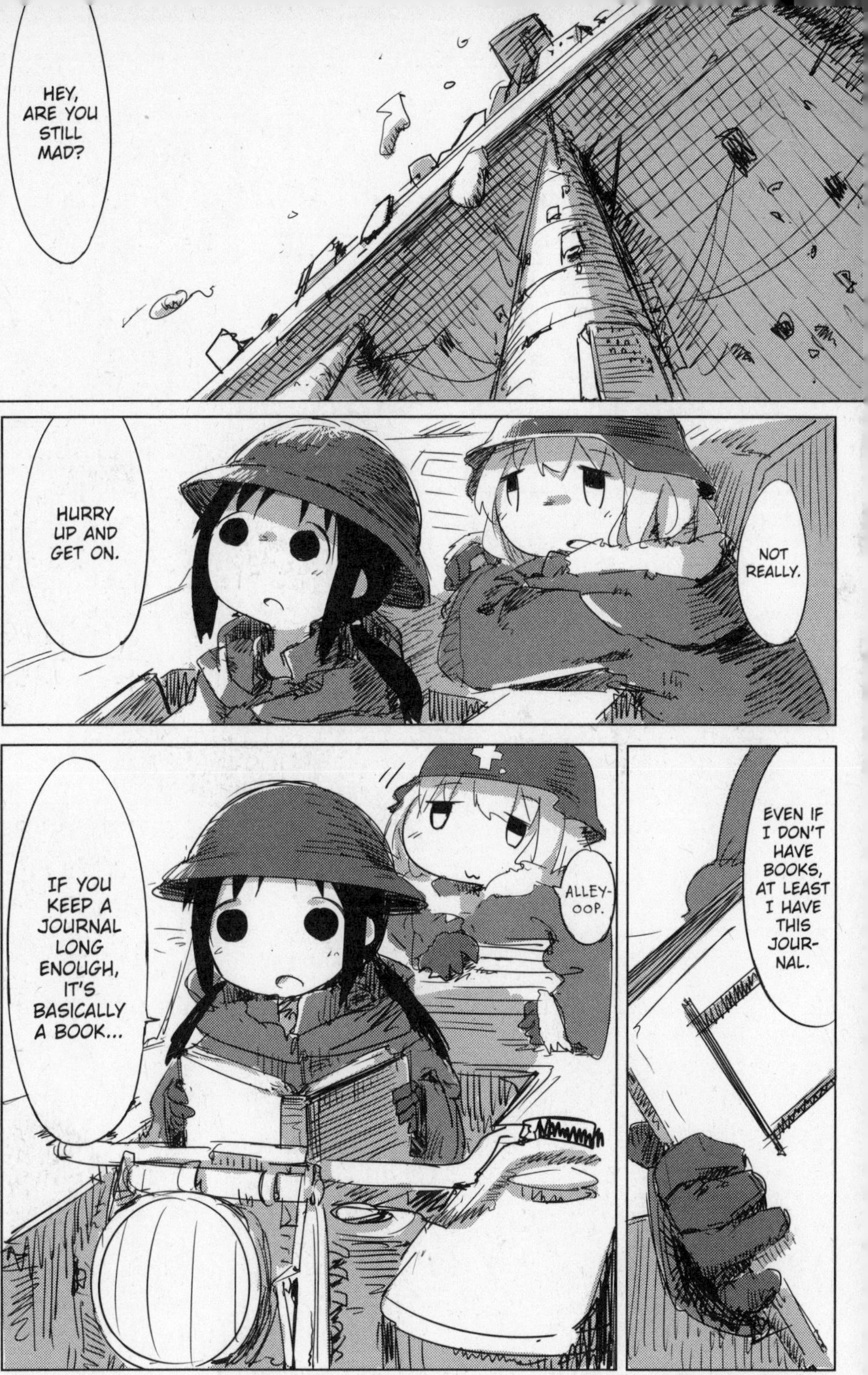
HEY, ARE YOU STILL MAD?
NOT REALLY.
HURRY UP AND GET ON.
EVEN IF I DON'T HAVE BOOKS, AT LEAST I HAVE THIS JOUR-NAL.
ALLEY-OOP.
IF YOU KEEP A JOURNAL LONG ENOUGH, IT'S BASICALLY A BOOK...

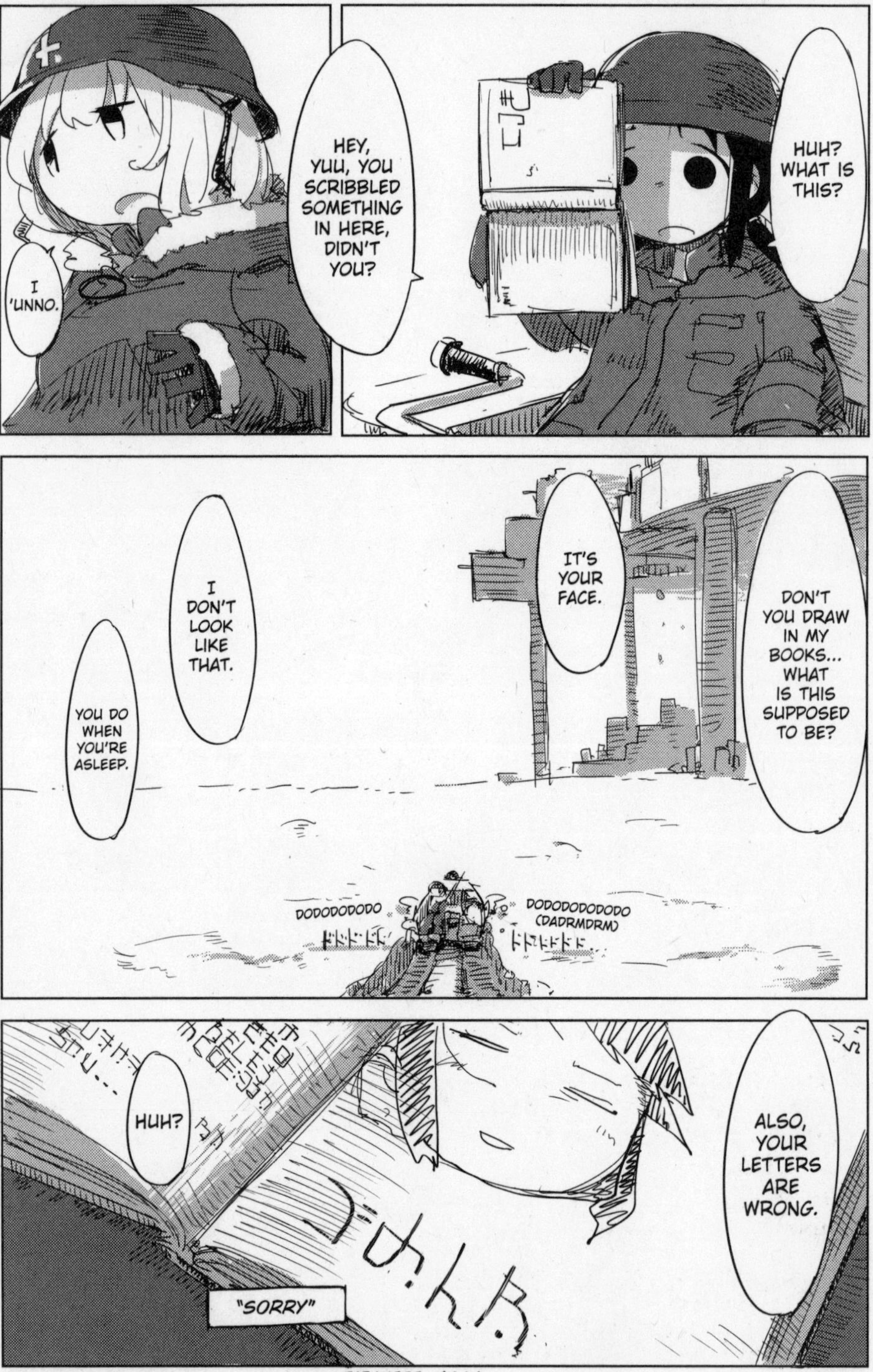
HUH? WHAT IS THIS?
HEY, YUU, YOU SCRIBBLED SOMETHING IN HERE, DIDN'T YOU?
I 'UNNO.
DON'T YOU DRAW IN MY BOOKS... WHAT IS THIS SUPPOSED TO BE?
IT'S YOUR FACE.
I DON'T LOOK LIKE THAT.
YOU DO WHEN YOU'RE ASLEEP.
DODODODODODO (DADRMDRM)
DODODODODO
ALSO, YOUR LETTERS ARE WRONG.
HUH?
"SORRY"

JAPANESE: ごめんね

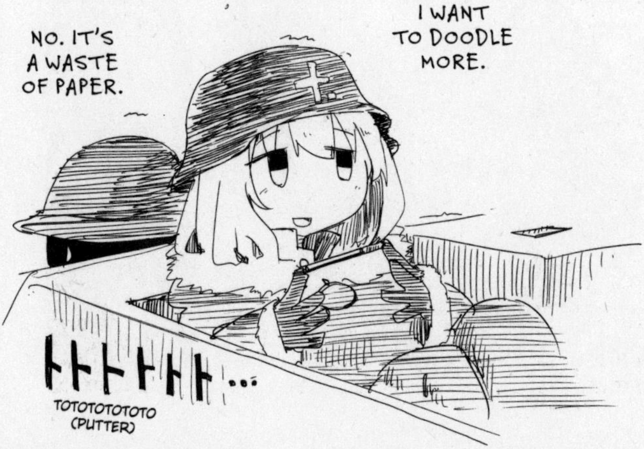
I WANT TO DOODLE MORE.
NO. IT'S A WASTE OF PAPER.
トトトトトト…
TOTOTOTOTOTO (PUTTER)

GIRLS' LAST TOUR

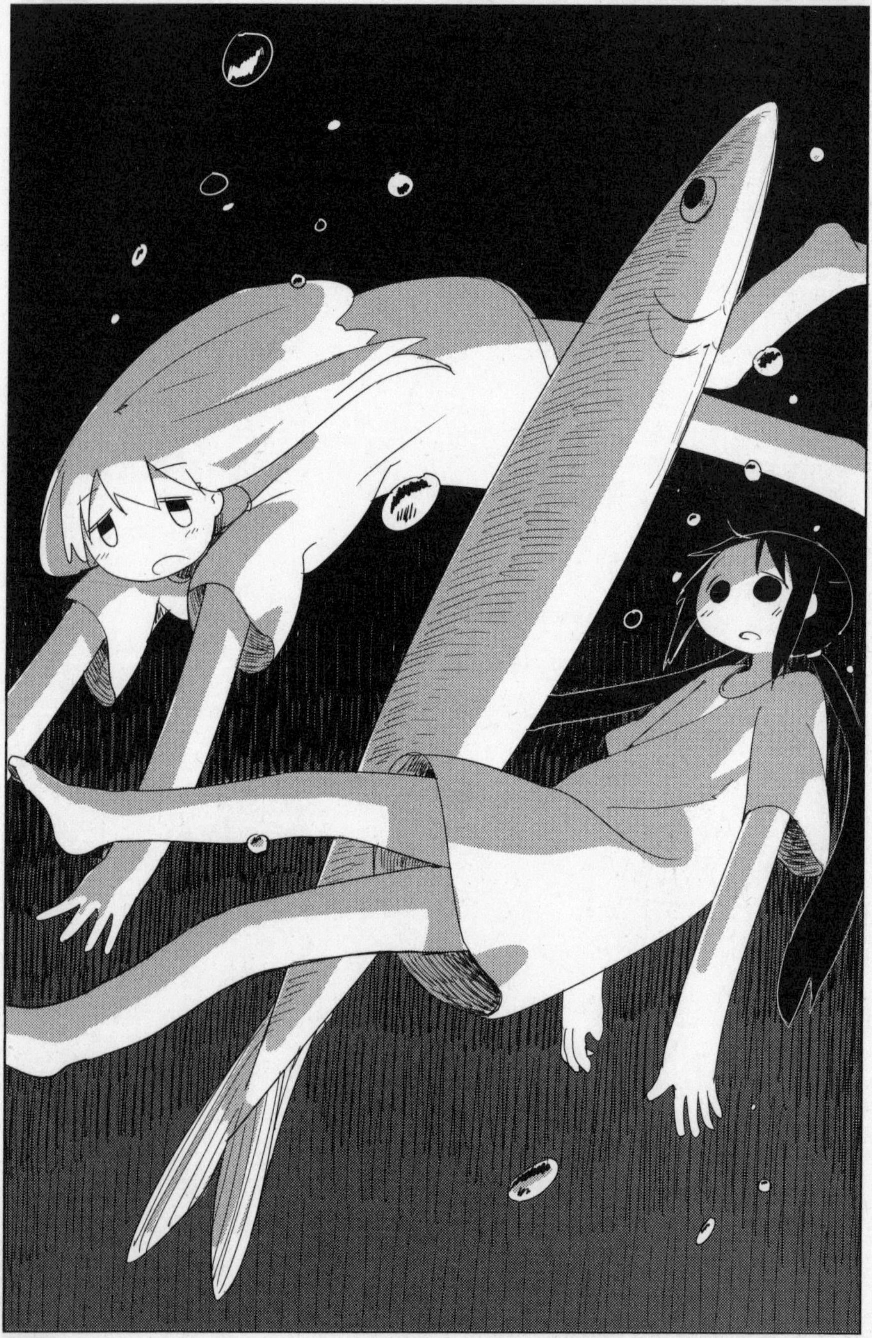

05

05 LAUNDRY

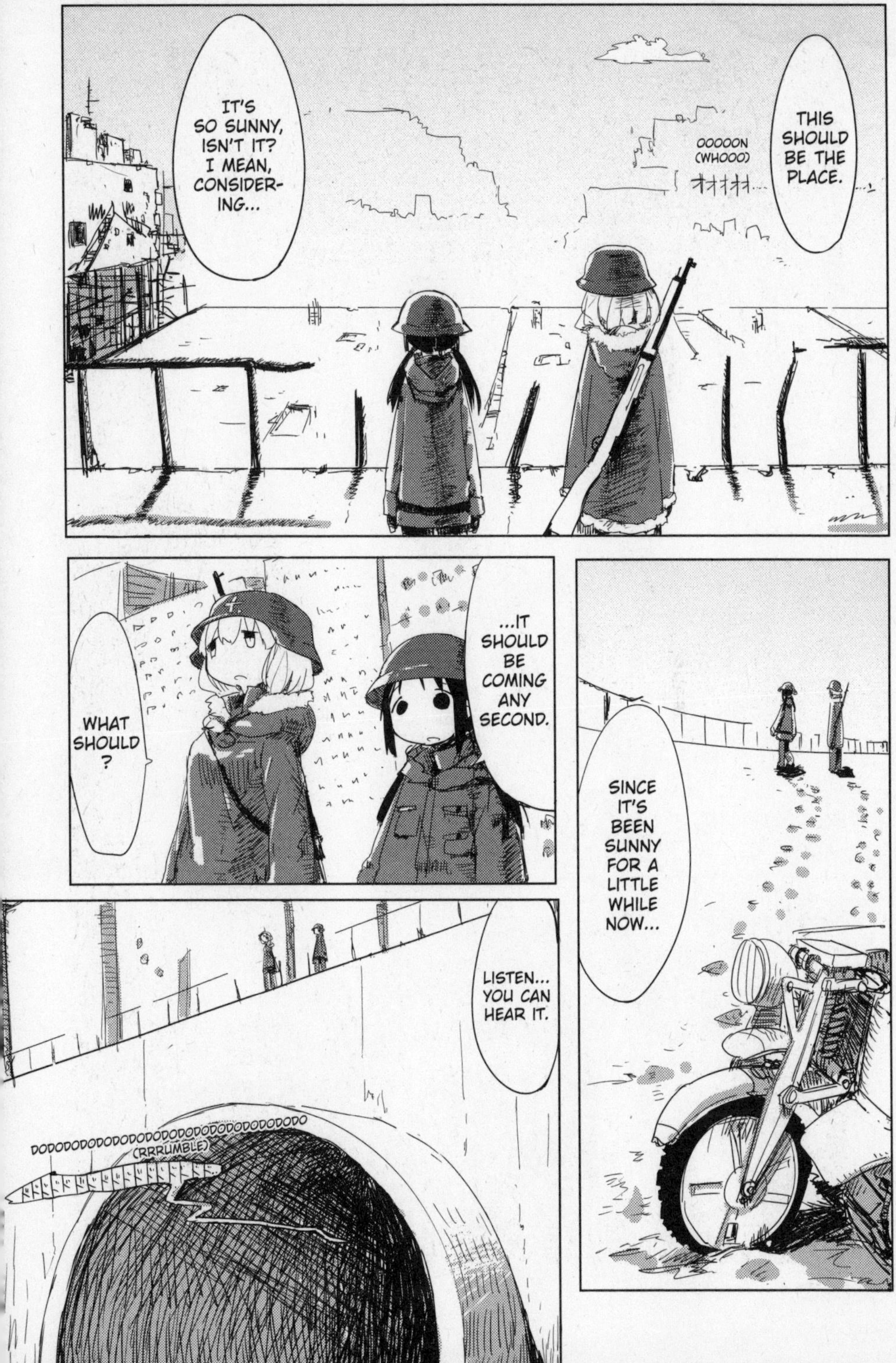
THIS SHOULD BE THE PLACE.
OOOOON (WHOOO)
オオオオオ…
IT'S SO SUNNY, ISN'T IT? I MEAN, CONSIDERING...
SINCE IT'S BEEN SUNNY FOR A LITTLE WHILE NOW...
...IT SHOULD BE COMING ANY SECOND.
WHAT SHOULD?
LISTEN... YOU CAN HEAR IT.
DODODODODODODODODODODODODODODODODODODODO
(RRRUMBLE)

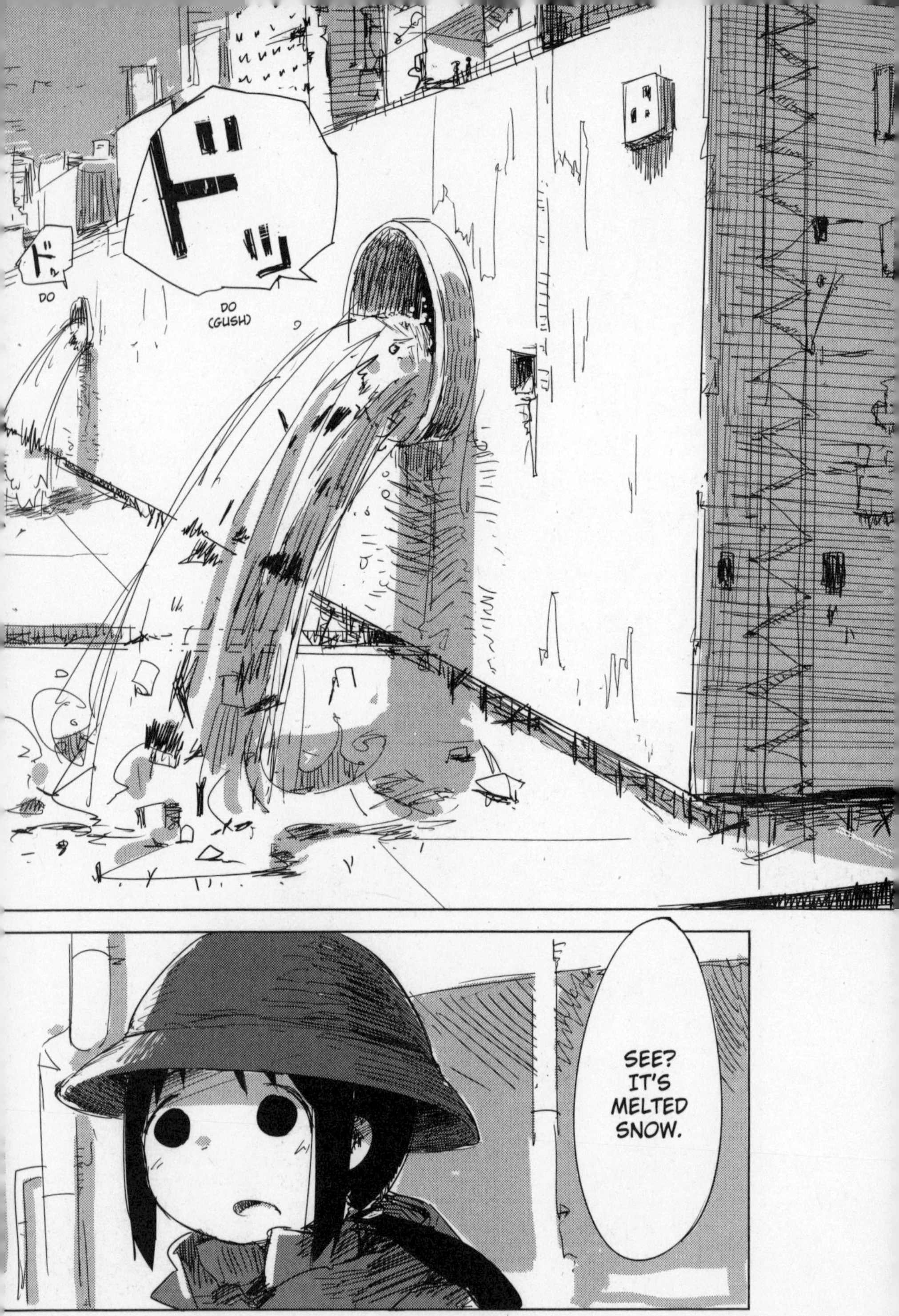
DO (GUSH)
DO
SEE? IT'S MELTED SNOW.

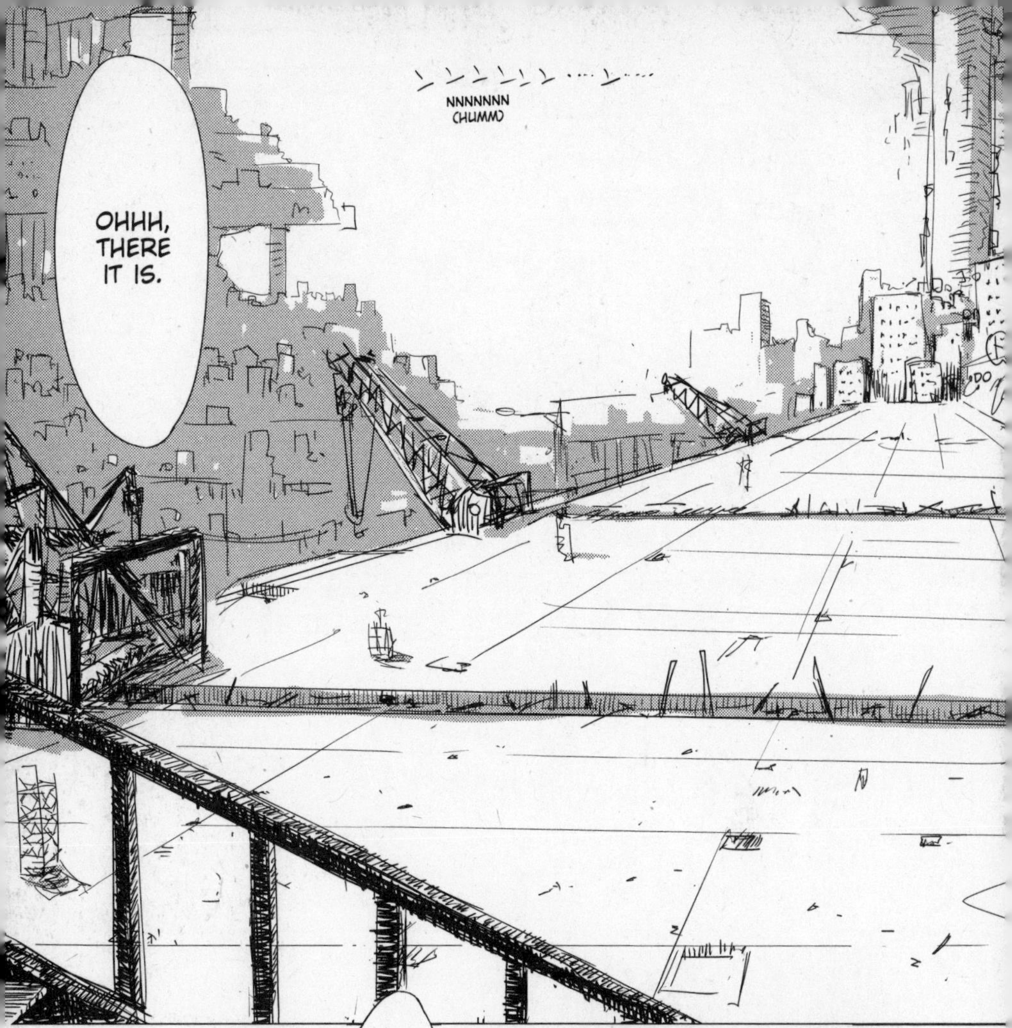
ンンンンンン……ン……
NNNNNNN
(HUMM)
OHHH, THERE IT IS.
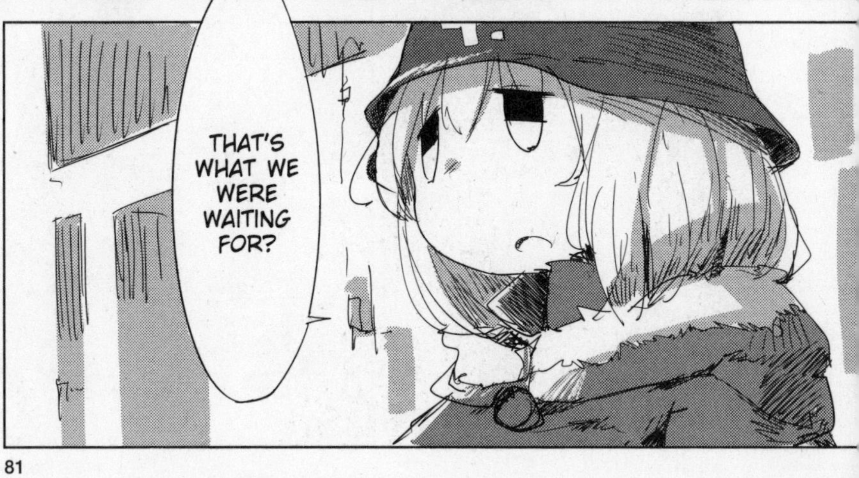
THAT'S WHAT WE WERE WAITING FOR?

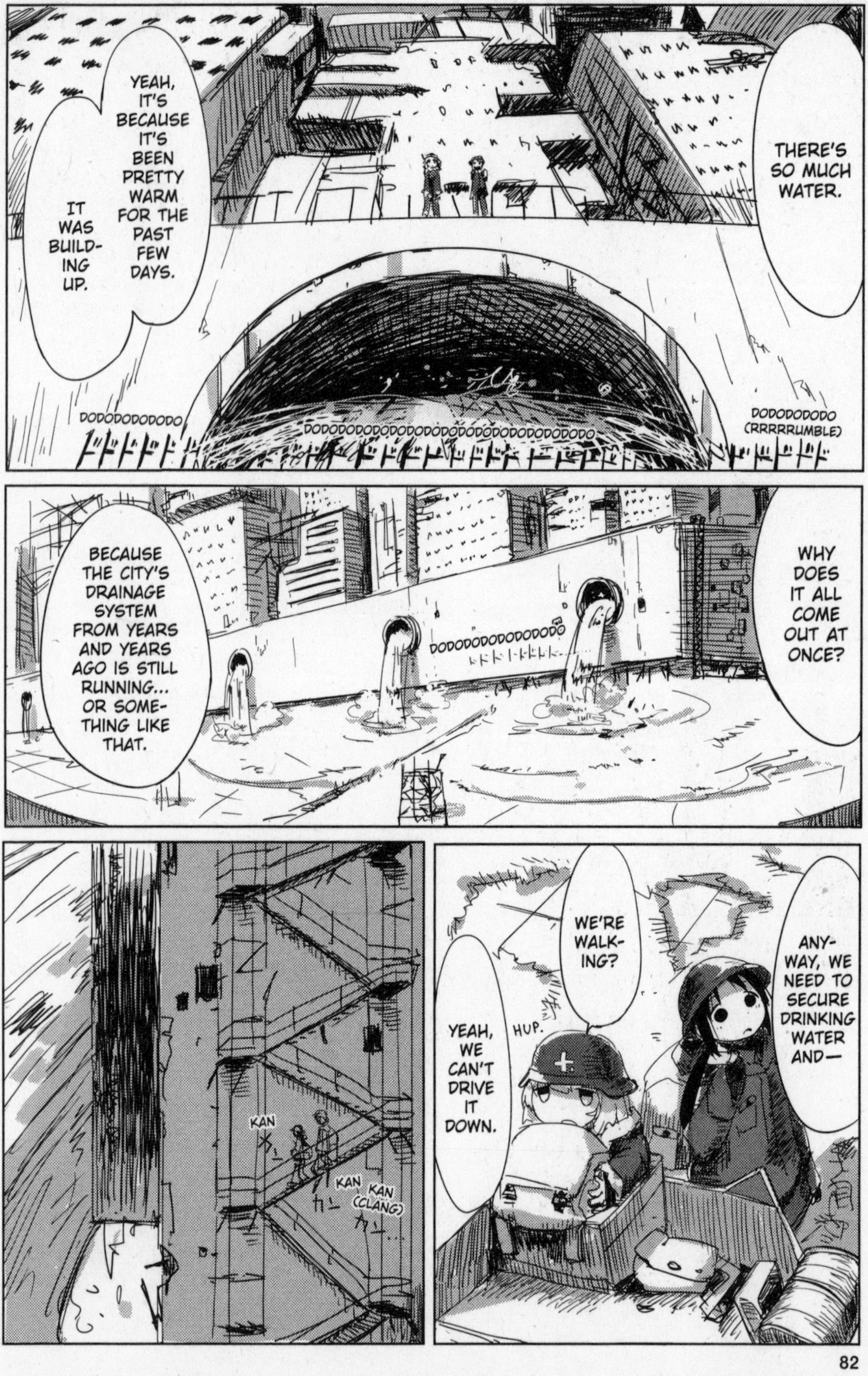
THERE'S SO MUCH WATER.
YEAH, IT'S BECAUSE IT'S BEEN PRETTY WARM FOR THE PAST FEW DAYS.
IT WAS BUILDING-ING UP.
DODODODODO (RRRRRUMBLE)
DODODODODODODODODODODODODODODODODODODODO
DODODODODODO
WHY DOES IT ALL COME OUT AT ONCE?
BECAUSE THE CITY'S DRAINAGE SYSTEM FROM YEARS AND YEARS AGO IS STILL RUNNING... OR SOME-THING LIKE THAT.
DODODODODODODODO
ANY-WAY, WE NEED TO SECURE DRINKING WATER AND—
WE'RE WALK-ING?
HUP.
YEAH, WE CAN'T DRIVE IT DOWN.
KAN
KAN KAN (CLANG)

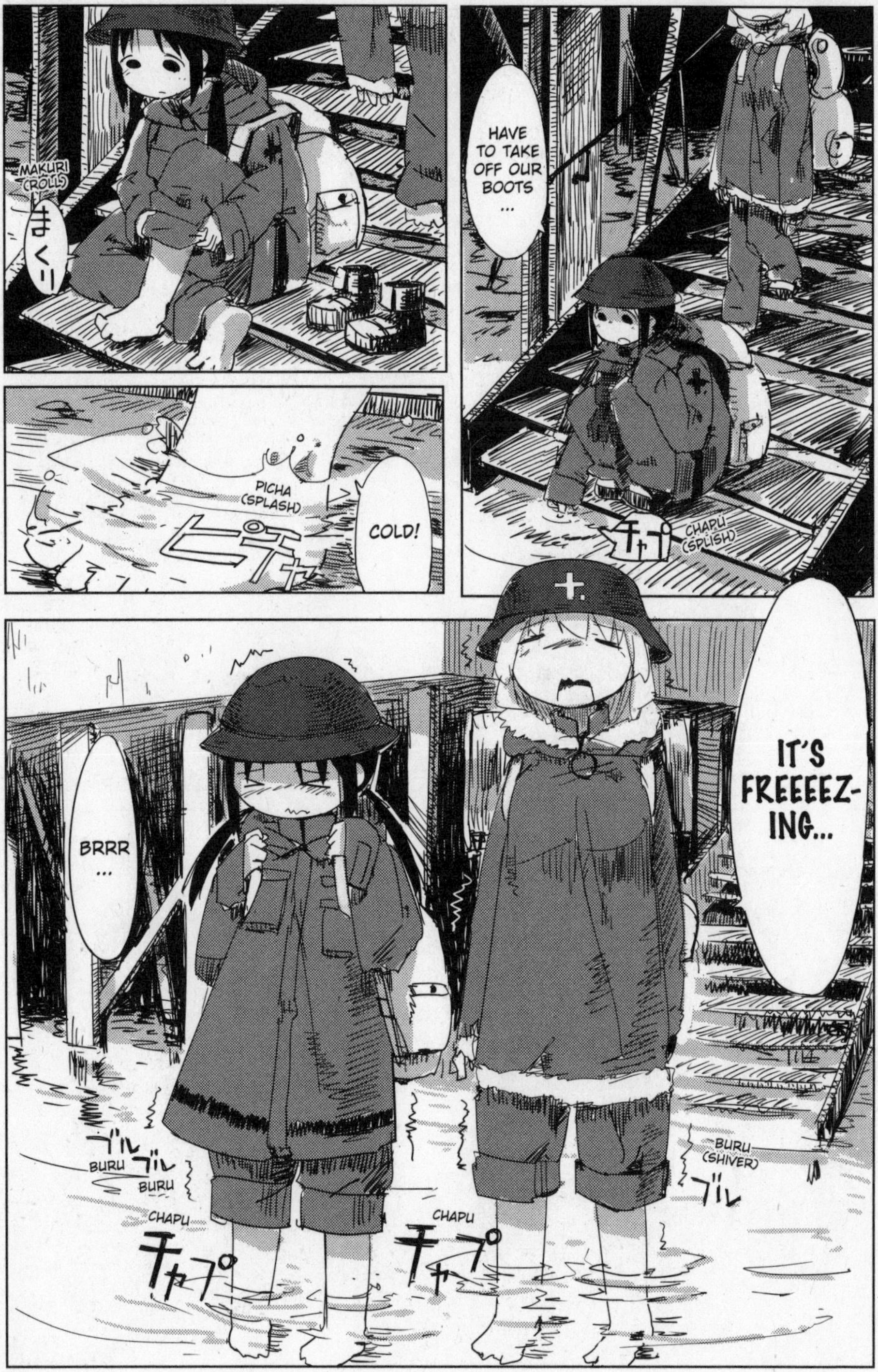
HAVE TO TAKE OFF OUR BOOTS ...
チャプ
CHAPU (SPLISH)
まくり
MAKURI (ROLL)
COLD!
ピチャ
PICHA (SPLASH)
IT'S FREEEEZ-ING...
BURU (SHIVER)
ブル
CHAPU
チャプ
BRRR ...
ブル
BURU
ブル
BURU
CHAPU
チャプ

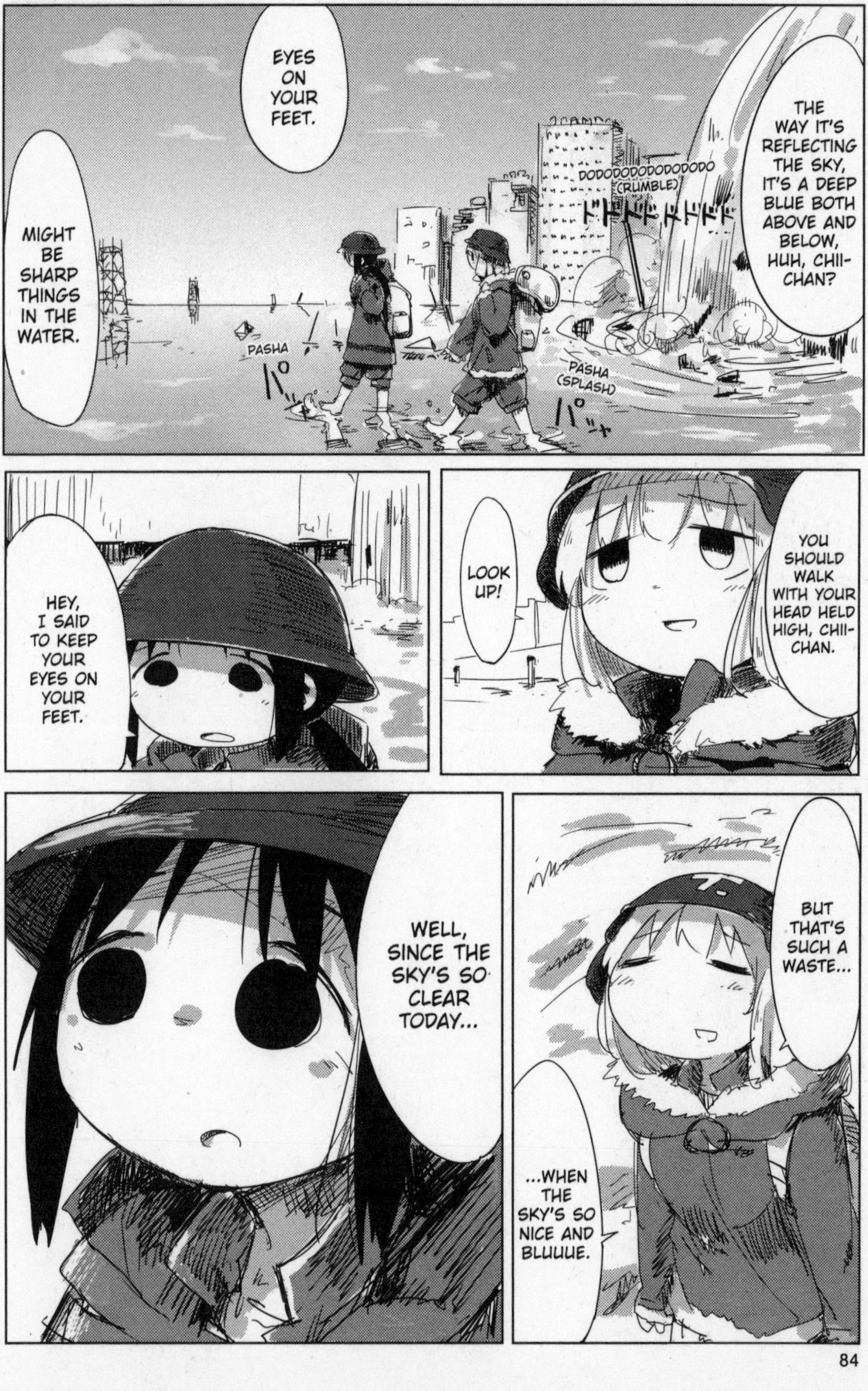
THE WAY IT'S REFLECTING THE SKY, IT'S A DEEP BLUE BOTH ABOVE AND BELOW, HUH, CHII-CHAN?
EYES ON YOUR FEET.
DODODODODODODODO (RUMBLE)
MIGHT BE SHARP THINGS IN THE WATER.
PASHA (SPLASH)
PASHA
YOU SHOULD WALK WITH YOUR HEAD HELD HIGH, CHII-CHAN.
LOOK UP!
HEY, I SAID TO KEEP YOUR EYES ON YOUR FEET.
BUT THAT'S SUCH A WASTE...
...WHEN THE SKY'S SO NICE AND BLUUUE.
WELL, SINCE THE SKY'S SO CLEAR TODAY...

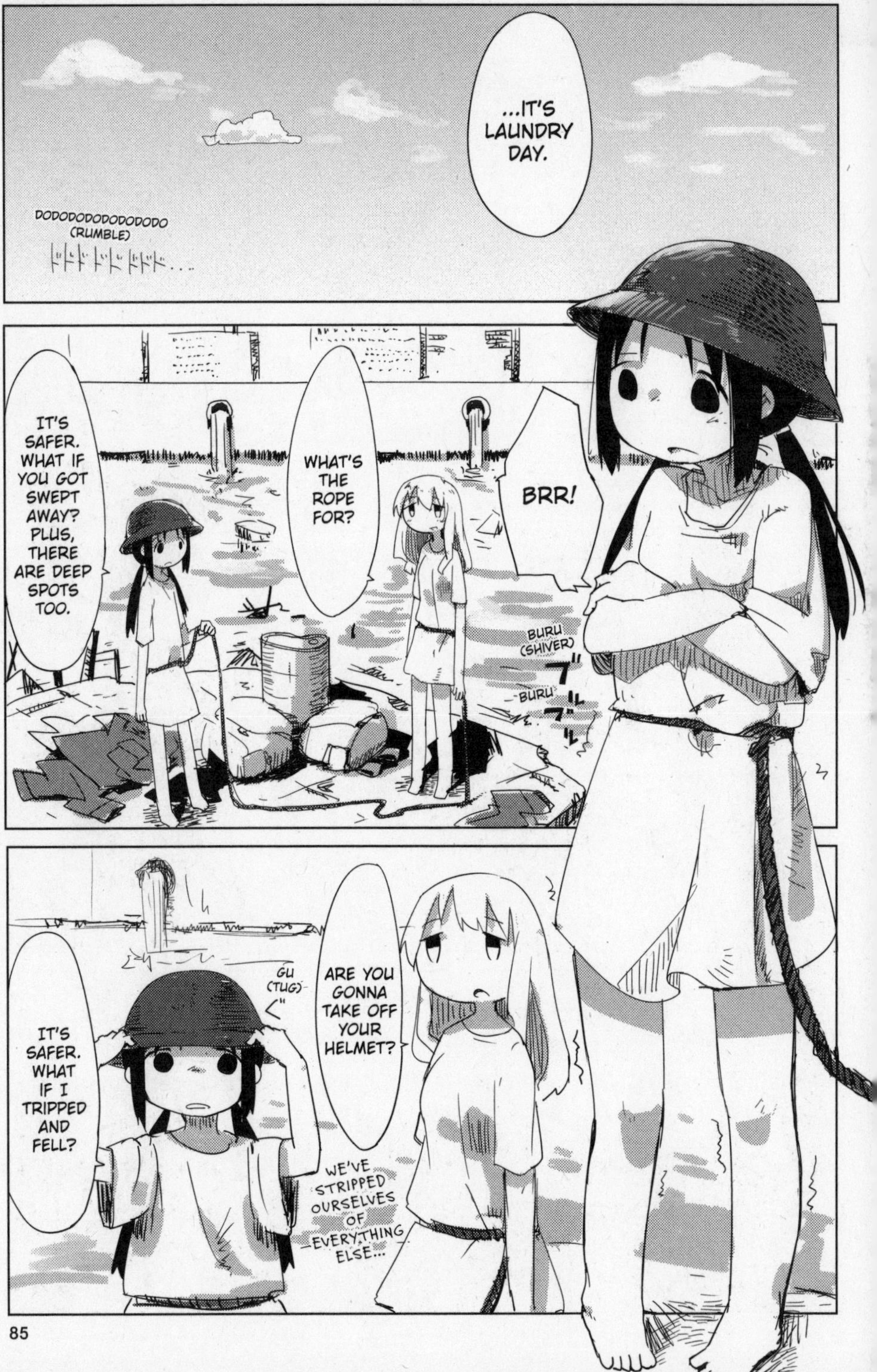
...IT'S LAUNDRY DAY.
DODODODODODODODO (RUMBLE)
BRR!
BURU (SHIVER) BURU
WHAT'S THE ROPE FOR?
IT'S SAFER. WHAT IF YOU GOT SWEPT AWAY? PLUS, THERE ARE DEEP SPOTS TOO.
ARE YOU GONNA TAKE OFF YOUR HELMET?
GU (TUG)
IT'S SAFER. WHAT IF I TRIPPED AND FELL?
WE'VE STRIPPED OURSELVES OF EVERYTHING ELSE...

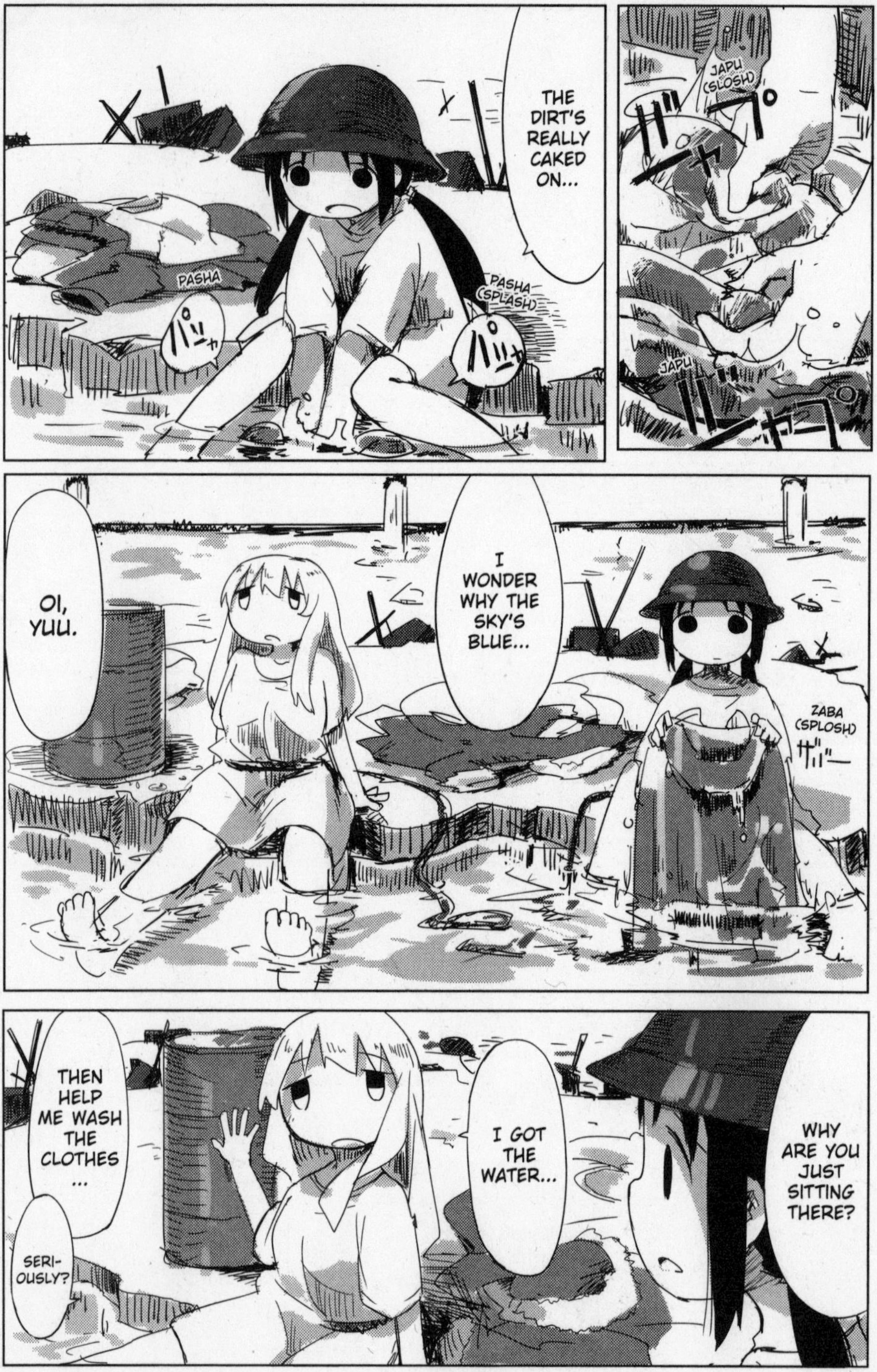

JAPU (SLOSH)
JAPU
THE DIRT'S REALLY CAKED ON...
PASHA (SPLASH)
PASHA
ZABA (SPLOSH)
I WONDER WHY THE SKY'S BLUE...
OI, YUU.
WHY ARE YOU JUST SITTING THERE?
I GOT THE WATER...
THEN HELP ME WASH THE CLOTHES ...
SERI-OUSLY?

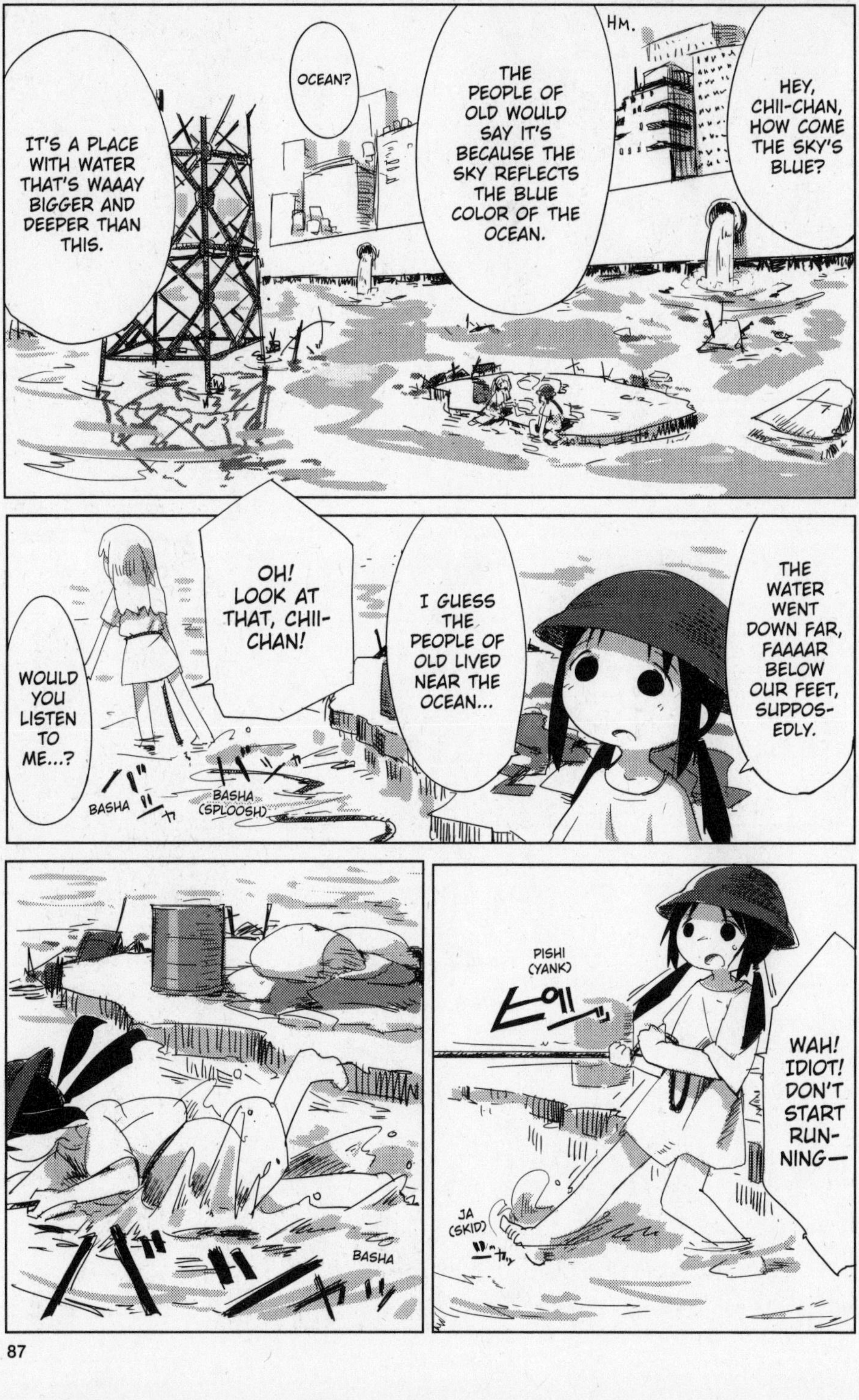
HEY, CHII-CHAN, HOW COME THE SKY'S BLUE?
HM.
THE PEOPLE OF OLD WOULD SAY IT'S BECAUSE THE SKY REFLECTS THE BLUE COLOR OF THE OCEAN.
OCEAN?
IT'S A PLACE WITH WATER THAT'S WAAAY BIGGER AND DEEPER THAN THIS.
THE WATER WENT DOWN FAR, FAAAAR BELOW OUR FEET, SUPPOS-EDLY.
I GUESS THE PEOPLE OF OLD LIVED NEAR THE OCEAN...
OH! LOOK AT THAT, CHII-CHAN!
WOULD YOU LISTEN TO ME...?
BASHA (SPLOOSH)
BASHA
WAH! IDIOT! DON'T START RUN-NING—
PISHI (YANK)
JA (SKID)
BASHA

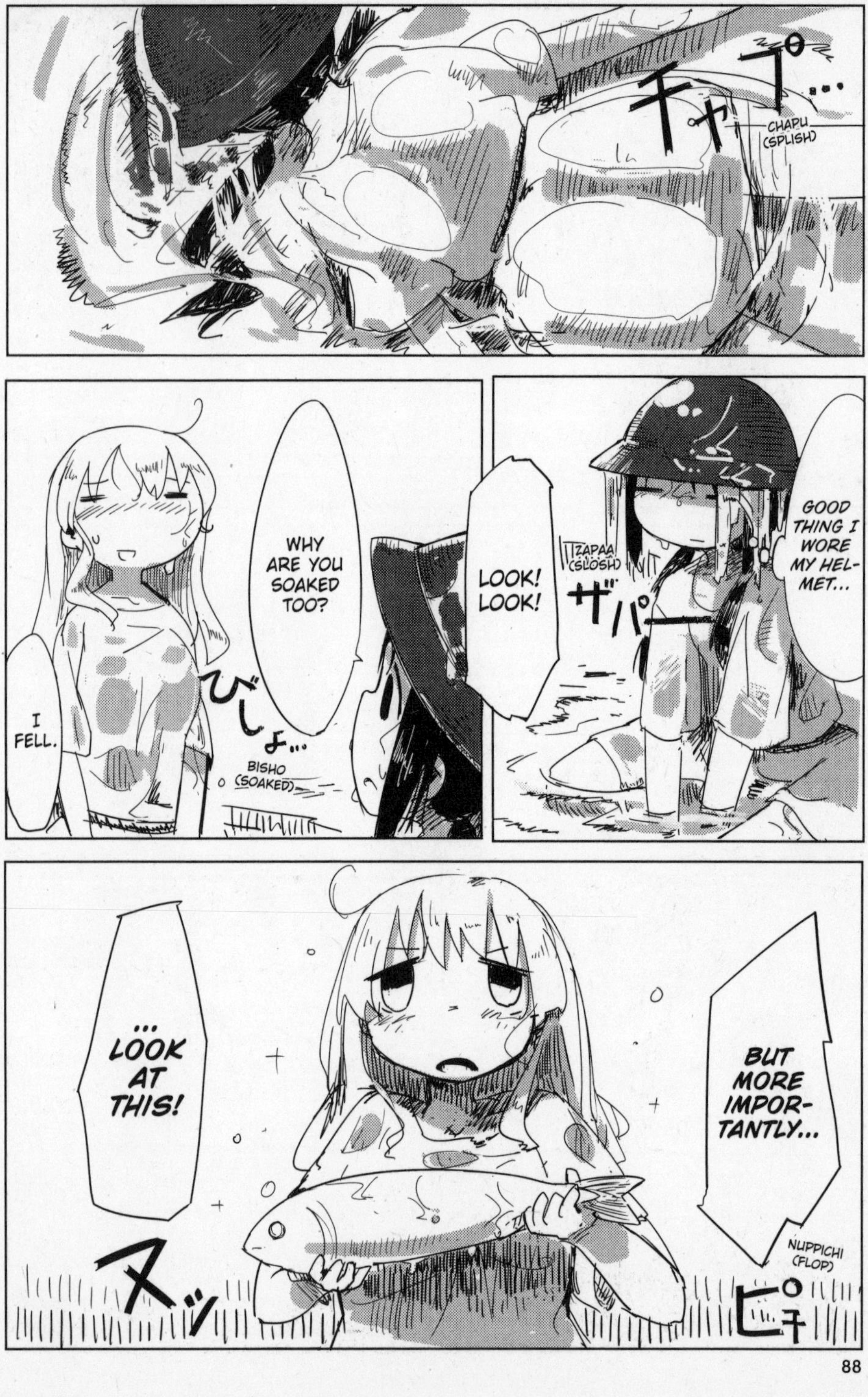
CHAPU (SPLISH)
GOOD THING I WORE MY HEL-MET...
ZAPAA (SLOSH)
LOOK! LOOK!
WHY ARE YOU SOAKED TOO?
BISHO (SOAKED)
I FELL.
BUT MORE IMPOR-TANTLY...
NUPPICHI (FLOP)
... LOOK AT THIS!

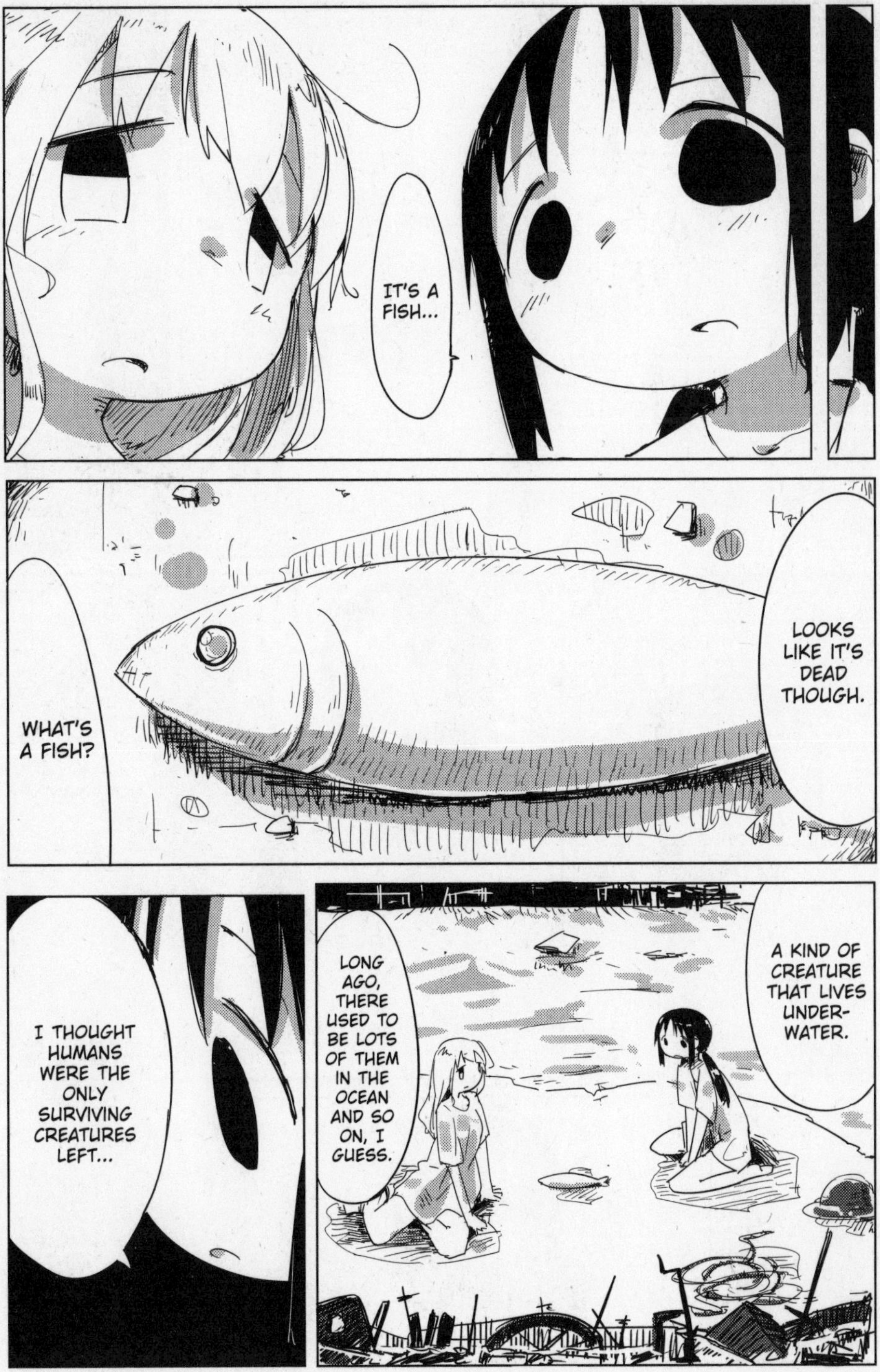
IT'S A FISH...
LOOKS LIKE IT'S DEAD THOUGH.
WHAT'S A FISH?
A KIND OF CREATURE THAT LIVES UNDER-WATER.
LONG AGO, THERE USED TO BE LOTS OF THEM IN THE OCEAN AND SO ON, I GUESS.
I THOUGHT HUMANS WERE THE ONLY SURVIVING CREATURES LEFT...

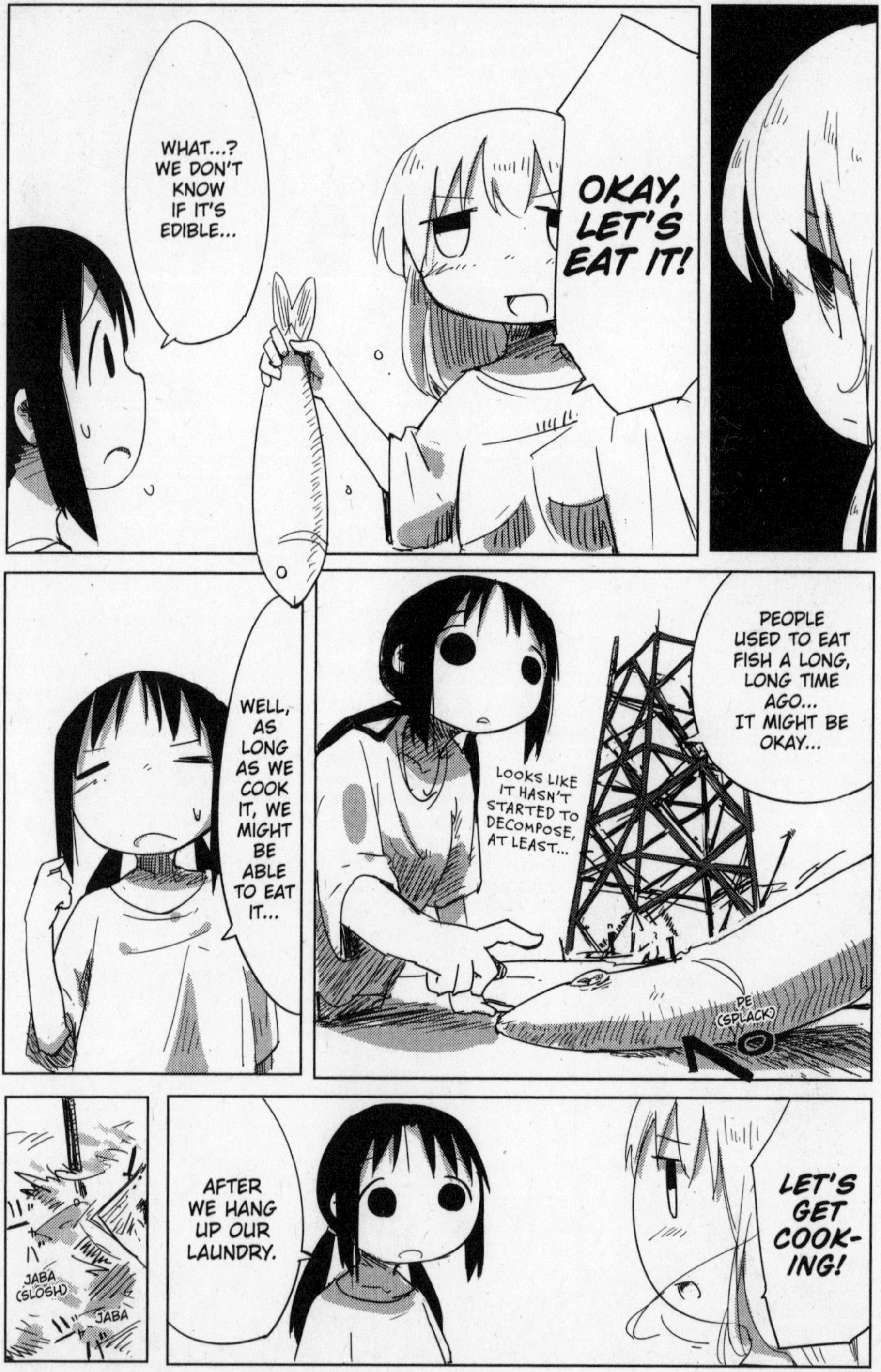
OKAY, LET'S EAT IT!
WHAT...? WE DON'T KNOW IF IT'S EDIBLE...
PEOPLE USED TO EAT FISH A LONG, LONG TIME AGO... IT MIGHT BE OKAY...
LOOKS LIKE IT HASN'T STARTED TO DECOMPOSE, AT LEAST...
PE (SPLACK)
WELL, AS LONG AS WE COOK IT, WE MIGHT BE ABLE TO EAT IT...
LET'S GET COOK-ING!
AFTER WE HANG UP OUR LAUNDRY.
JABA (SLOSH)
JABA

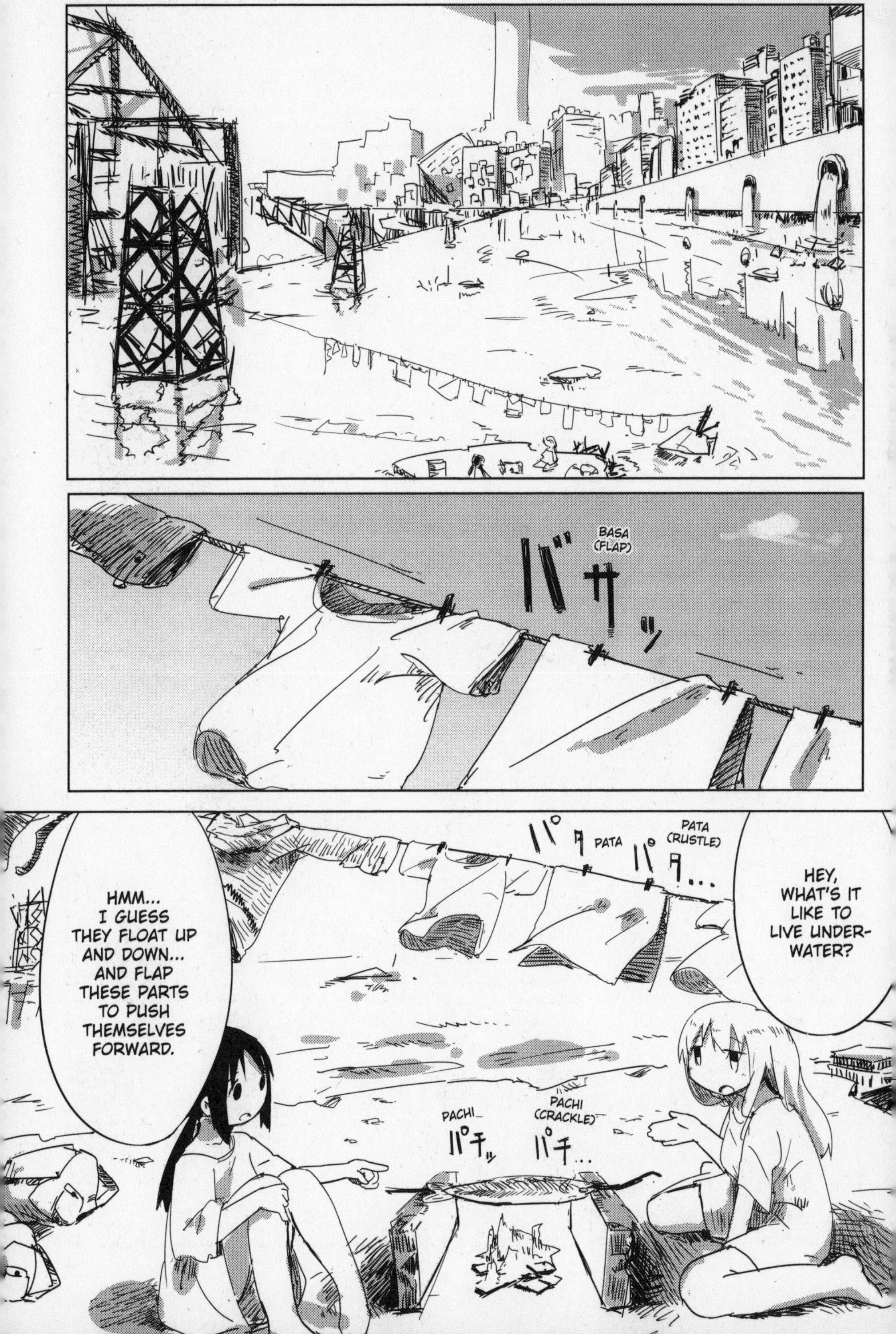
BASA (FLAP)
バサッ
HEY, WHAT'S IT LIKE TO LIVE UNDER-WATER?
PATA (RUSTLE)
パタ...
PATA
パタ
HMM... I GUESS THEY FLOAT UP AND DOWN... AND FLAP THESE PARTS TO PUSH THEMSELVES FORWARD.
PACHI (CRACKLE)
パチ...
PACHI
パチッ

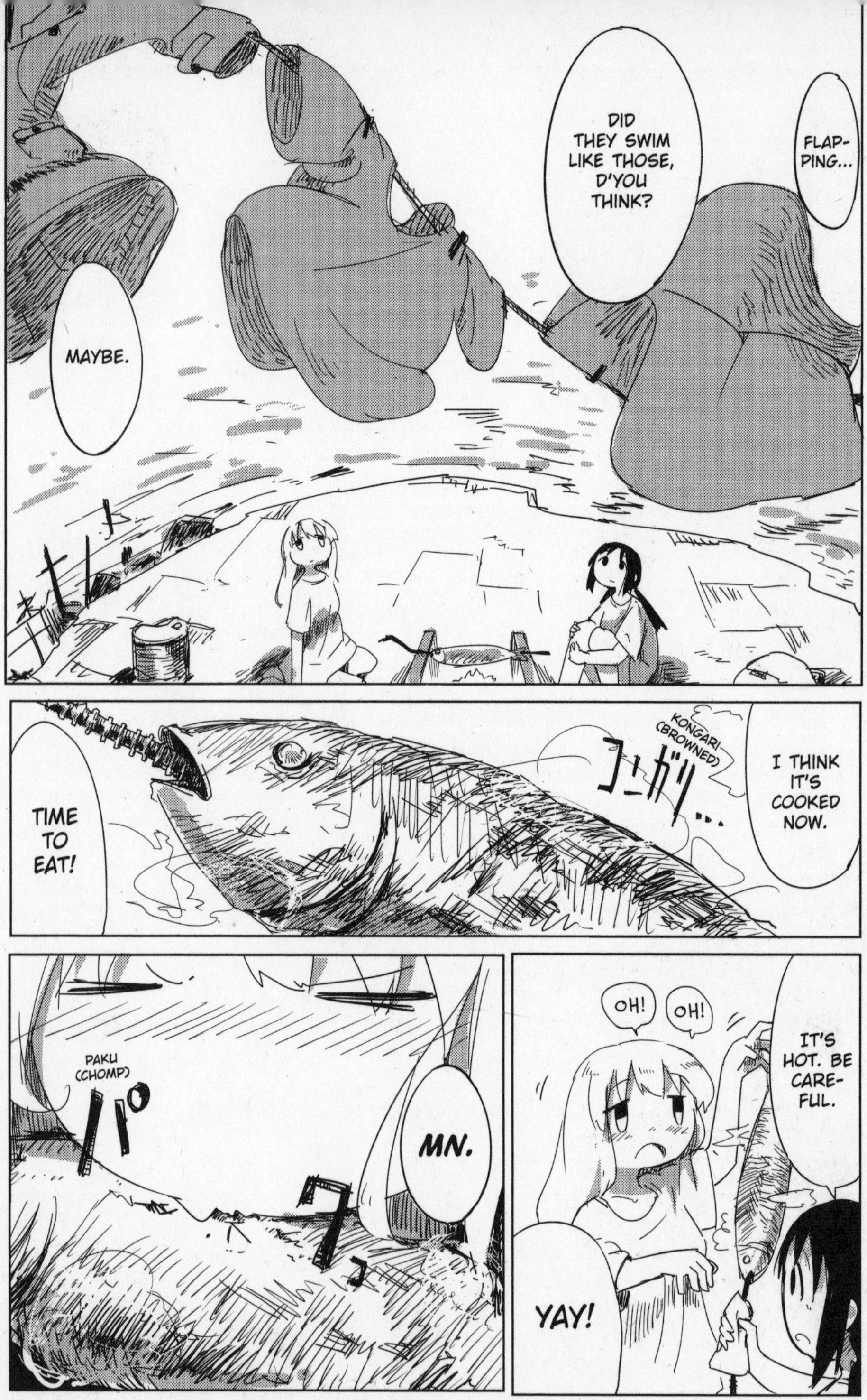
FLAP-PING...
DID THEY SWIM LIKE THOSE, D'YOU THINK?
MAYBE.
I THINK IT'S COOKED NOW.
KONGARI (BROWNED)
TIME TO EAT!
IT'S HOT. BE CARE-FUL.
OH!
OH!
YAY!
MN.
PAKU (CHOMP)

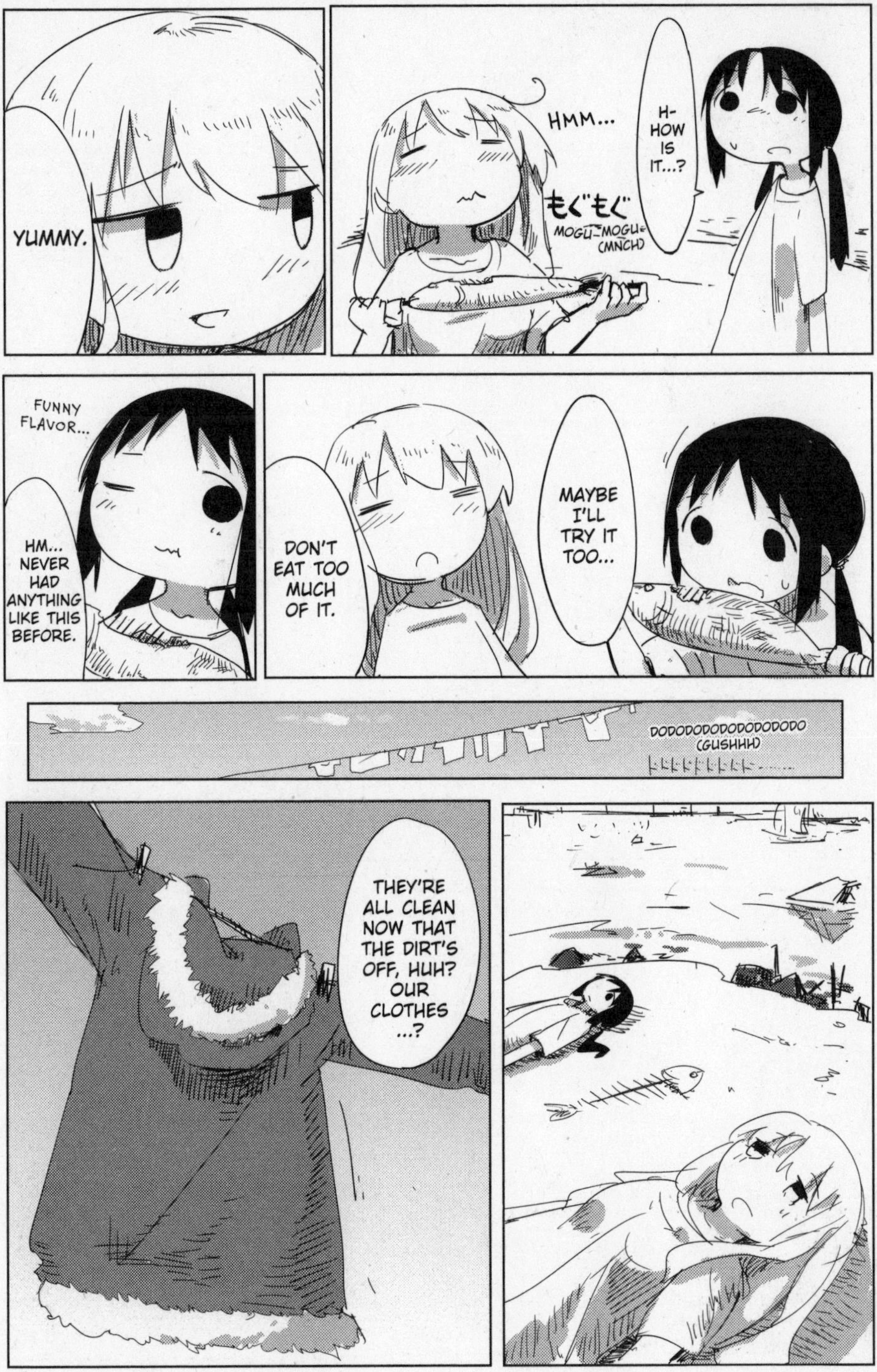

H-HOW IS IT...?
HMM...
もぐもぐ
MOGU-MOGU (MNCH)
YUMMY.
MAYBE I'LL TRY IT TOO...
DON'T EAT TOO MUCH OF IT.
FUNNY FLAVOR...
HM... NEVER HAD ANYTHING LIKE THIS BEFORE.
DODODODODODODODODO (GUSHHH)
THEY'RE ALL CLEAN NOW THAT THE DIRT'S OFF, HUH? OUR CLOTHES ...?

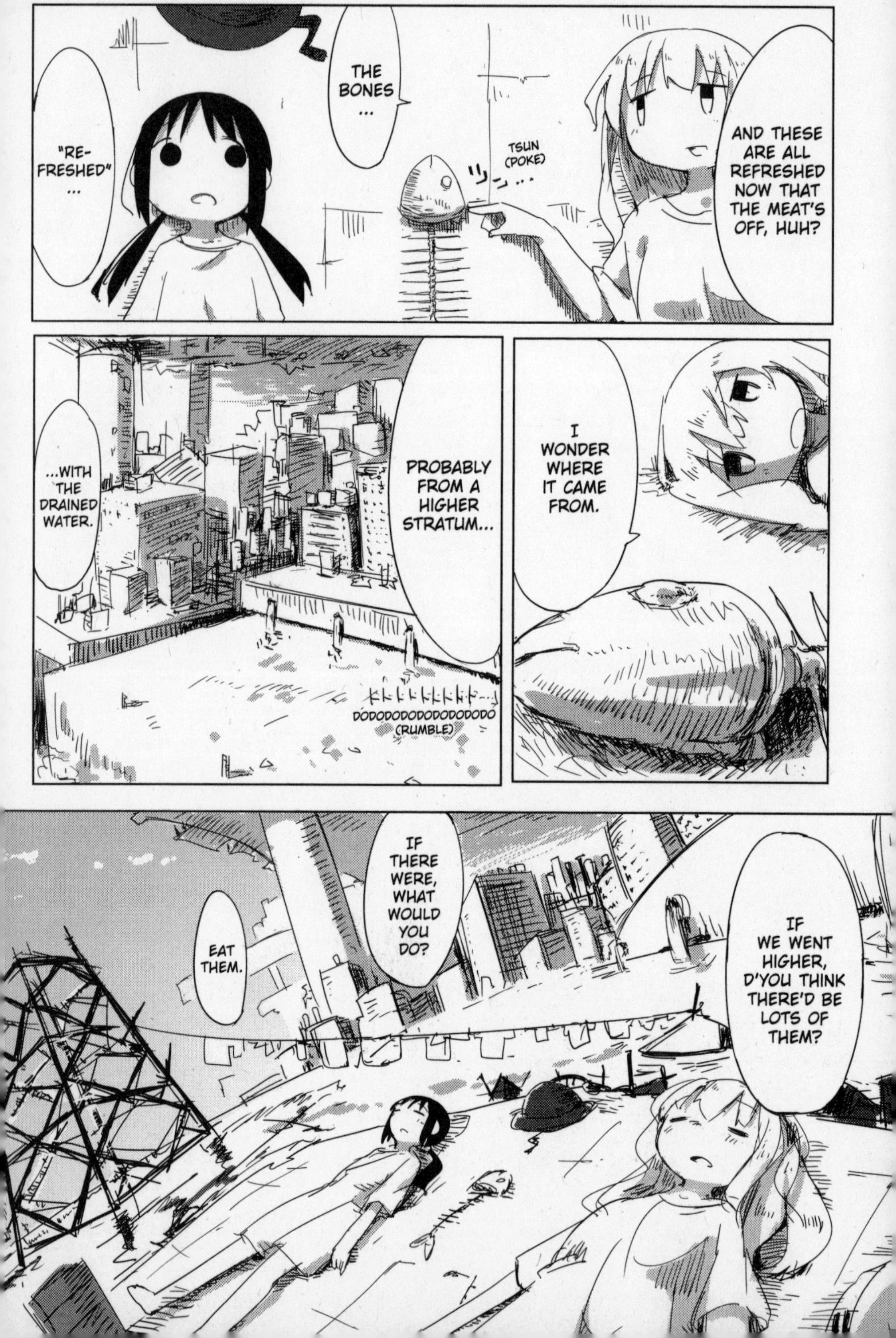
AND THESE ARE ALL REFRESHED NOW THAT THE MEAT'S OFF, HUH?
TSUN (POKE)
THE BONES ...
"RE-FRESHED" ...
I WONDER WHERE IT CAME FROM.
PROBABLY FROM A HIGHER STRATUM...
...WITH THE DRAINED WATER.
DODODODODODODODODO (RUMBLE)
IF WE WENT HIGHER, D'YOU THINK THERE'D BE LOTS OF THEM?
IF THERE WERE, WHAT WOULD YOU DO?
EAT THEM.

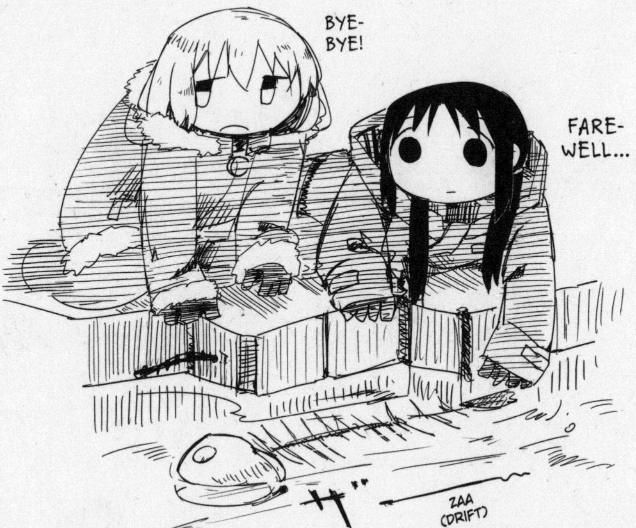
FARE-
WELL...
BYE-
BYE!
ZAA
(DRIFT)

GIRLS' LAST TOUR

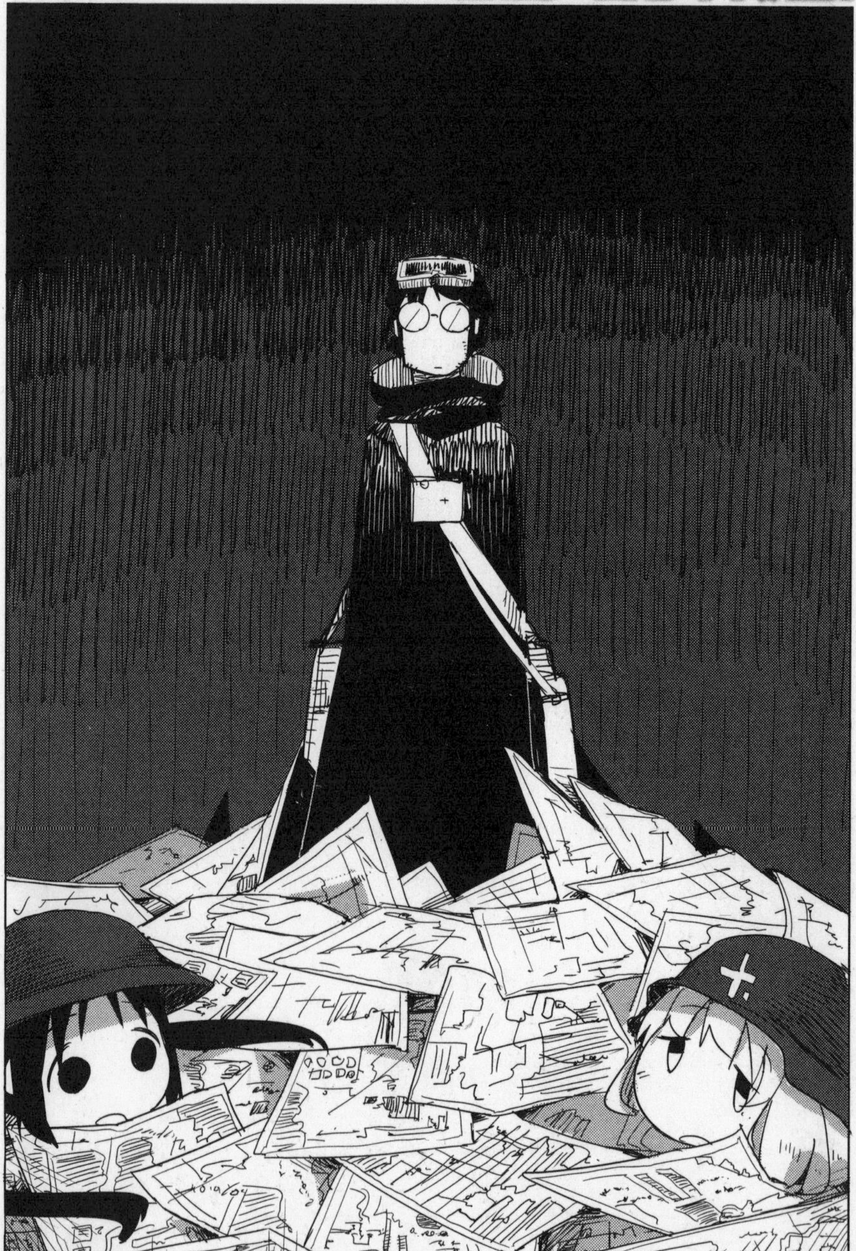

06/07/08

06 ENCOUNTER

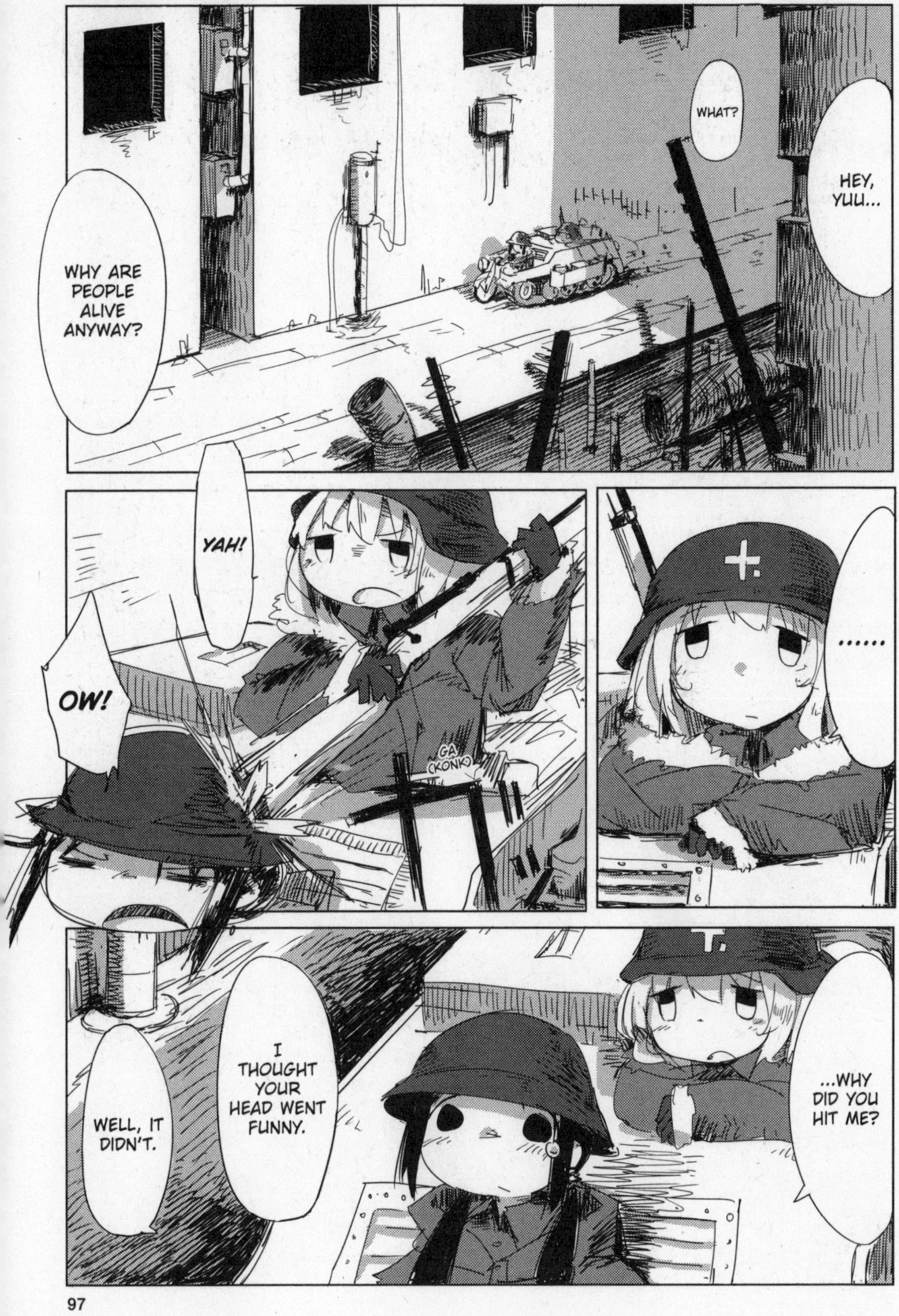
HEY, YUU...
WHAT?
WHY ARE PEOPLE ALIVE ANYWAY?
......
YAH!
GA (KONK)
OW!
...WHY DID YOU HIT ME?
I THOUGHT YOUR HEAD WENT FUNNY.
WELL, IT DIDN'T.

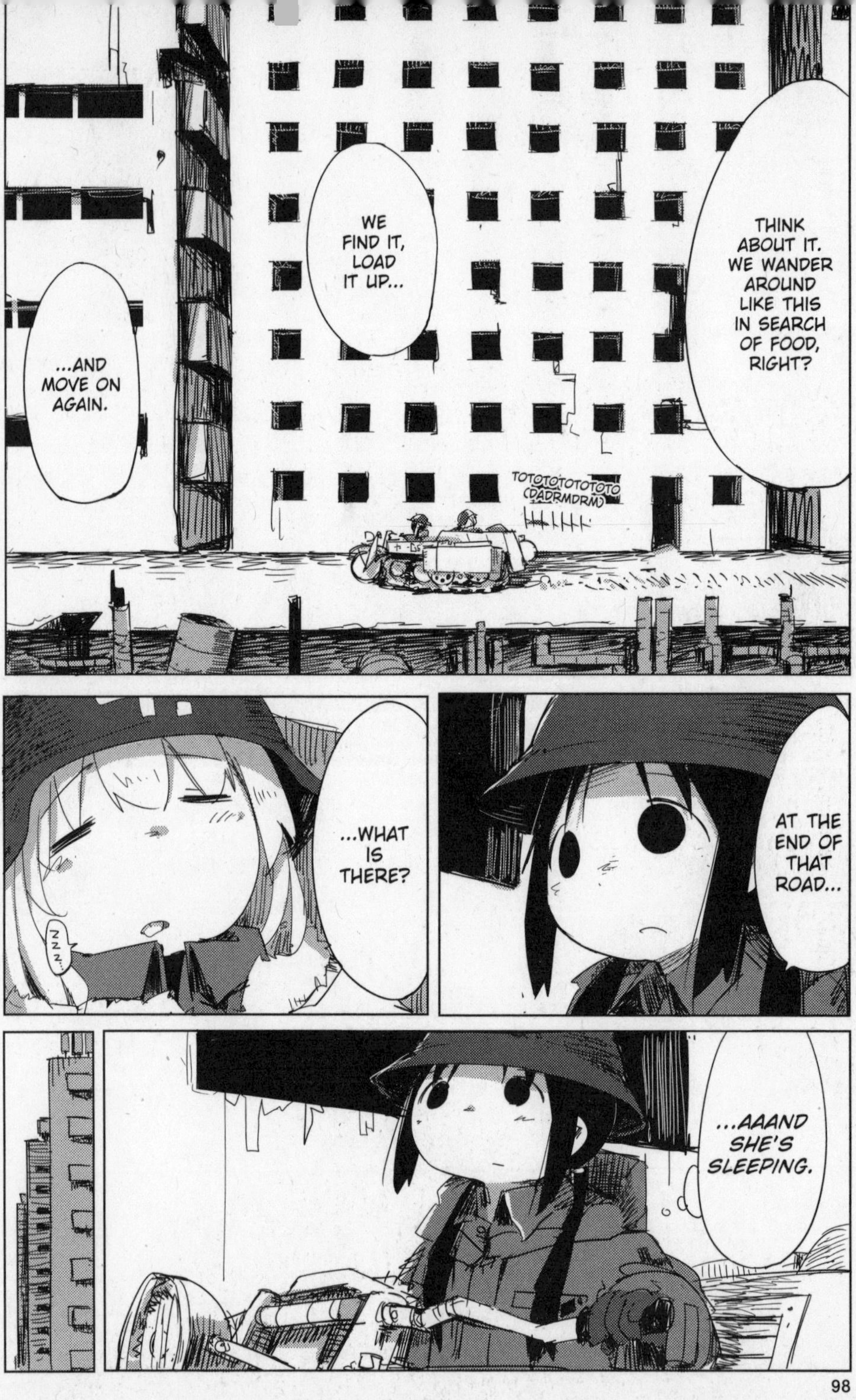
THINK ABOUT IT. WE WANDER AROUND LIKE THIS IN SEARCH OF FOOD, RIGHT?
WE FIND IT, LOAD IT UP...
...AND MOVE ON AGAIN.
TOTOTOTOTOTOTO (DADRMDRM)
AT THE END OF THAT ROAD...
...WHAT IS THERE?
ZZZ...
...AAAND SHE'S SLEEPING.

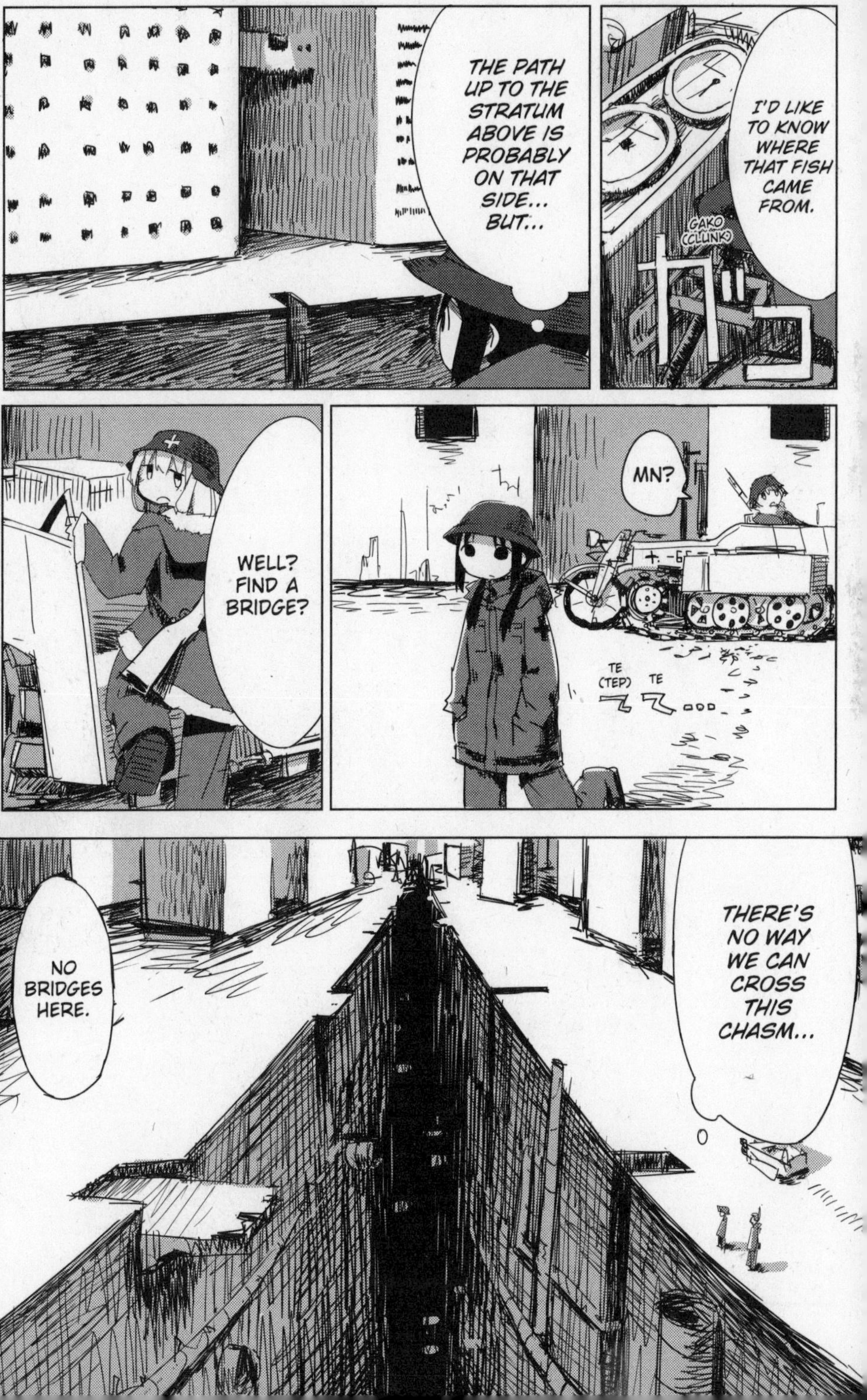
I'D LIKE TO KNOW WHERE THAT FISH CAME FROM.
GAKO (CLUNK)
THE PATH UP TO THE STRATUM ABOVE IS PROBABLY ON THAT SIDE... BUT...
MN?
TE (TEP) TE
WELL? FIND A BRIDGE?
THERE'S NO WAY WE CAN CROSS THIS CHASM...
NO BRIDGES HERE.

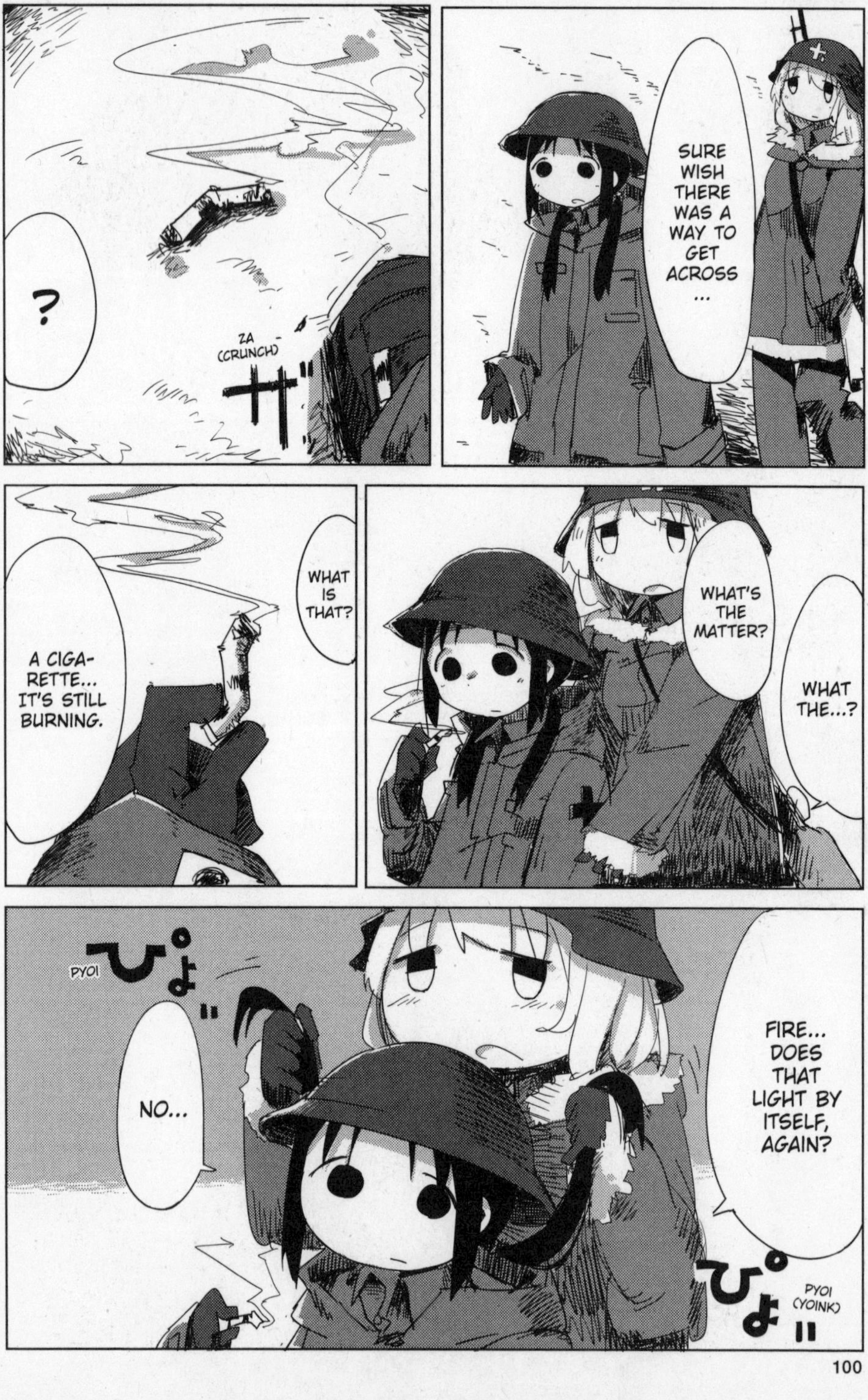
SURE WISH THERE WAS A WAY TO GET ACROSS ...
ZA (CRUNCH)
?
WHAT THE...?
WHAT'S THE MATTER?
WHAT IS THAT?
A CIGARETTE... IT'S STILL BURNING.
FIRE... DOES THAT LIGHT BY ITSELF, AGAIN?
PYOI
NO...
PYOI (YOINK)

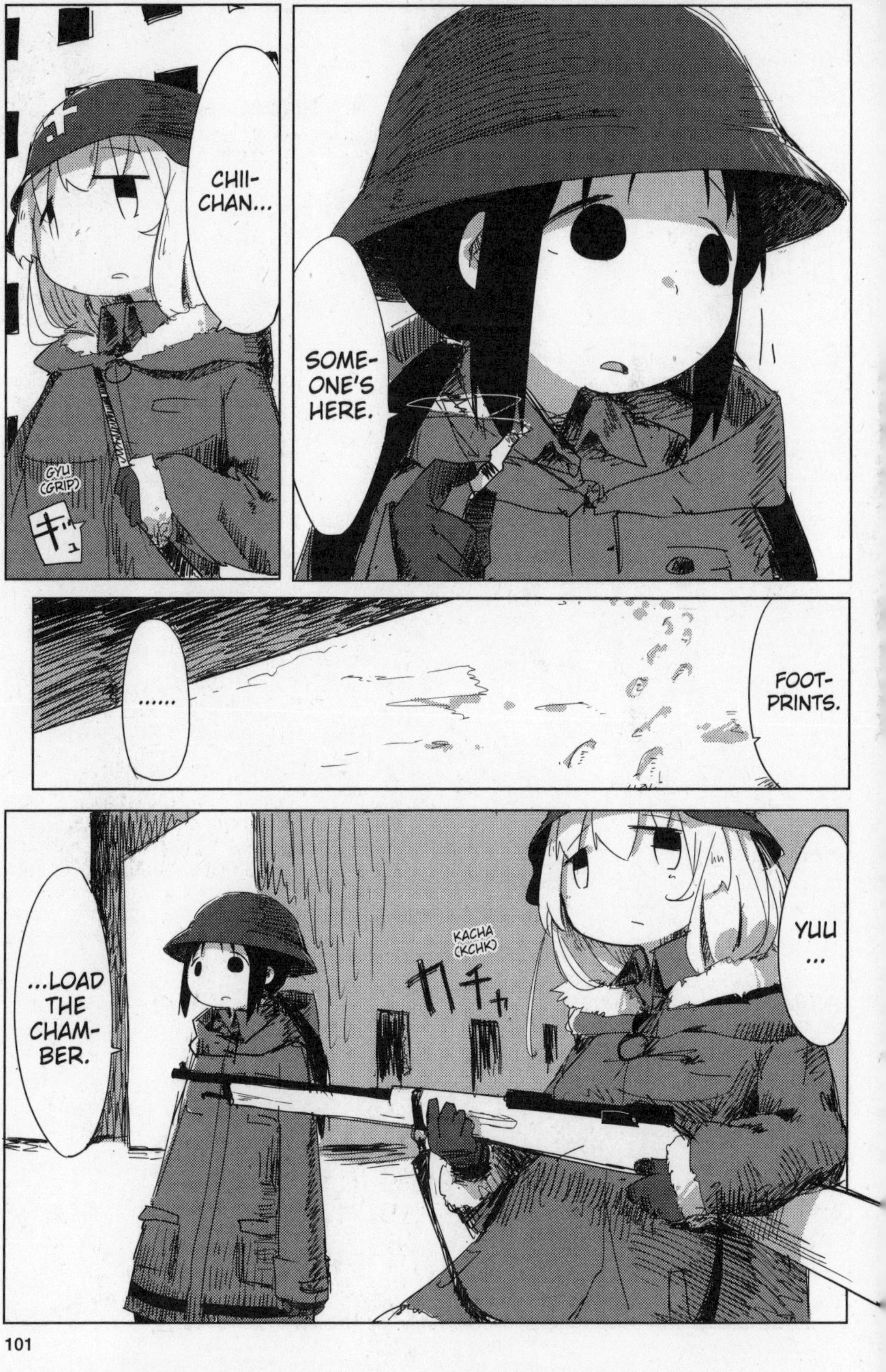
SOME-ONE'S HERE.
CHII-CHAN...
GYU (GRIP)
ギュ
FOOT-PRINTS.
......
YUU ...
KACHA (KCHK)
カチャ
...LOAD THE CHAM-BER.

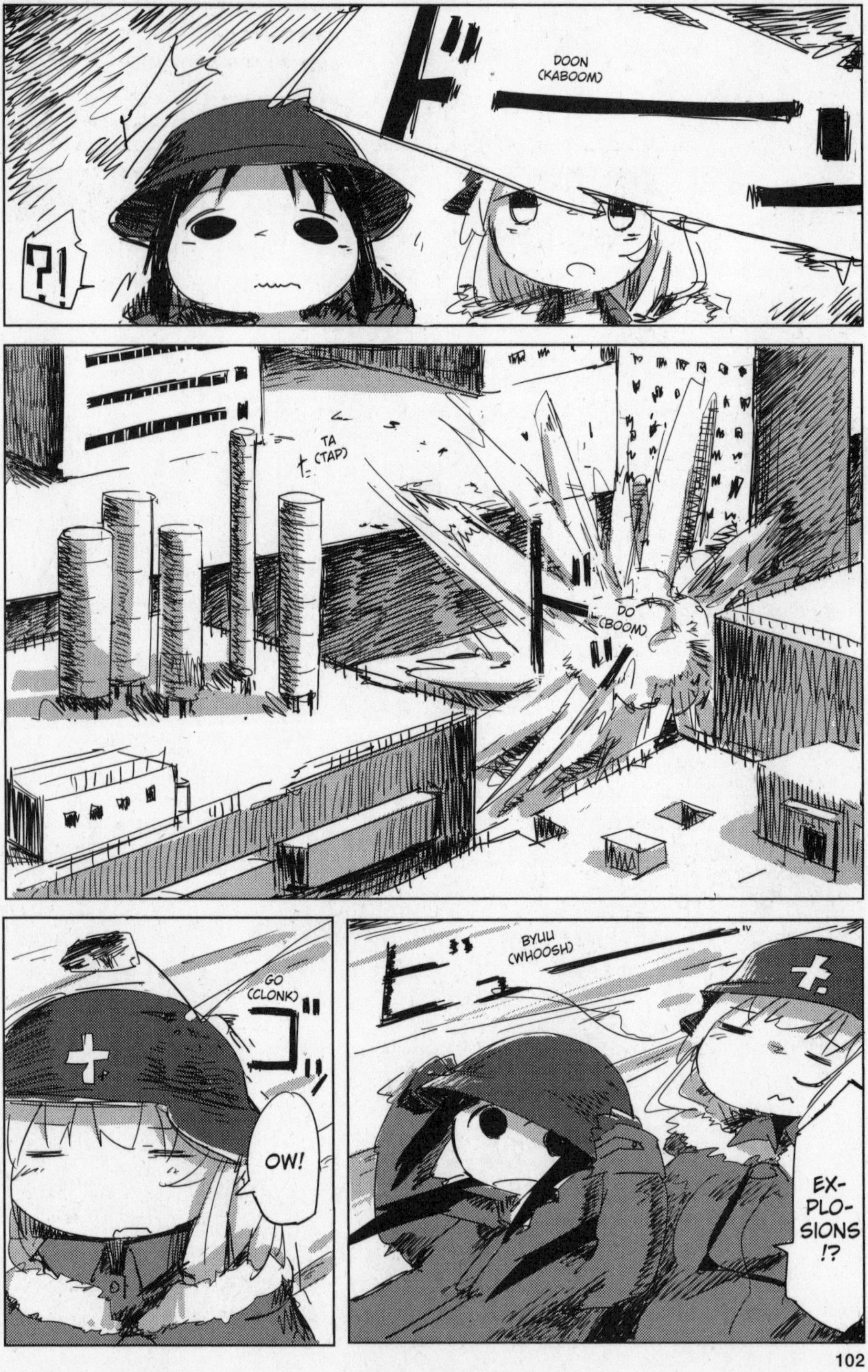
DOON (KABOOM)
?!
TA (TAP)
DO (BOOM)
BYUU (WHOOSH)
EX-PLO-SIONS!?
GO (CLONK)
OW!

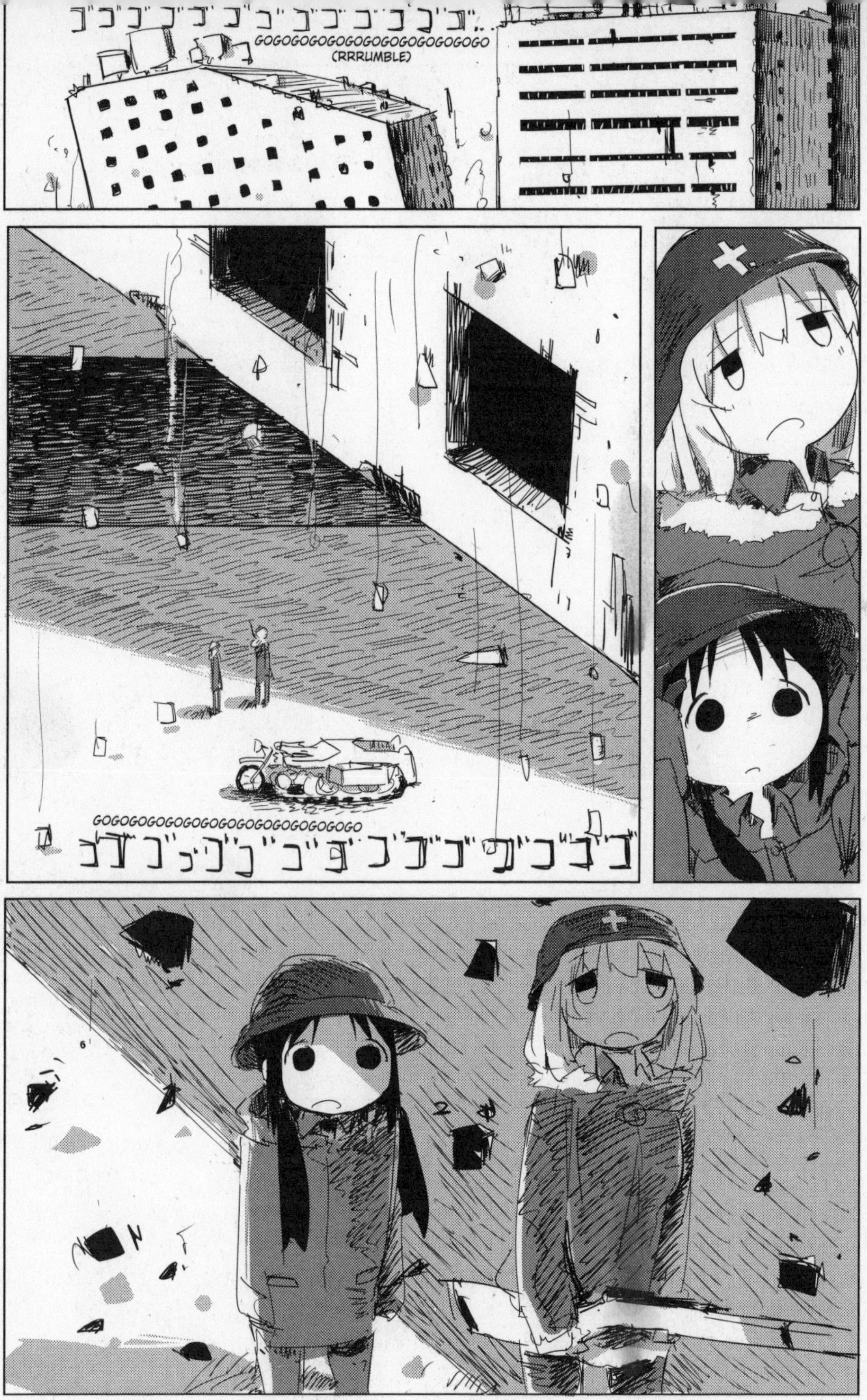
ゴゴゴゴゴゴゴゴゴゴゴゴゴ…
GOGOGOGOGOGOGOGOGOGOGOGOGO
(RRRUMBLE)
GOGOGOGOGOGOGOGOGOGOGOGOGOGO
ゴゴゴゴゴゴゴゴゴゴゴゴゴゴゴ

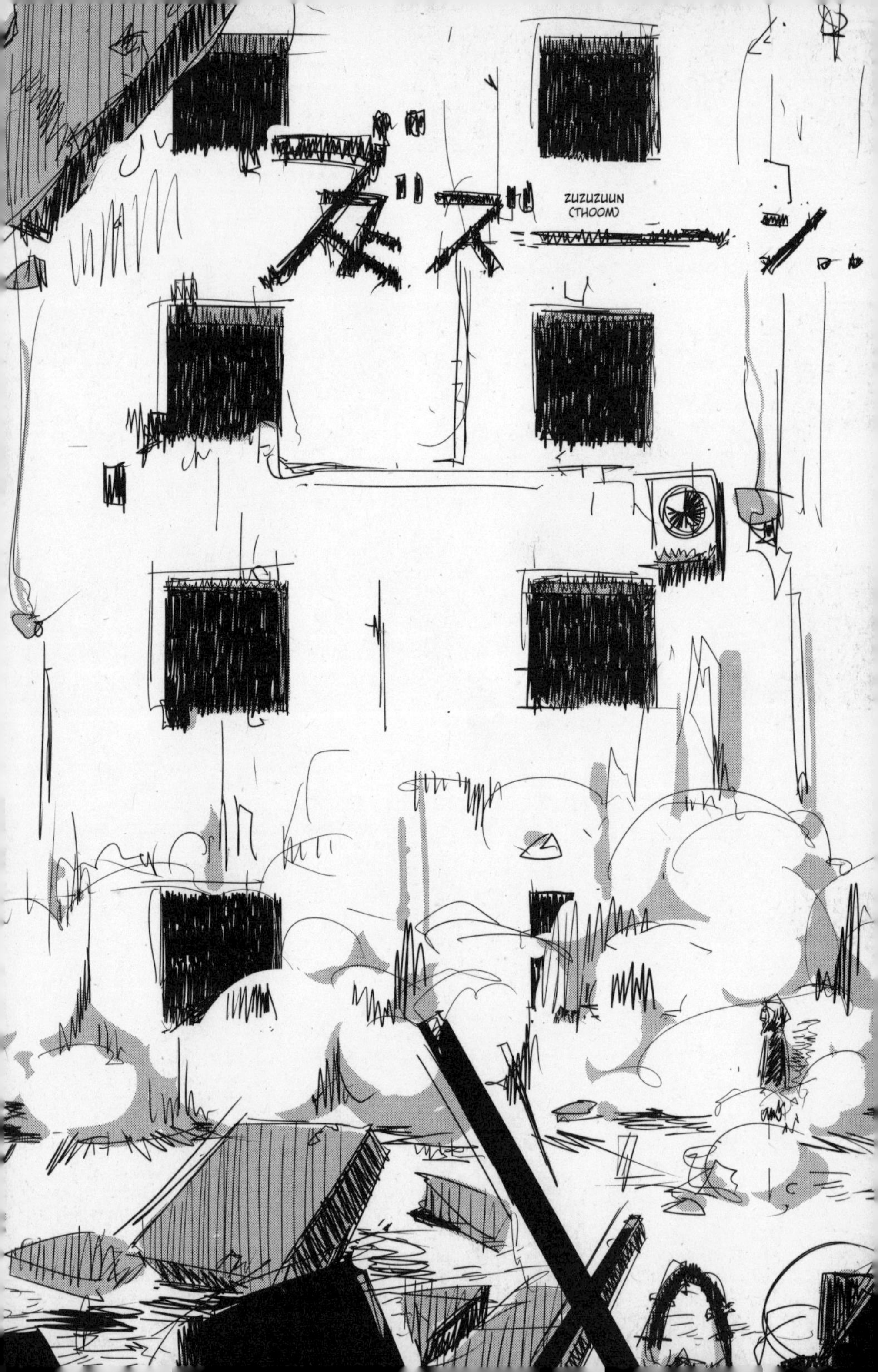
ズズズーン
ZUZUZUUN
(THOOM)

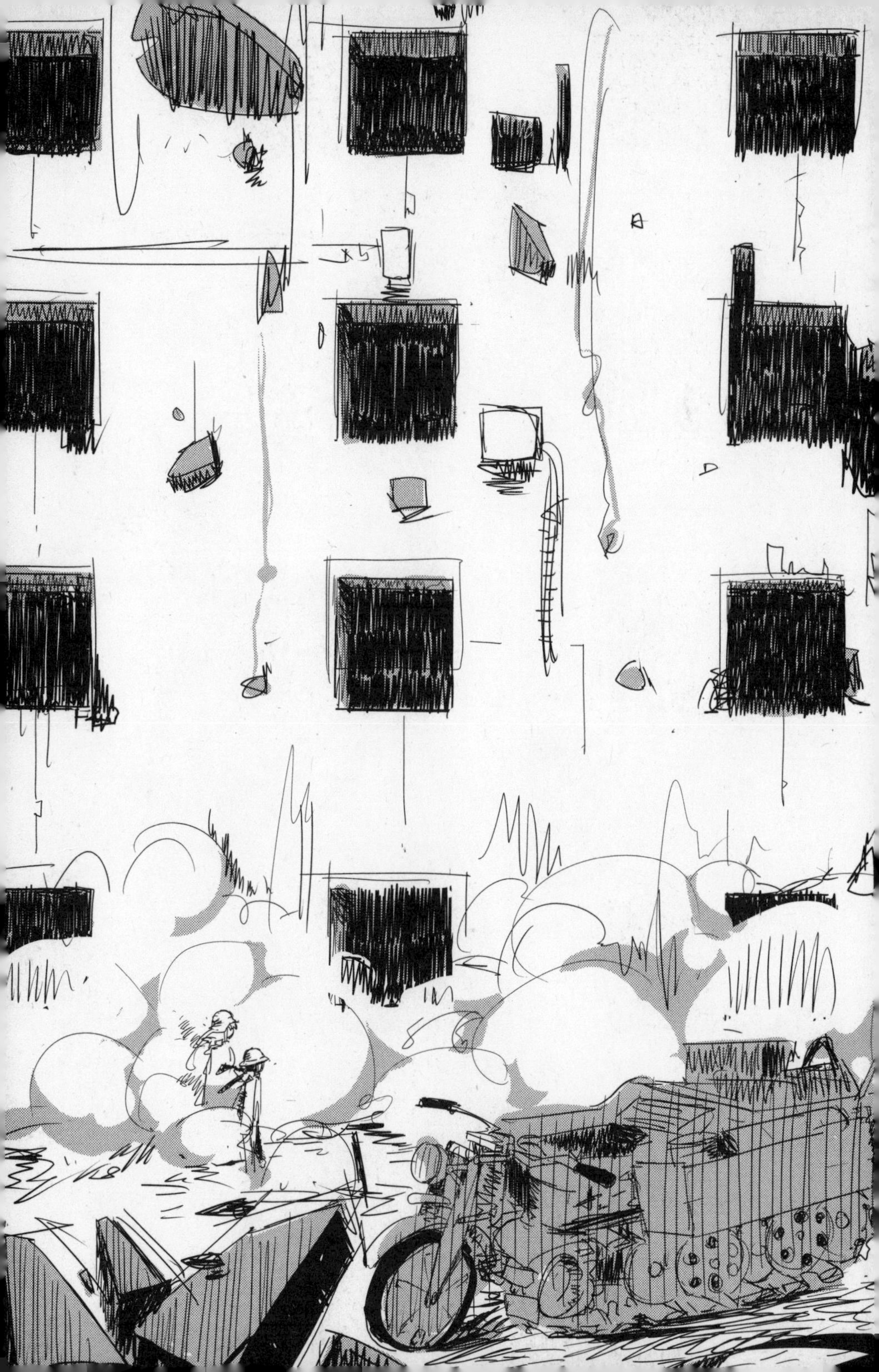

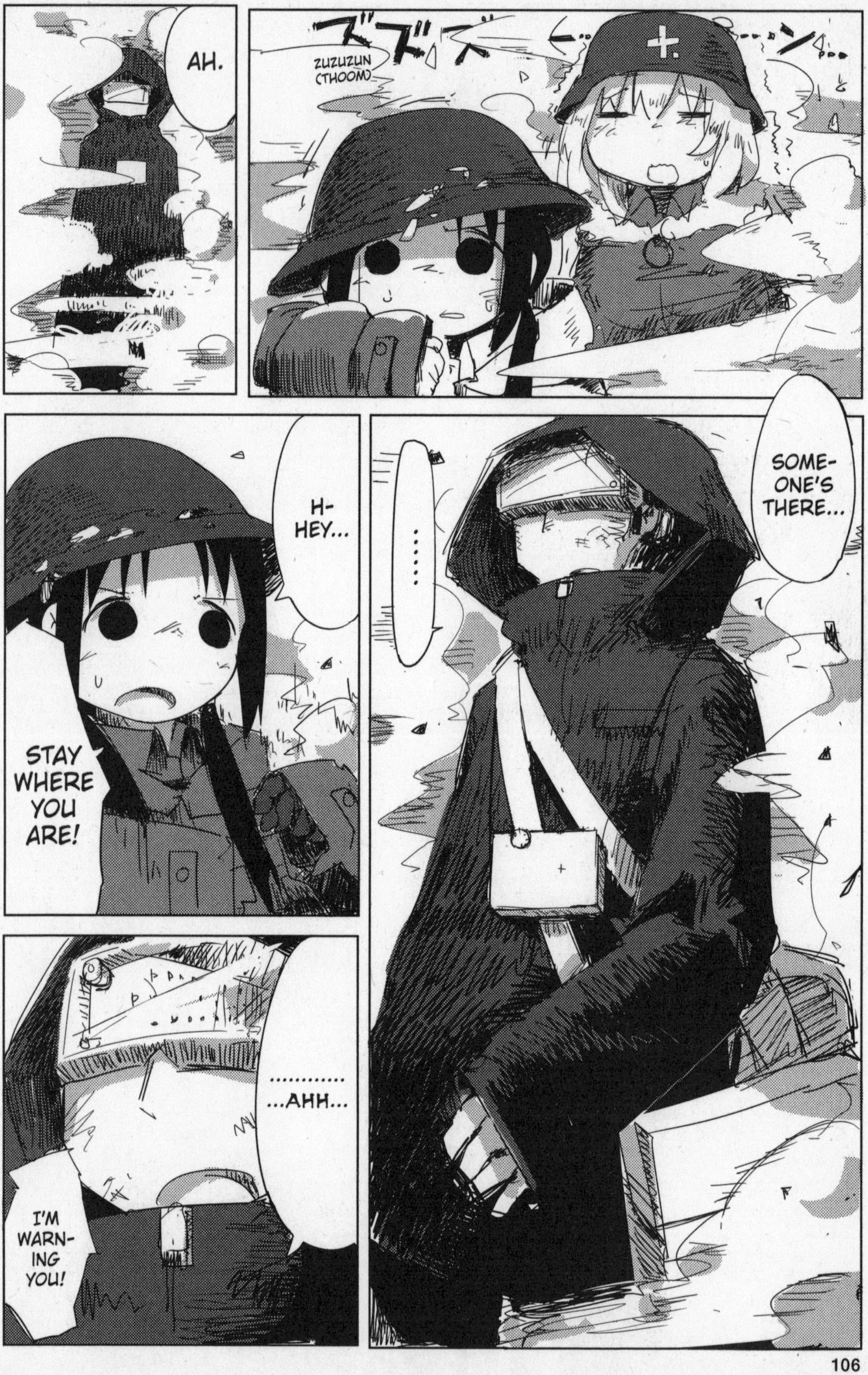
ZUZUZUN (THOOM)
AH.
SOME-ONE'S THERE...
......
H-HEY...
STAY WHERE YOU ARE!
....AHH...
I'M WARNING YOU!

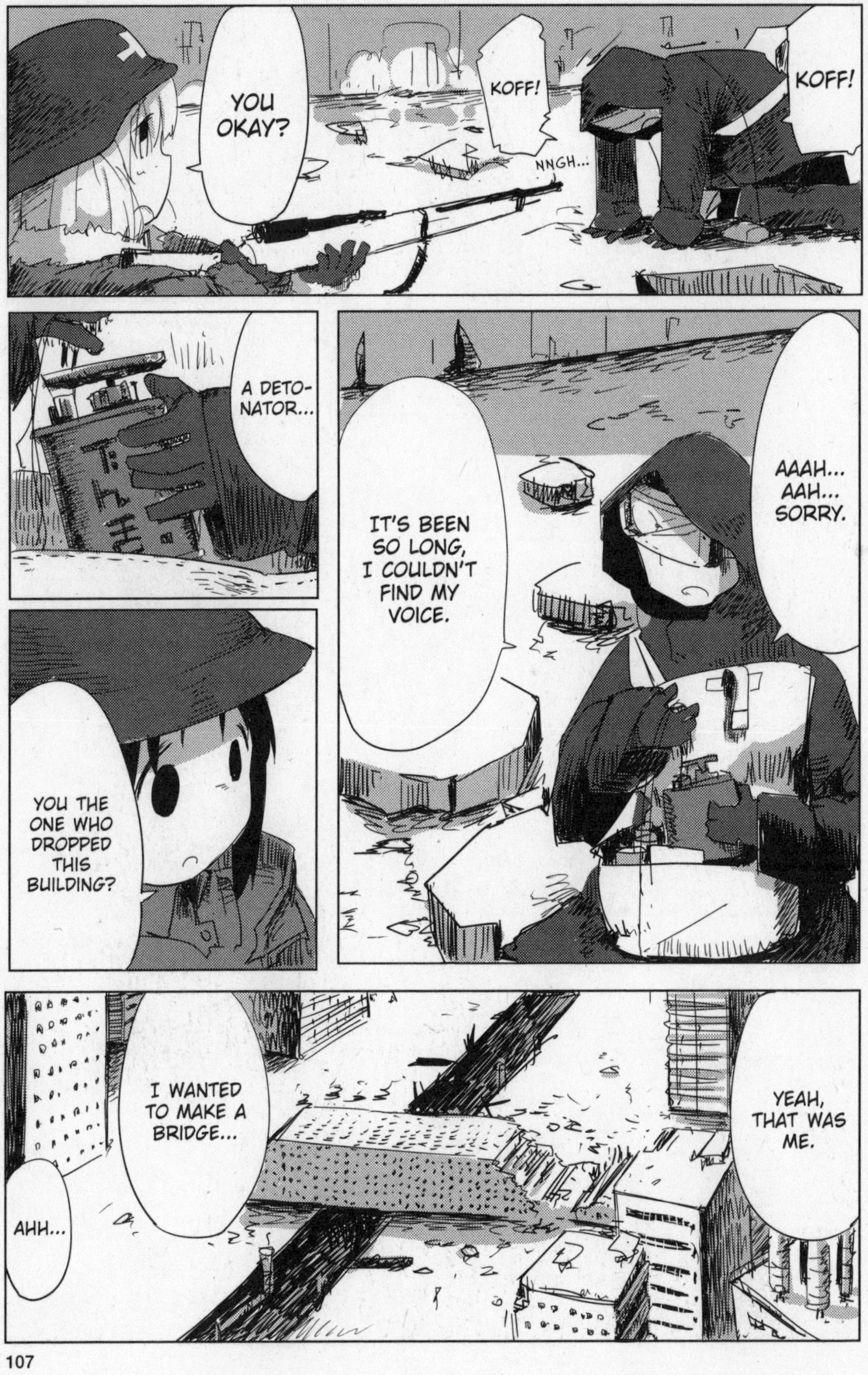
KOFF!
KOFF!
NNGH...
YOU OKAY?
AAAH... AAH... SORRY.
IT'S BEEN SO LONG, I COULDN'T FIND MY VOICE.
A DETO-NATOR...
YOU THE ONE WHO DROPPED THIS BUILDING?
YEAH, THAT WAS ME.
I WANTED TO MAKE A BRIDGE...
AHH...

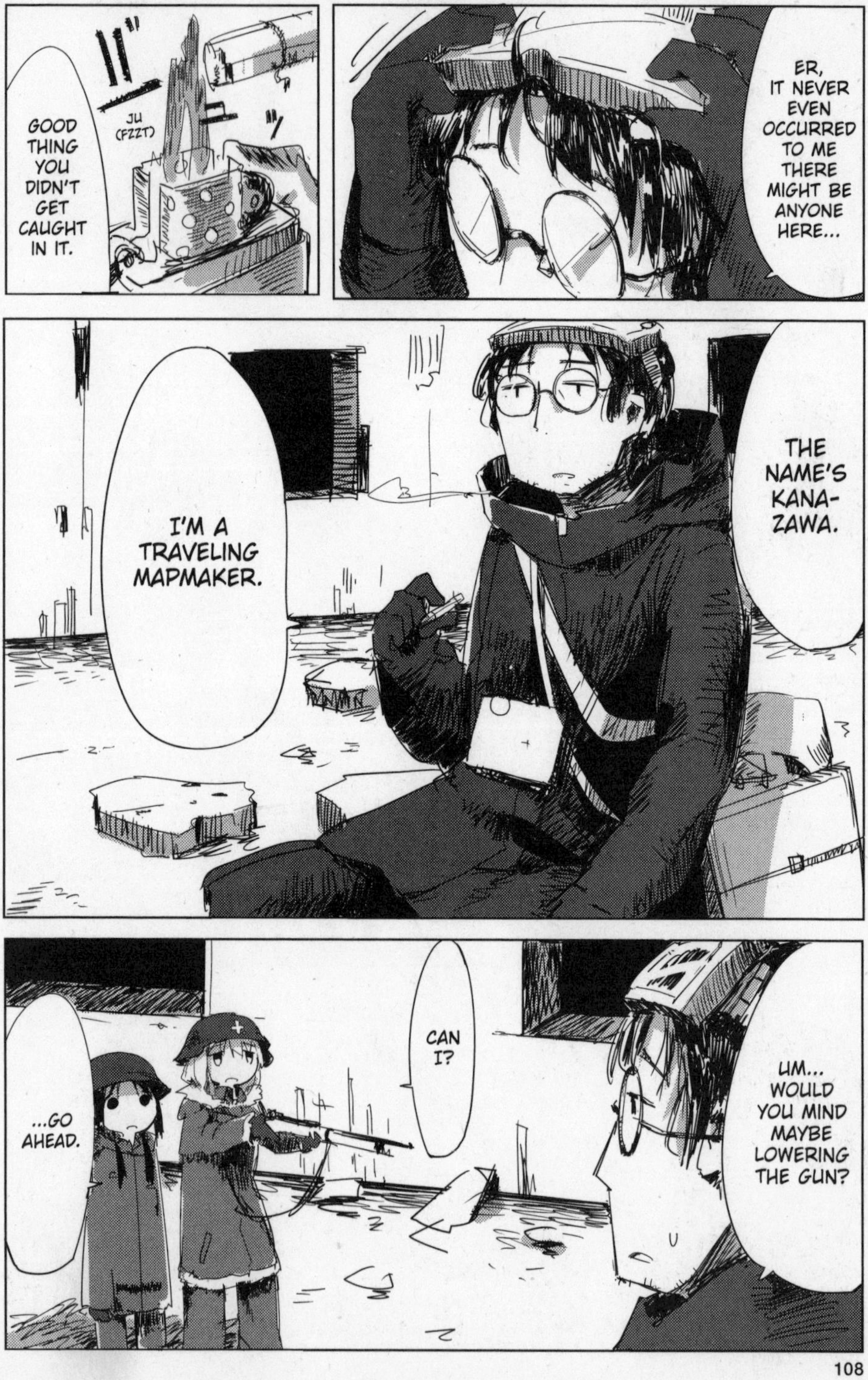
ER, IT NEVER EVEN OCCURRED TO ME THERE MIGHT BE ANYONE HERE...
JU (FZZT)
GOOD THING YOU DIDN'T GET CAUGHT IN IT.
THE NAME'S KANA-ZAWA.
I'M A TRAVELING MAPMAKER.
UM... WOULD YOU MIND MAYBE LOWERING THE GUN?
CAN I?
...GO AHEAD.

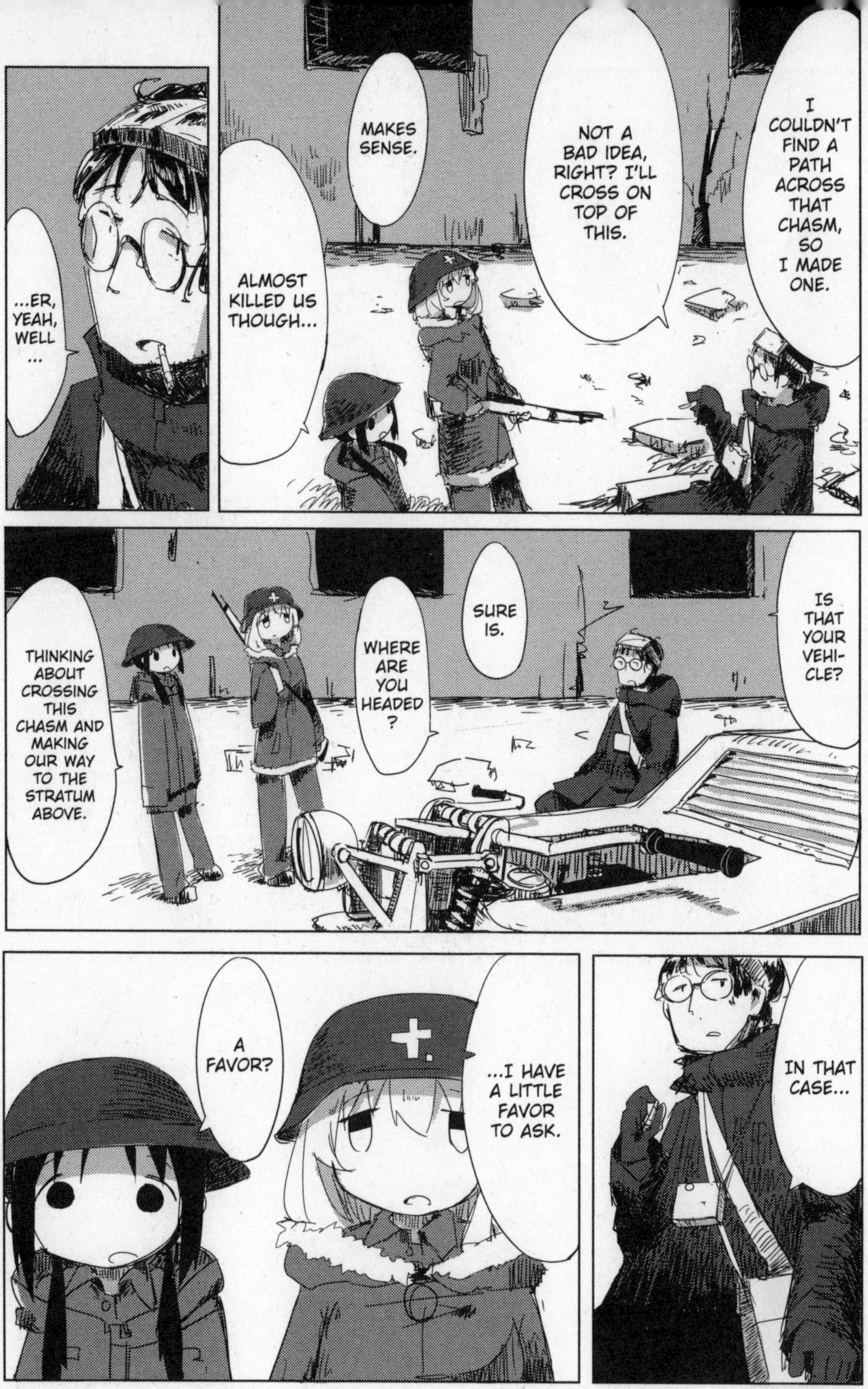
I COULDN'T FIND A PATH ACROSS THAT CHASM, SO I MADE ONE.
NOT A BAD IDEA, RIGHT? I'LL CROSS ON TOP OF THIS.
MAKES SENSE.
ALMOST KILLED US THOUGH...
...ER, YEAH, WELL ...
IS THAT YOUR VEHICLE?
SURE IS.
WHERE ARE YOU HEADED?
THINKING ABOUT CROSSING THIS CHASM AND MAKING OUR WAY TO THE STRATUM ABOVE.
IN THAT CASE...
...I HAVE A LITTLE FAVOR TO ASK.
A FAVOR?

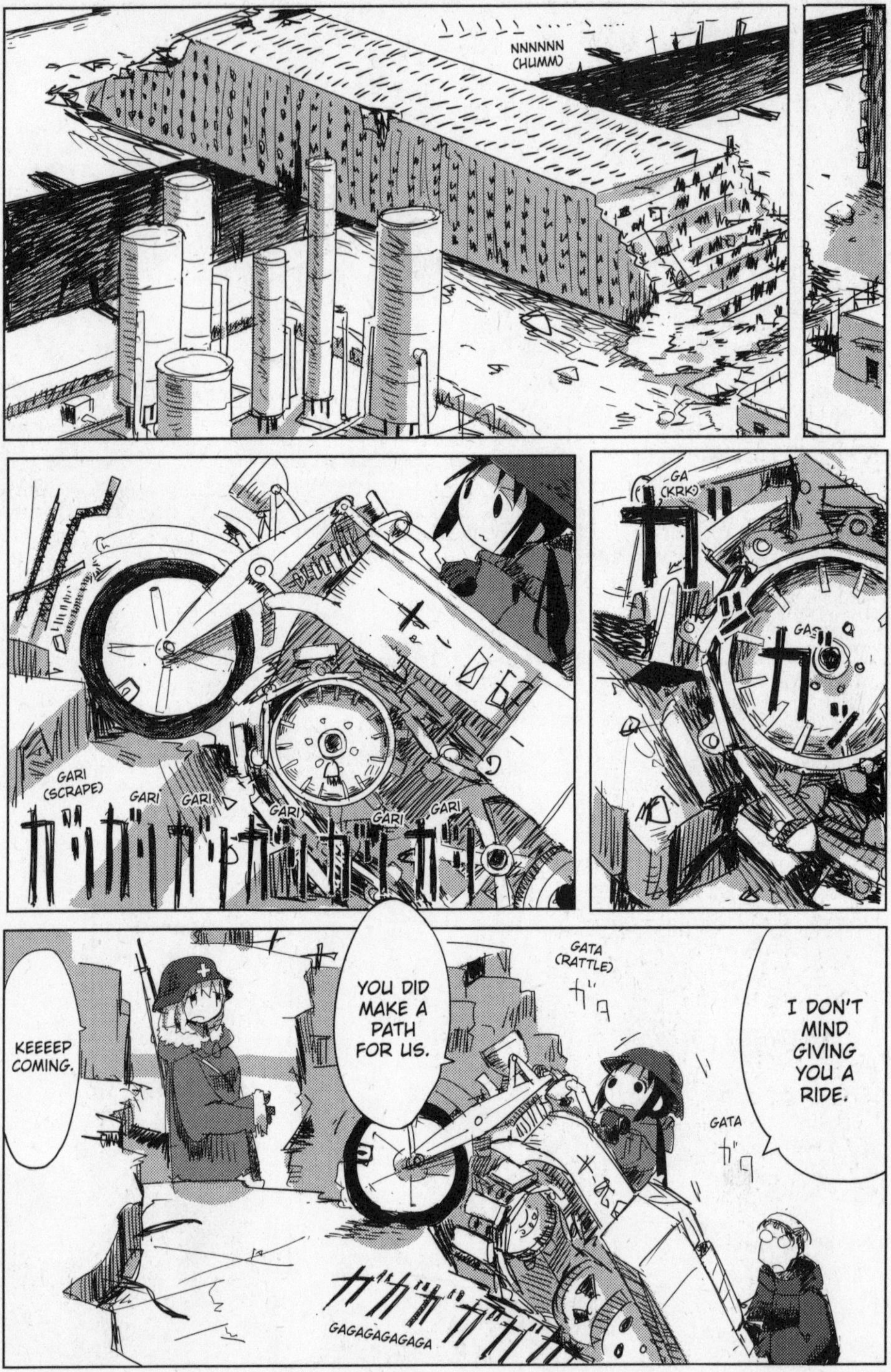

NNNNNN (HUMM)
GA (KRK)
GA
GARI (SCRAPE)
GARI
GARI
GARI
GARI
GARI
I DON'T MIND GIVING YOU A RIDE.
GATA
GATA (RATTLE)
YOU DID MAKE A PATH FOR US.
GAGAGAGAGAGA
KEEEEP COMING.

BUT GETTING UP IS NOT GONNA BE EASY...

TOTOTOTOTOTO
(PUTTER)

HUP...

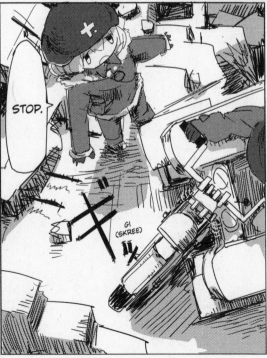

STOP.

GI
(SKREE)

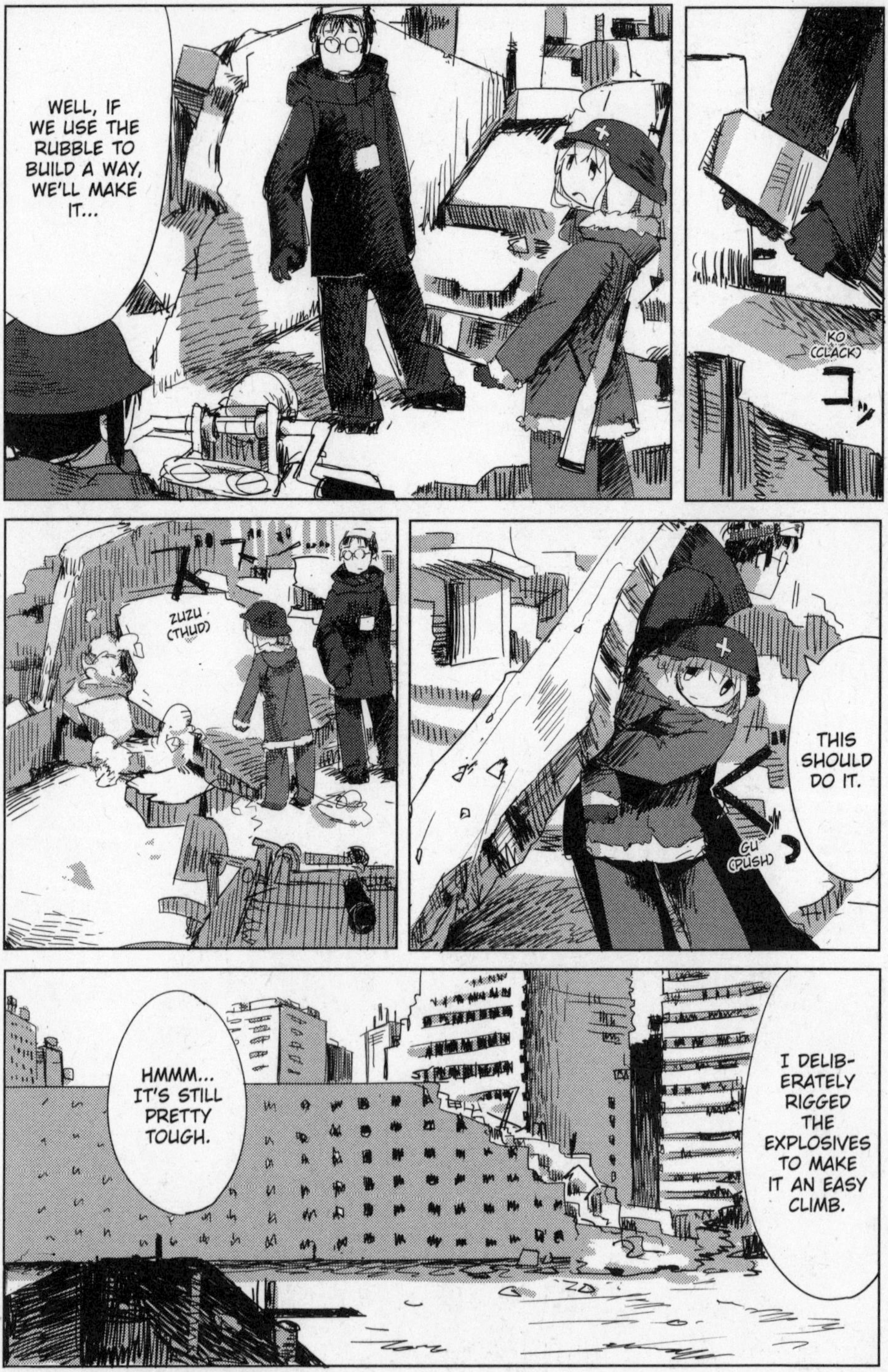
KO (CLACK)
コッ
WELL, IF WE USE THE RUBBLE TO BUILD A WAY, WE'LL MAKE IT...
THIS SHOULD DO IT.
GU (PUSH)
ZUZU (THUD)
I DELIB-ERATELY RIGGED THE EXPLOSIVES TO MAKE IT AN EASY CLIMB.
HMMM... IT'S STILL PRETTY TOUGH.

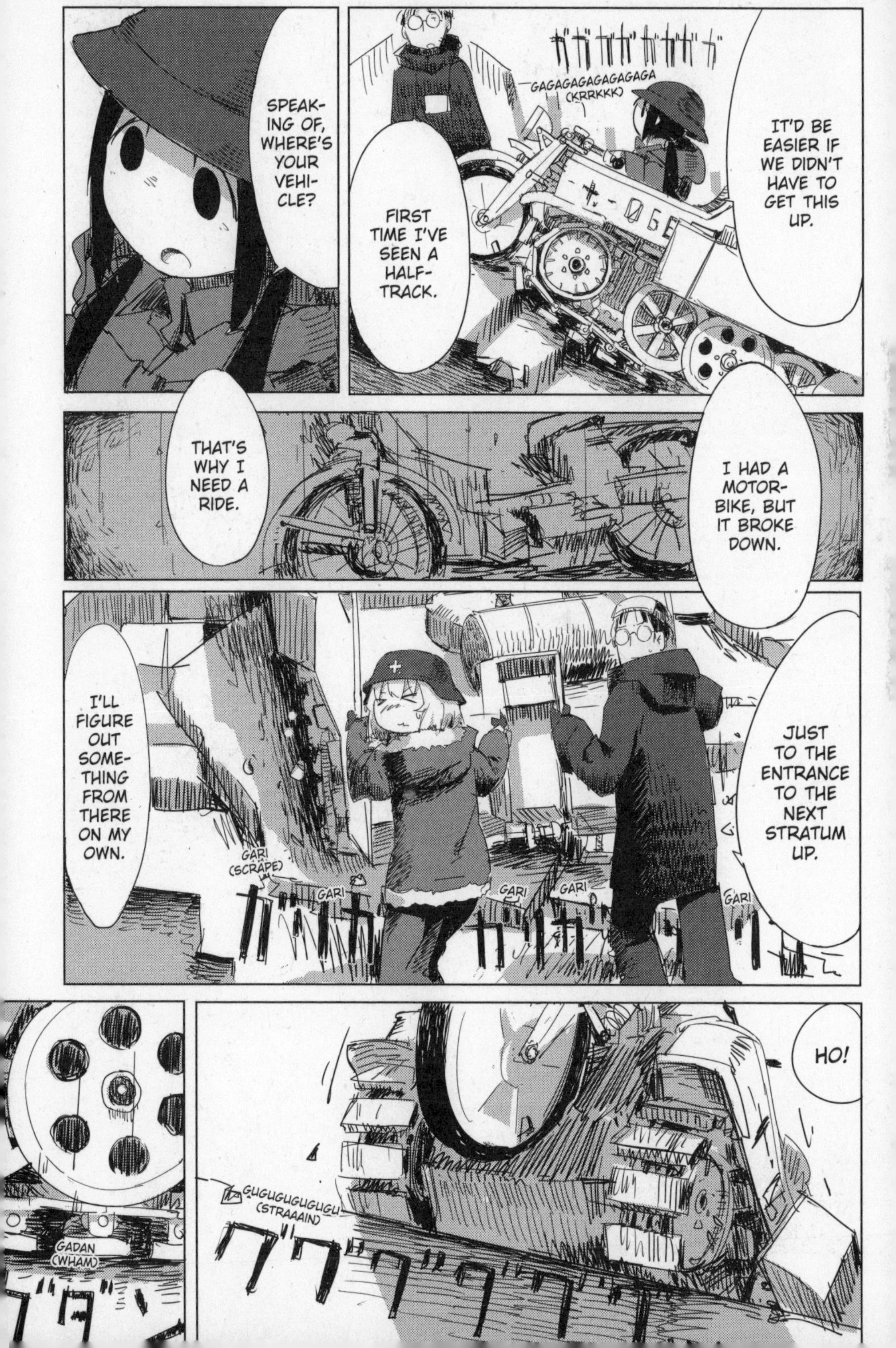
IT'D BE EASIER IF WE DIDN'T HAVE TO GET THIS UP.
GAGAGAGAGAGAGAGA (KRRKKK)
FIRST TIME I'VE SEEN A HALF-TRACK.
SPEAKING OF, WHERE'S YOUR VEHICLE?
I HAD A MOTORBIKE, BUT IT BROKE DOWN.
THAT'S WHY I NEED A RIDE.
JUST TO THE ENTRANCE TO THE NEXT STRATUM UP.
GARI
GARI
GARI
GARI
GARI (SCRAPE)
I'LL FIGURE OUT SOMETHING FROM THERE ON MY OWN.
HO!
GUGUGUGUGUGU (STRAAAIND)
GADAN (WHAM)

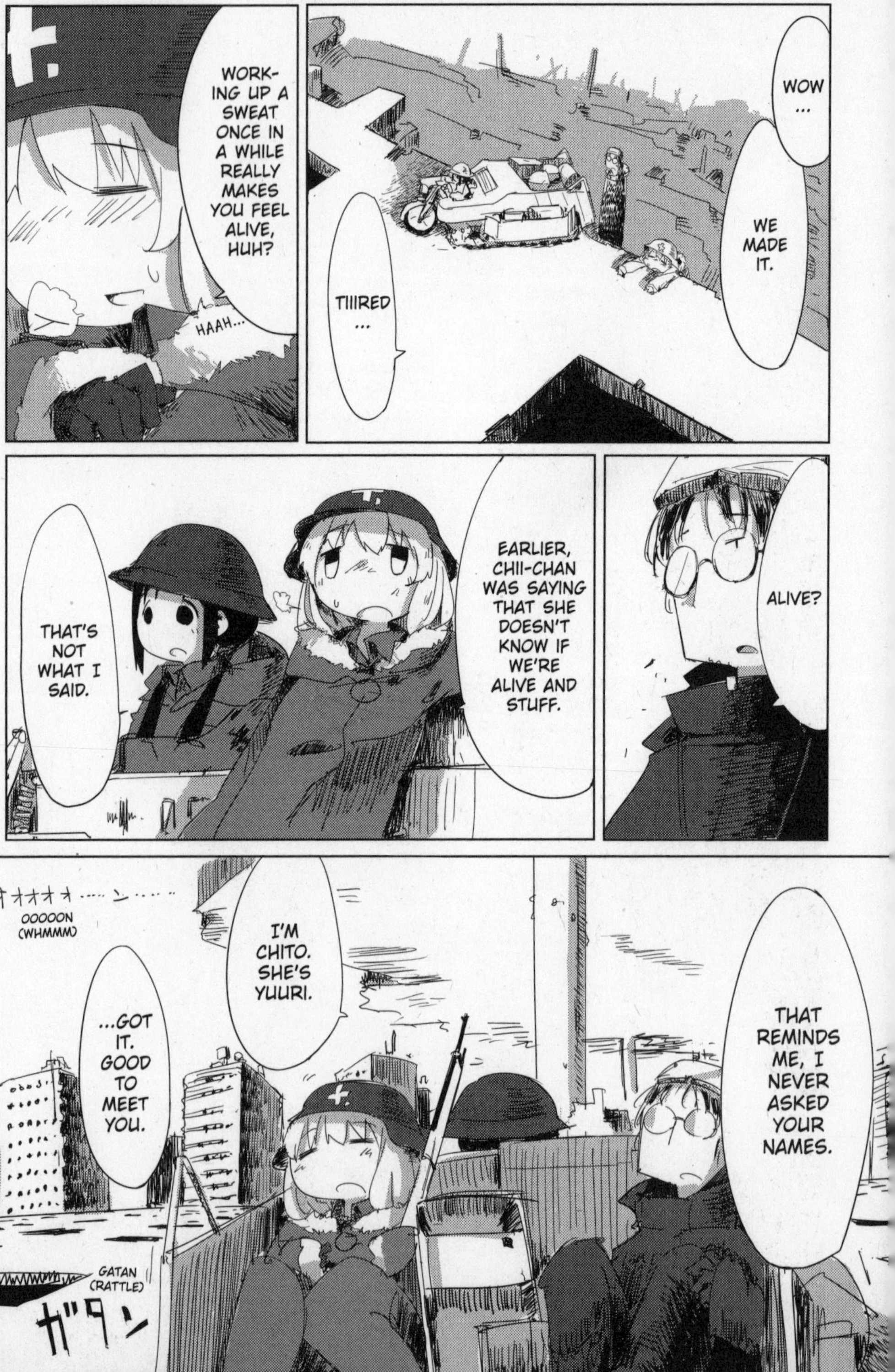
WOW ...
WE MADE IT.
TIIIRED ...
WORKING UP A SWEAT ONCE IN A WHILE REALLY MAKES YOU FEEL ALIVE, HUH?
HAAH...
ALIVE?
EARLIER, CHII-CHAN WAS SAYING THAT SHE DOESN'T KNOW IF WE'RE ALIVE AND STUFF.
THAT'S NOT WHAT I SAID.
THAT REMINDS ME, I NEVER ASKED YOUR NAMES.
I'M CHITO. SHE'S YUURI.
...GOT IT. GOOD TO MEET YOU.
オオオオオ……ン……
OOOOON (WHMMM)
ガタン
GATAN (RATTLE)

07 CITY

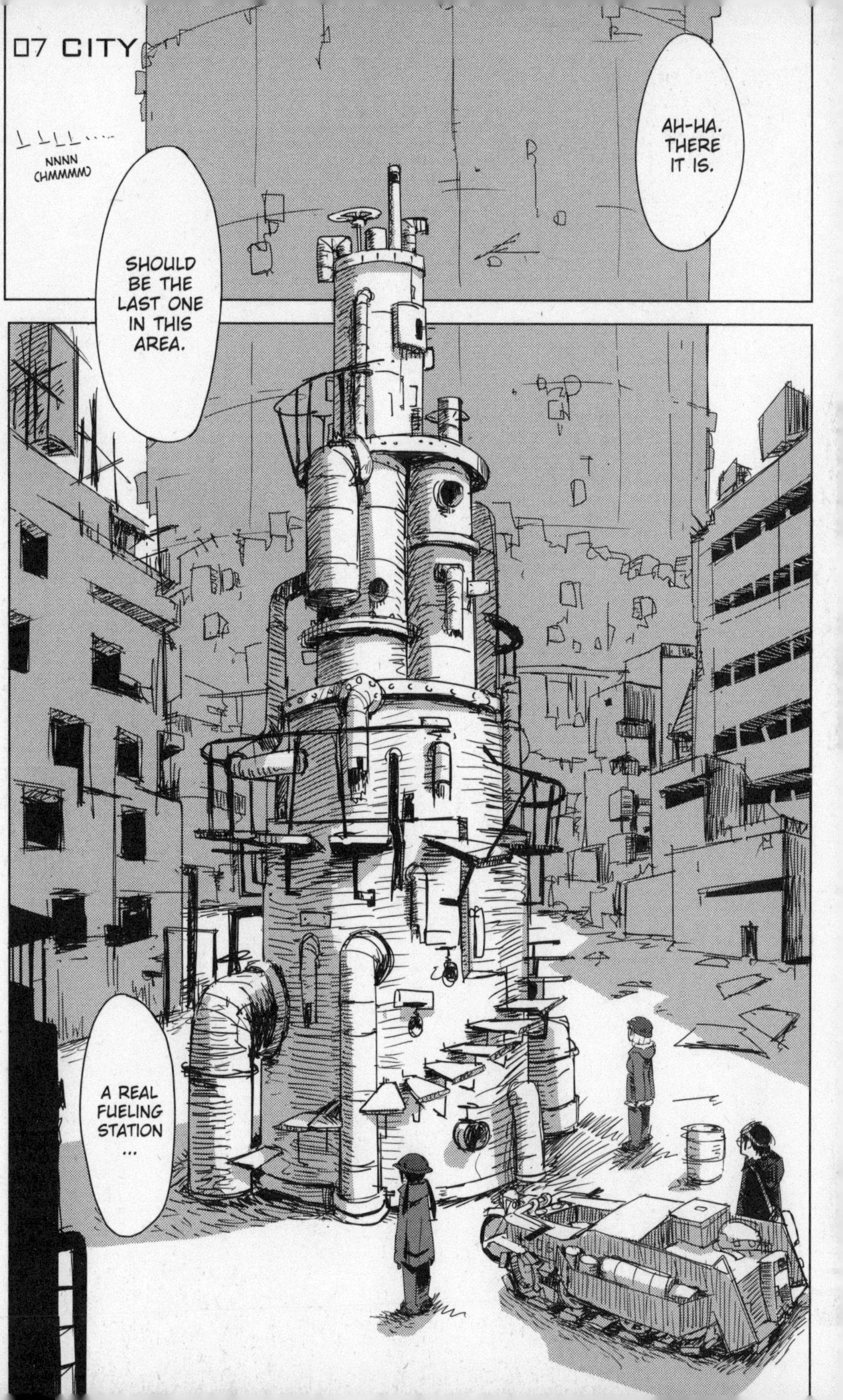
AH-HA. THERE IT IS.
NNNN (HMMMM)
SHOULD BE THE LAST ONE IN THIS AREA.
A REAL FUELING STATION ...

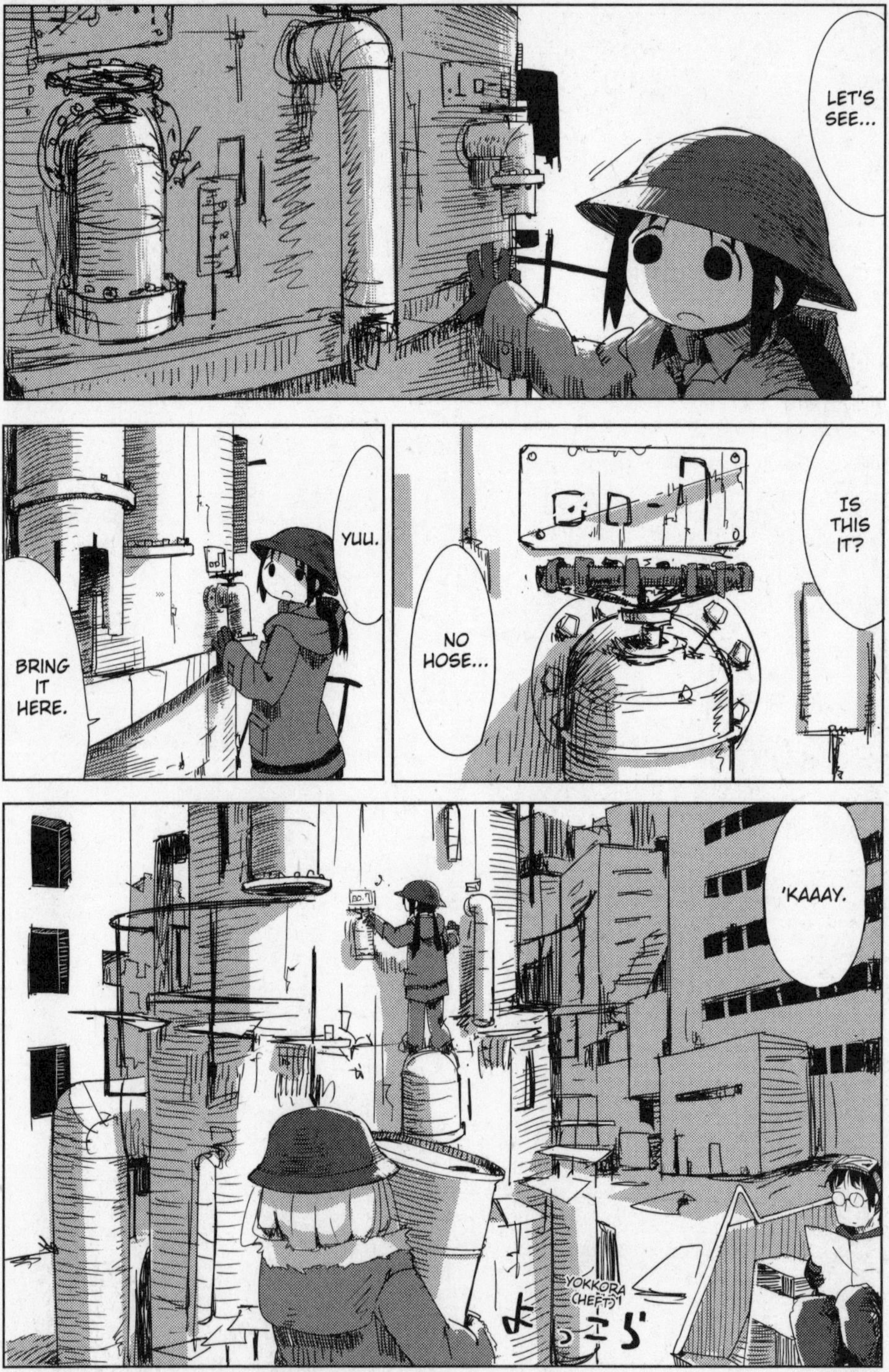
LET'S SEE...
IS THIS IT?
NO HOSE...
YUU.
BRING IT HERE.
'KAAAY.
YOKKORA (HEFT)
よっこら

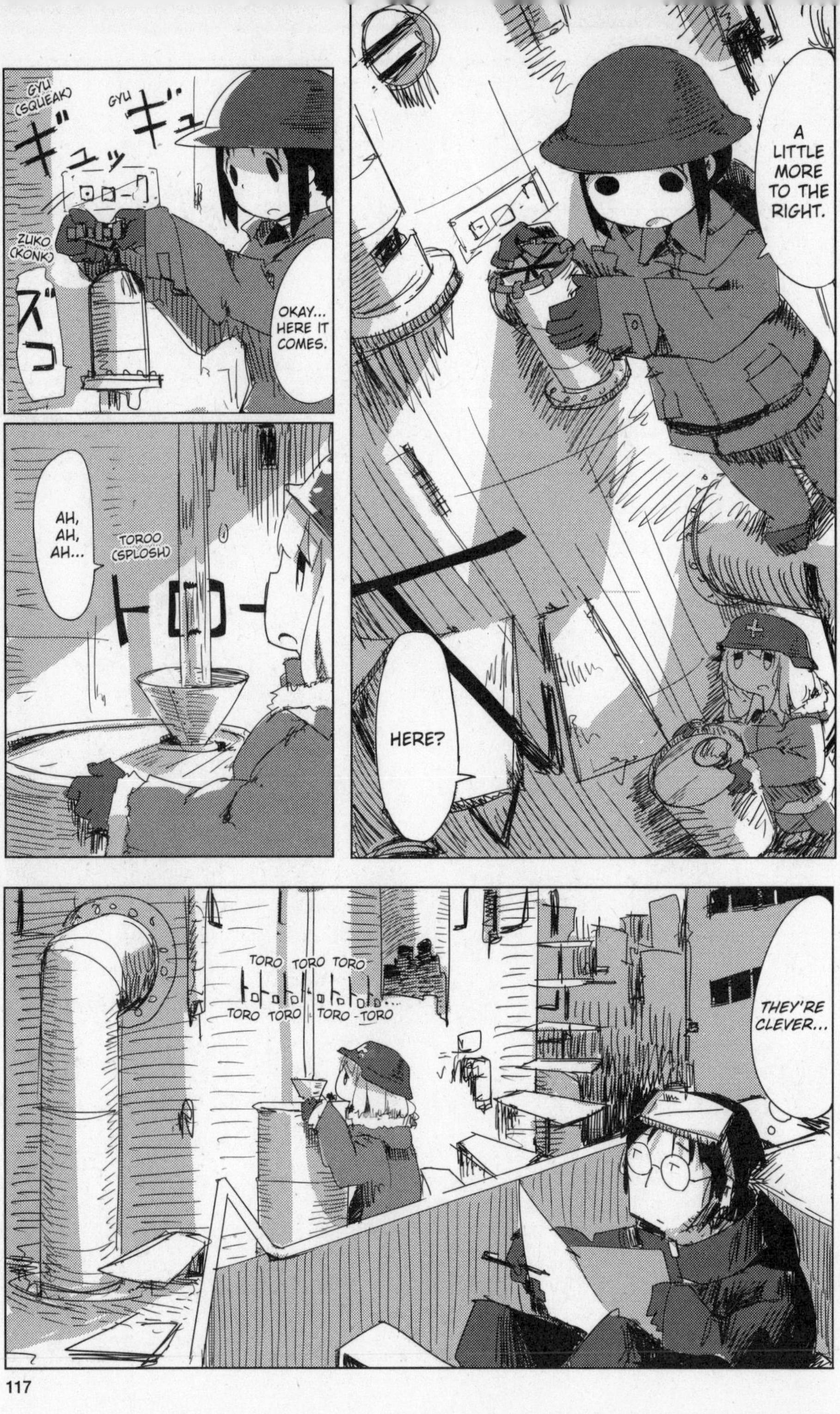
A LITTLE MORE TO THE RIGHT.
HERE?
GYU ギュ
GYU (SQUEAK) ギュッ
OKAY... HERE IT COMES.
ZUKO (KONK) ズコ
AH, AH, AH...
TOROO (SPLOSH) トロー
THEY'RE CLEVER...
TORO TORO TORO TORO TORO TORO-TORO トロトロトロトロトロトロトロ...

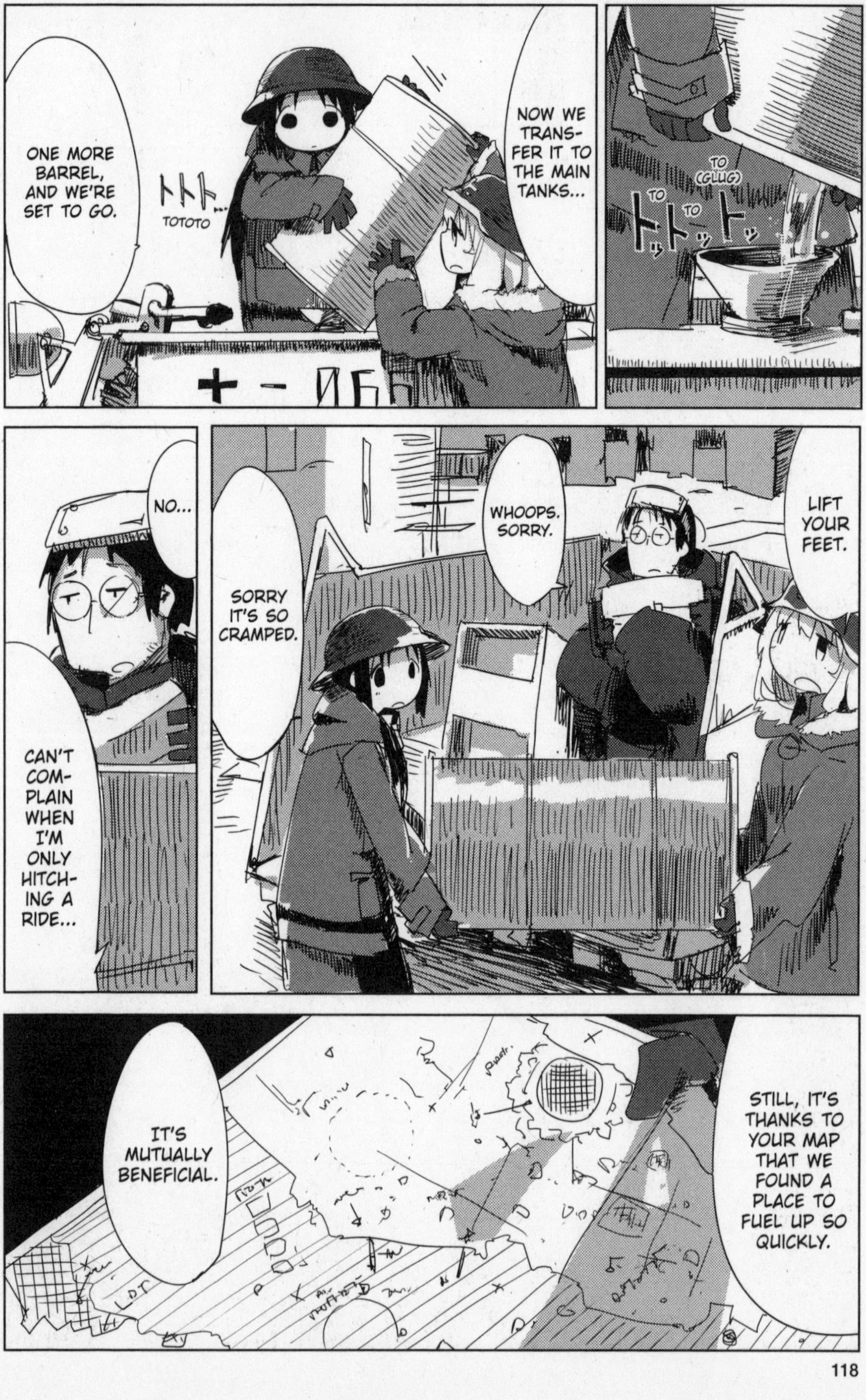
TO (GLUG) TO TO
トトッッ
NOW WE TRANSFER IT TO THE MAIN TANKS...
トトト...
TOTOTO
ONE MORE BARREL, AND WE'RE SET TO GO.
LIFT YOUR FEET.
WHOOPS. SORRY.
SORRY IT'S SO CRAMPED.
NO...
CAN'T COMPLAIN WHEN I'M ONLY HITCHING A RIDE...
STILL, IT'S THANKS TO YOUR MAP THAT WE FOUND A PLACE TO FUEL UP SO QUICKLY.
IT'S MUTUALLY BENEFICIAL.

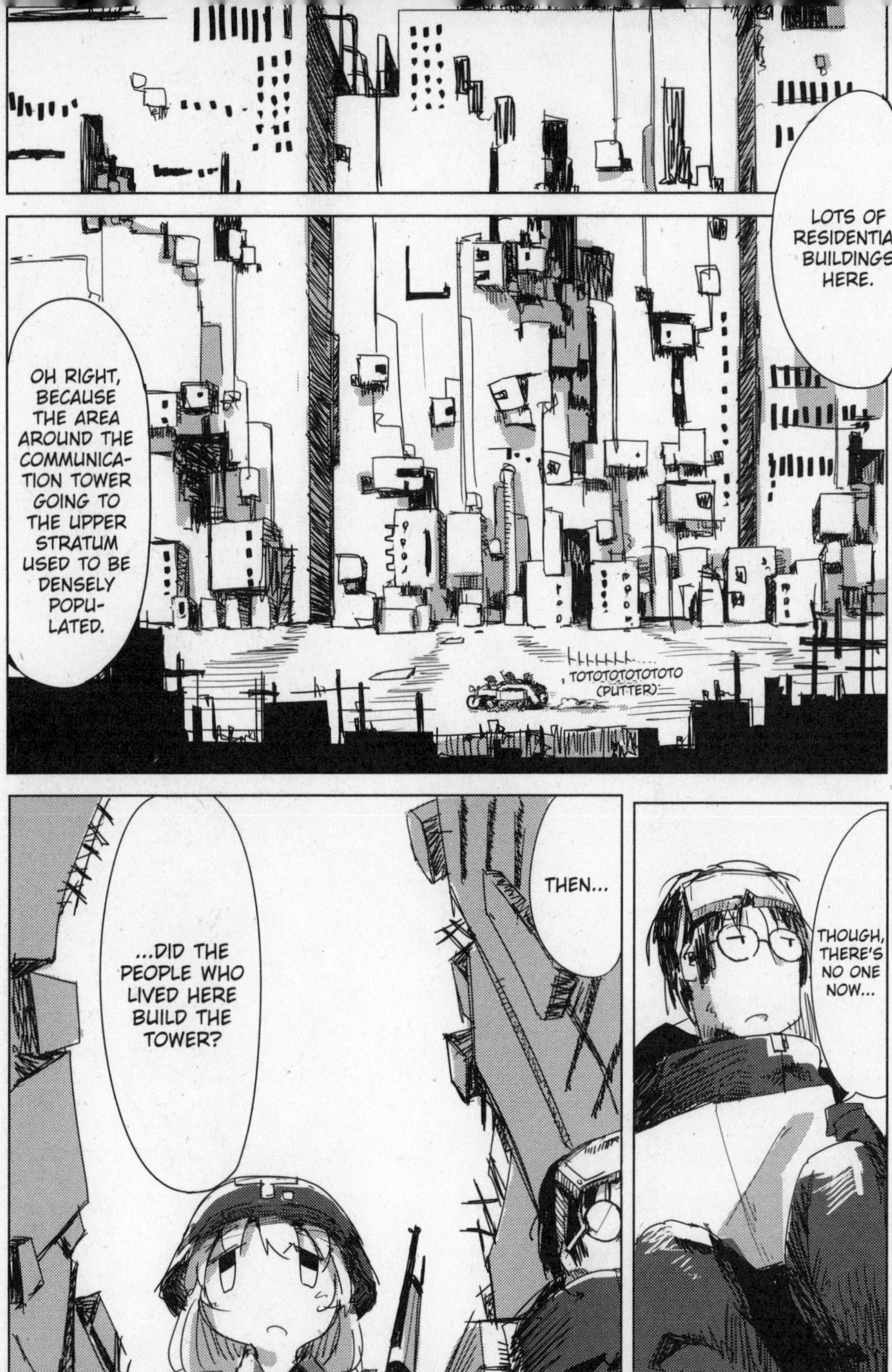
LOTS OF RESIDENTIAL BUILDINGS HERE.
OH RIGHT, BECAUSE THE AREA AROUND THE COMMUNICATION TOWER GOING TO THE UPPER STRATUM USED TO BE DENSELY POPULATED.
TOTOTOTOTOTOTOTO (PUTTER)
THOUGH, THERE'S NO ONE NOW...
THEN...
...DID THE PEOPLE WHO LIVED HERE BUILD THE TOWER?

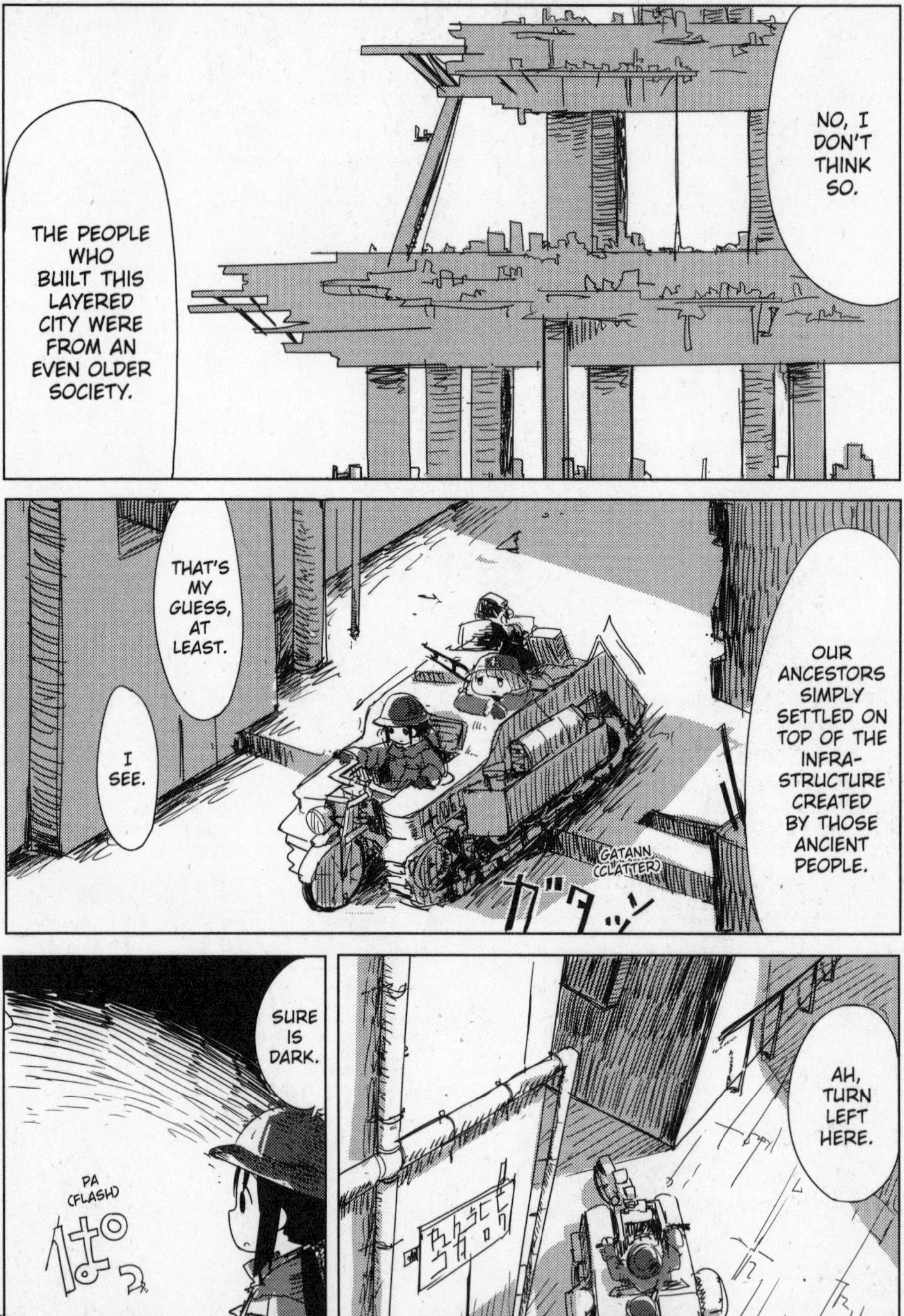
NO, I DON'T THINK SO.
THE PEOPLE WHO BUILT THIS LAYERED CITY WERE FROM AN EVEN OLDER SOCIETY.
OUR ANCESTORS SIMPLY SETTLED ON TOP OF THE INFRA-STRUCTURE CREATED BY THOSE ANCIENT PEOPLE.
THAT'S MY GUESS, AT LEAST.
I SEE.
GATANN (CLATTER)
ガタッ
AH, TURN LEFT HERE.
TOTOTOTOTOTO (PUTTER)
トトトトトト…
SURE IS DARK.
PA (FLASH)
ぱっ

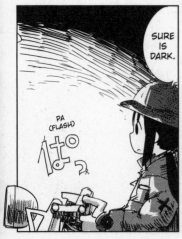

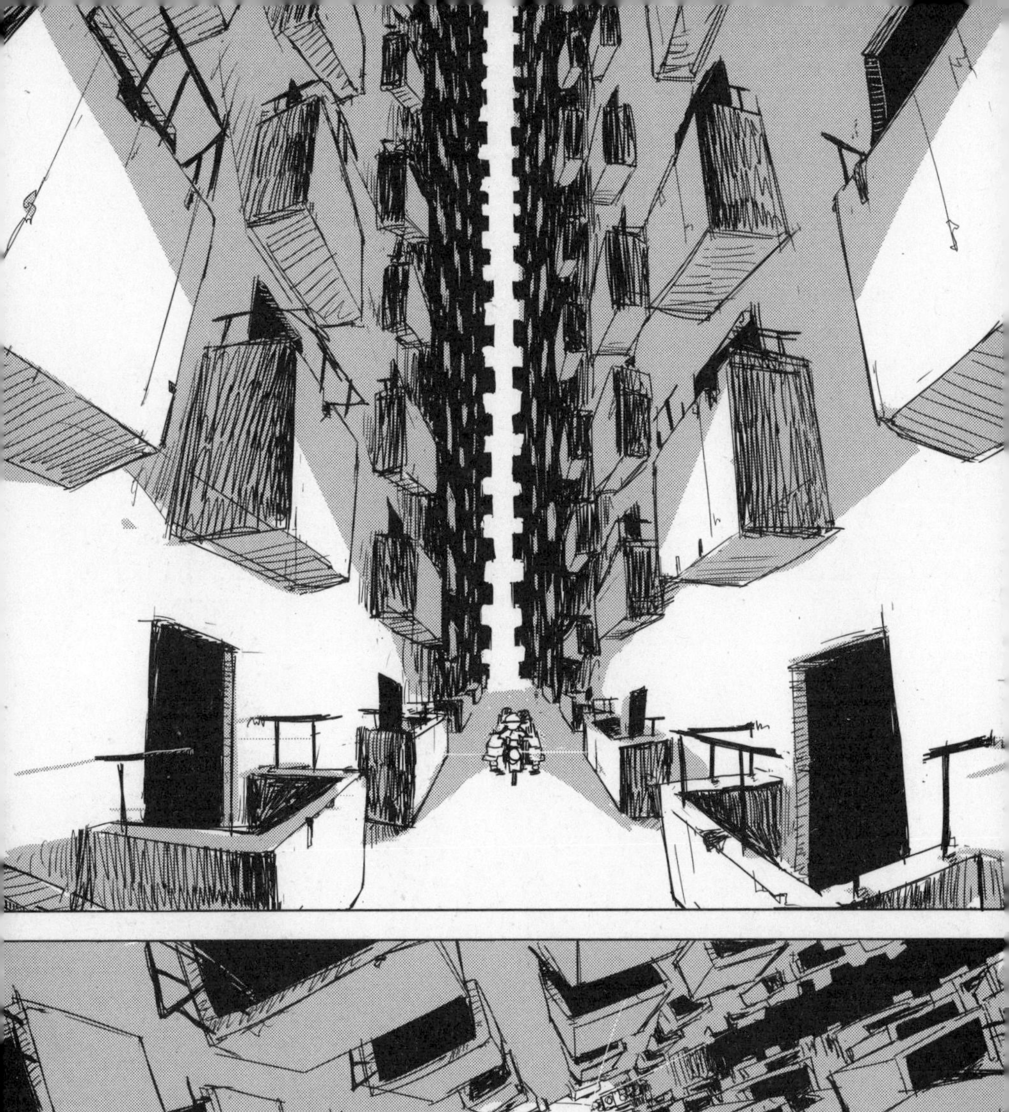
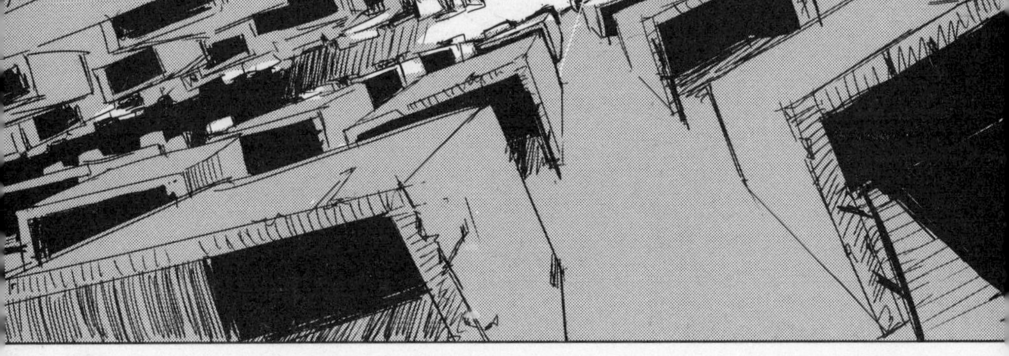

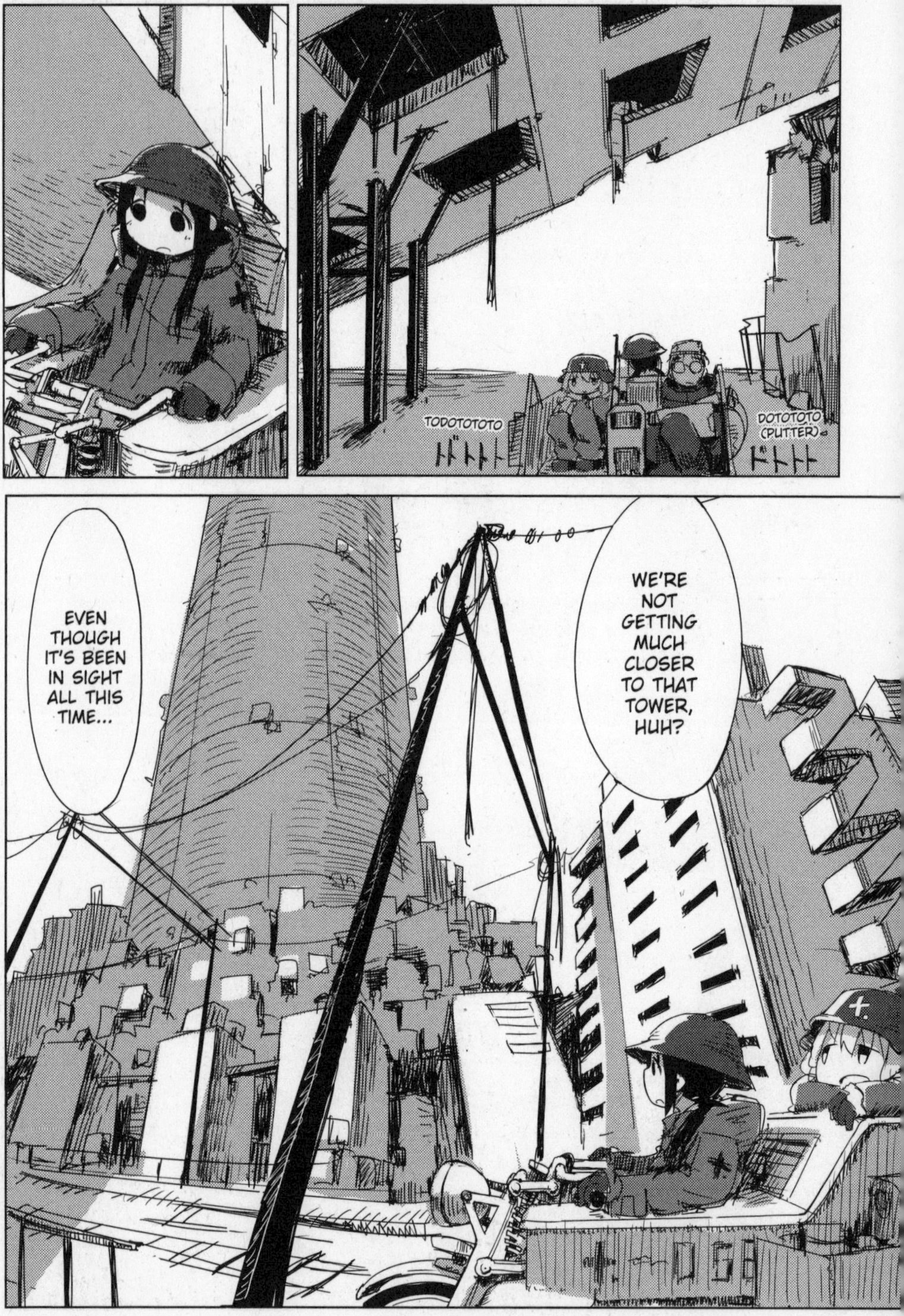
DOTOTOTO (PUTTER)
ドトトト
TODOTOTOTO
ドトトト
WE'RE NOT GETTING MUCH CLOSER TO THAT TOWER, HUH?
EVEN THOUGH IT'S BEEN IN SIGHT ALL THIS TIME...

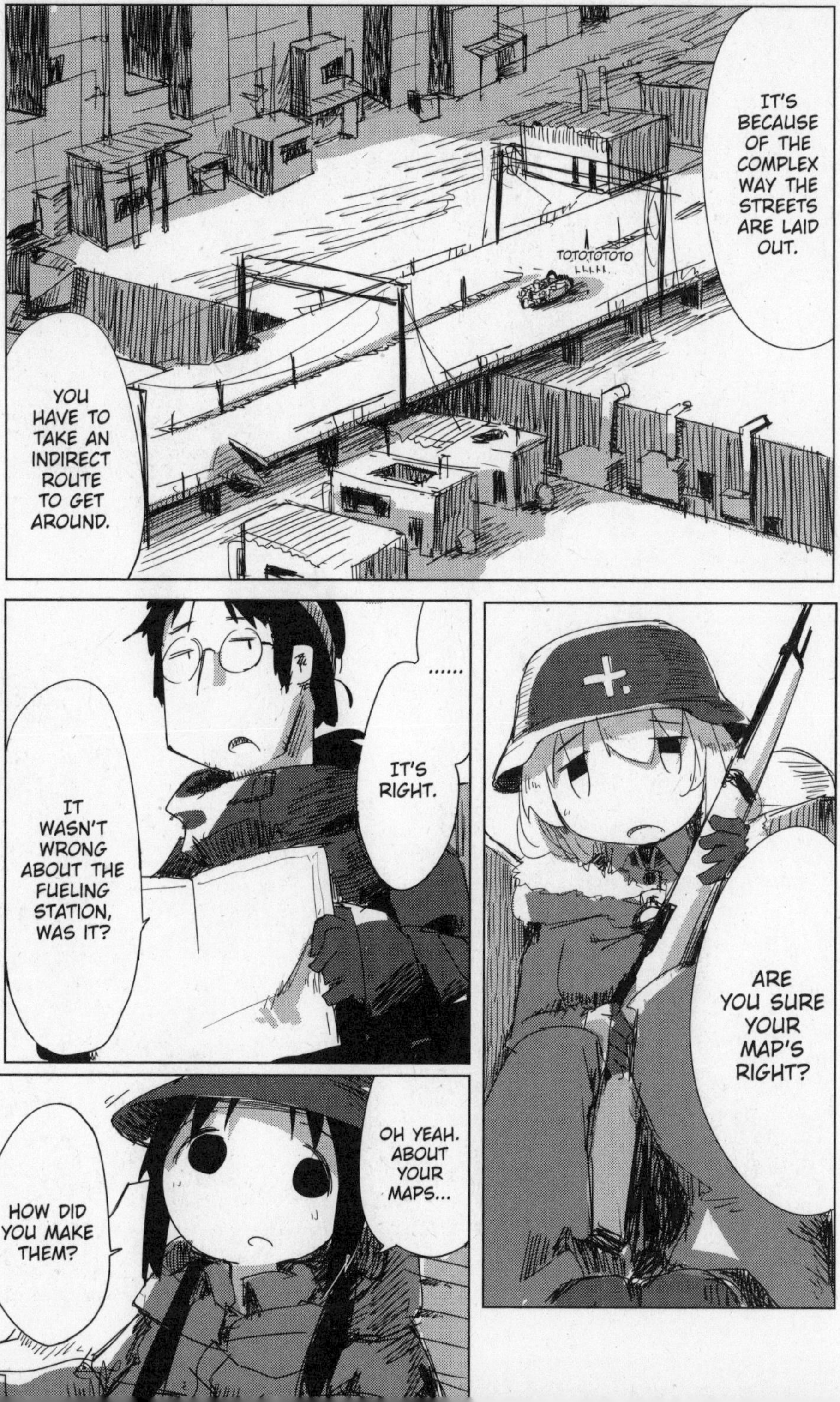
IT'S BECAUSE OF THE COMPLEX WAY THE STREETS ARE LAID OUT.
TOTOTOTOTO
YOU HAVE TO TAKE AN INDIRECT ROUTE TO GET AROUND.
ARE YOU SURE YOUR MAP'S RIGHT?
......
IT'S RIGHT.
IT WASN'T WRONG ABOUT THE FUELING STATION, WAS IT?
OH YEAH. ABOUT YOUR MAPS...
HOW DID YOU MAKE THEM?

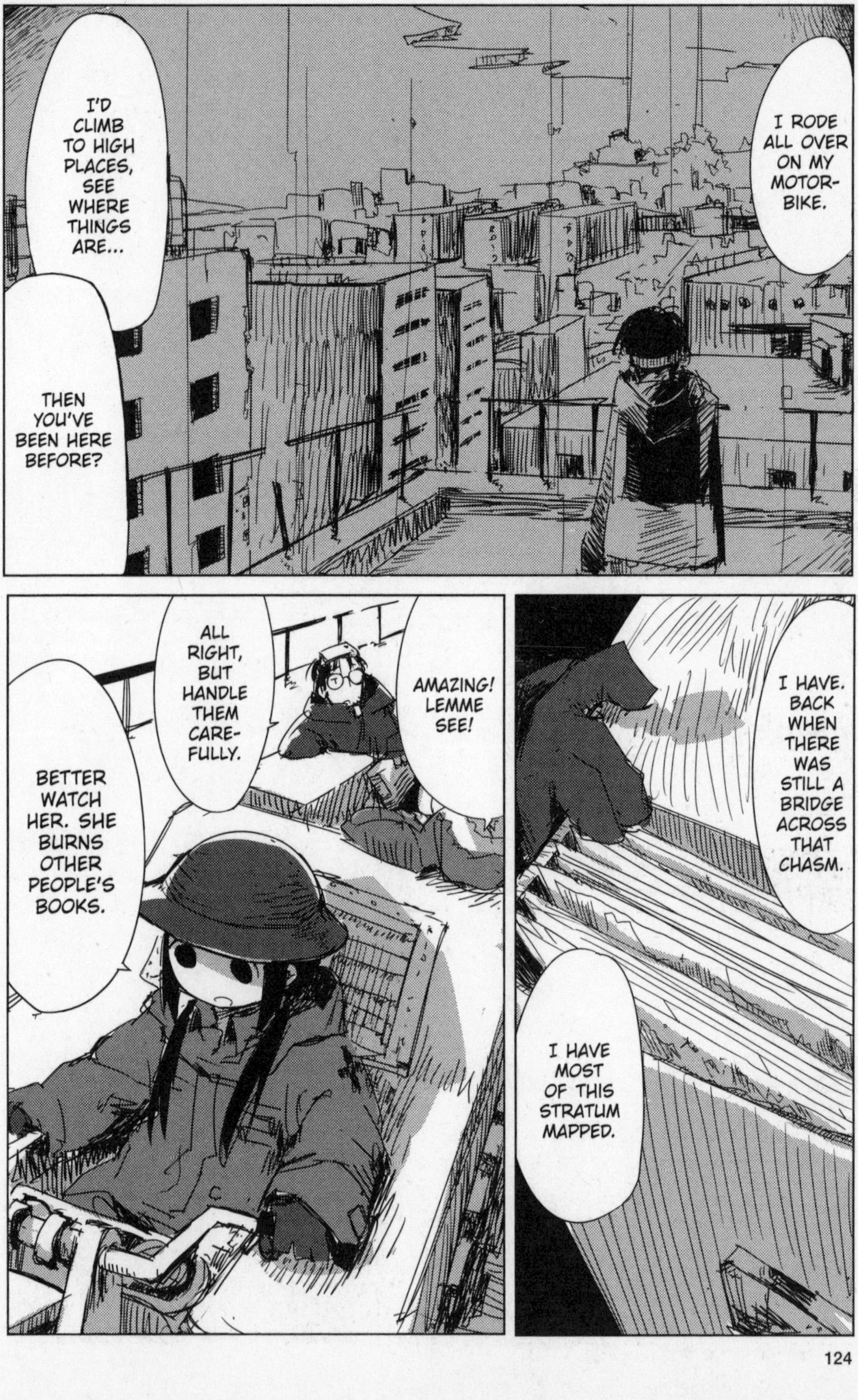
I RODE ALL OVER ON MY MOTOR-BIKE.
I'D CLIMB TO HIGH PLACES, SEE WHERE THINGS ARE...
THEN YOU'VE BEEN HERE BEFORE?
I HAVE. BACK WHEN THERE WAS STILL A BRIDGE ACROSS THAT CHASM.
I HAVE MOST OF THIS STRATUM MAPPED.
AMAZING! LEMME SEE!
ALL RIGHT, BUT HANDLE THEM CARE-FULLY.
BETTER WATCH HER. SHE BURNS OTHER PEOPLE'S BOOKS.

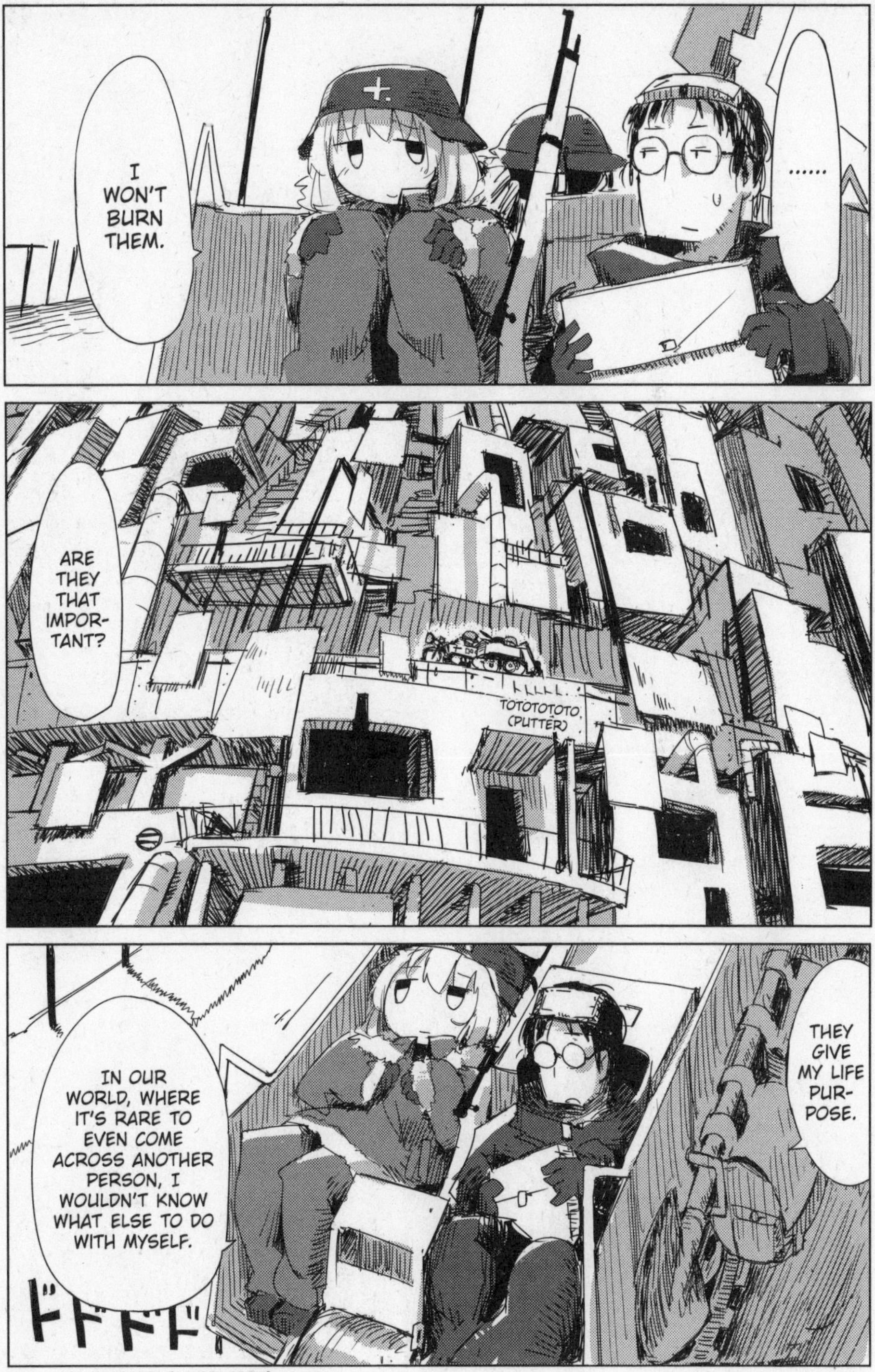
......
I WON'T BURN THEM.
ARE THEY THAT IMPOR-TANT?
TOTOTOTOTO (PUTTER)
THEY GIVE MY LIFE PUR-POSE.
IN OUR WORLD, WHERE IT'S RARE TO EVEN COME ACROSS ANOTHER PERSON, I WOULDN'T KNOW WHAT ELSE TO DO WITH MYSELF.
ドドドド
SFX: DODODODO (DADRRMDRRM)

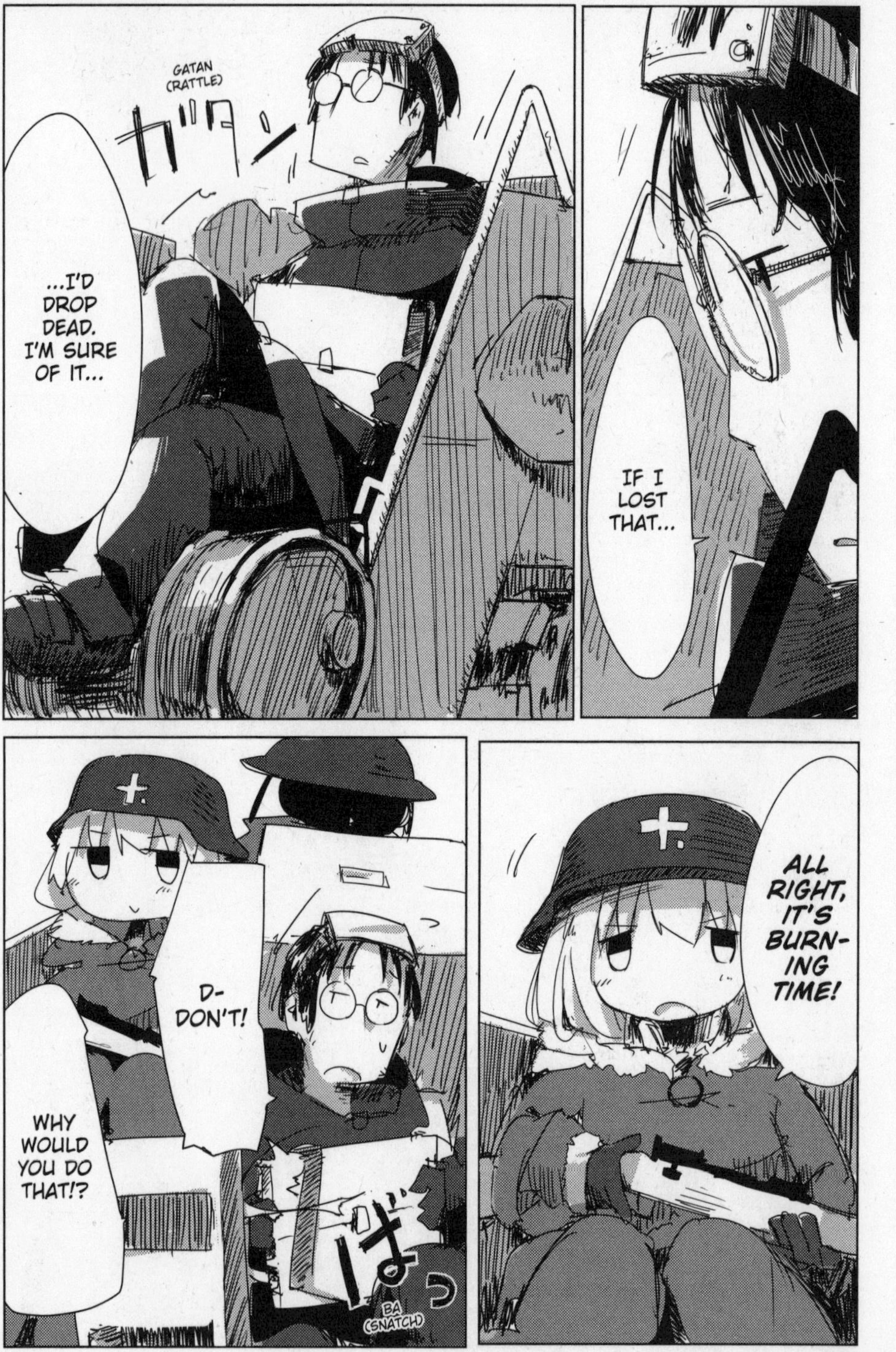
IF I LOST THAT...
GATAN (RATTLE)
...I'D DROP DEAD. I'M SURE OF IT...
ALL RIGHT, IT'S BURNING TIME!
D-DON'T!
WHY WOULD YOU DO THAT!?
BA (SNATCH)

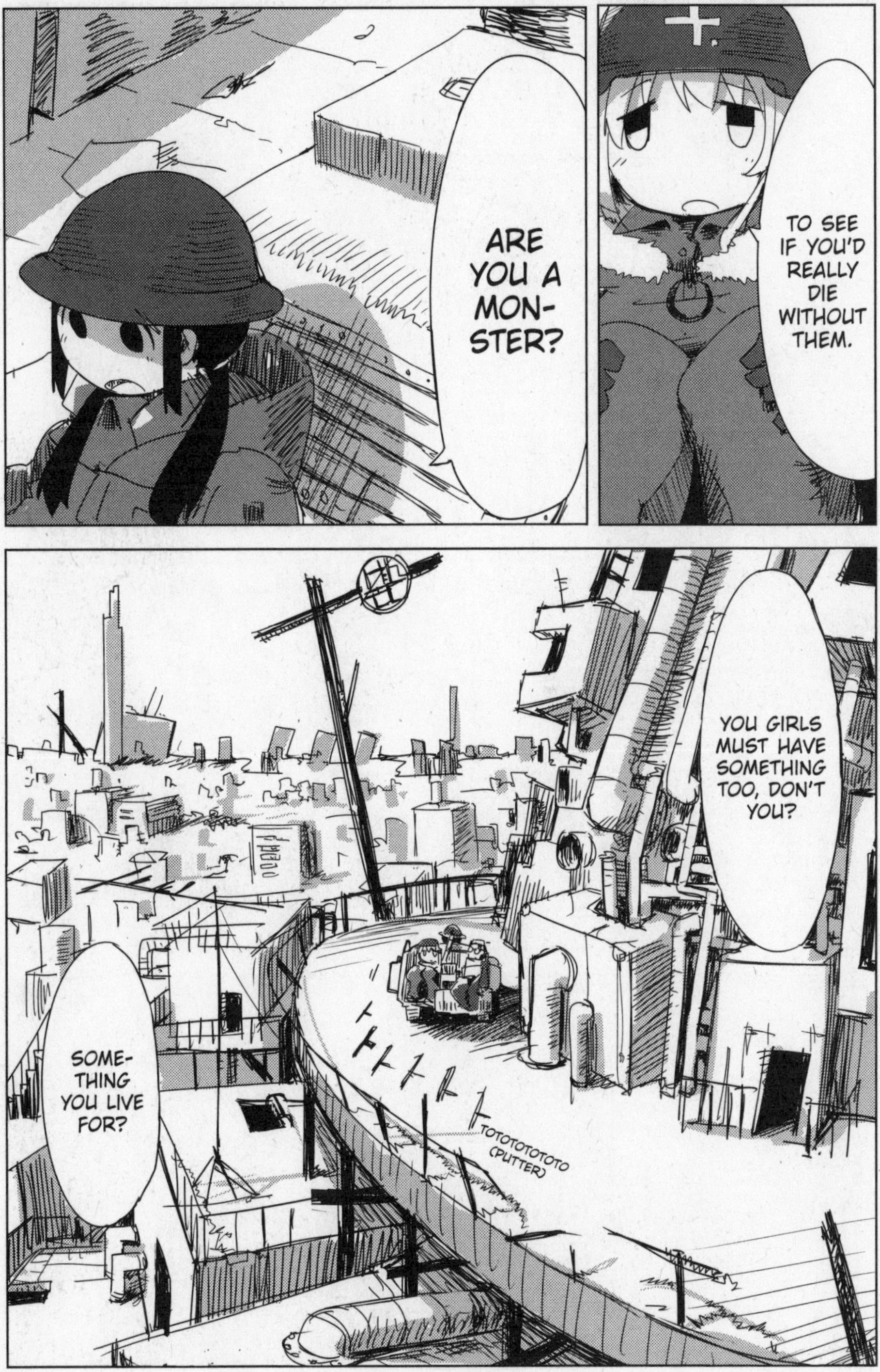
TO SEE IF YOU'D REALLY DIE WITHOUT THEM.
ARE YOU A MON-STER?
YOU GIRLS MUST HAVE SOMETHING TOO, DON'T YOU?
TOTOTOTOTOTO (PUTTER)
SOME-THING YOU LIVE FOR?

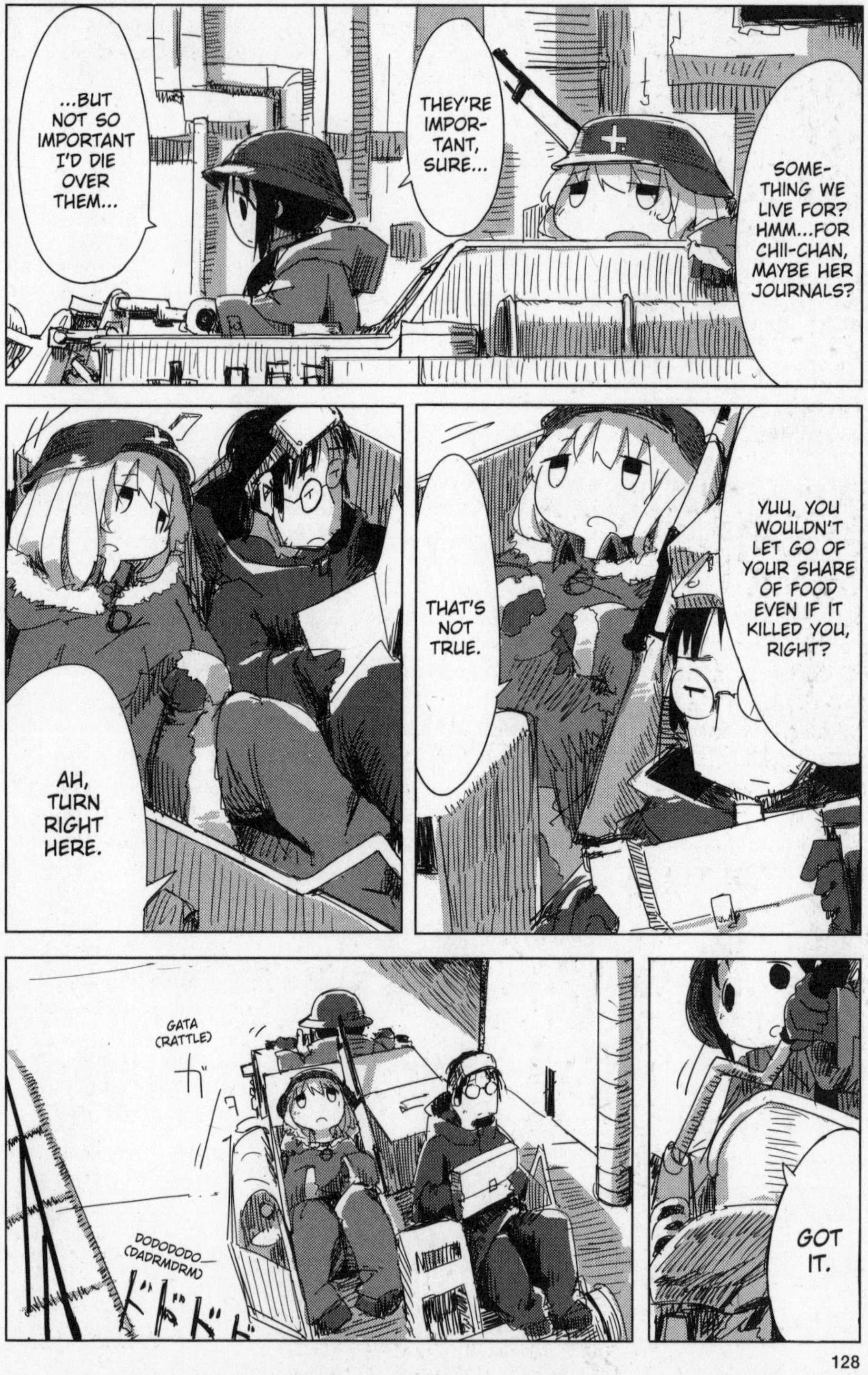
SOME-THING WE LIVE FOR? HMM...FOR CHII-CHAN, MAYBE HER JOURNALS?
THEY'RE IMPOR-TANT, SURE...
...BUT NOT SO IMPORTANT I'D DIE OVER THEM...
YUU, YOU WOULDN'T LET GO OF YOUR SHARE OF FOOD EVEN IF IT KILLED YOU, RIGHT?
THAT'S NOT TRUE.
AH, TURN RIGHT HERE.
GOT IT.
GATA (RATTLE)
DODODODO (DADRMDRM)
ドドドド

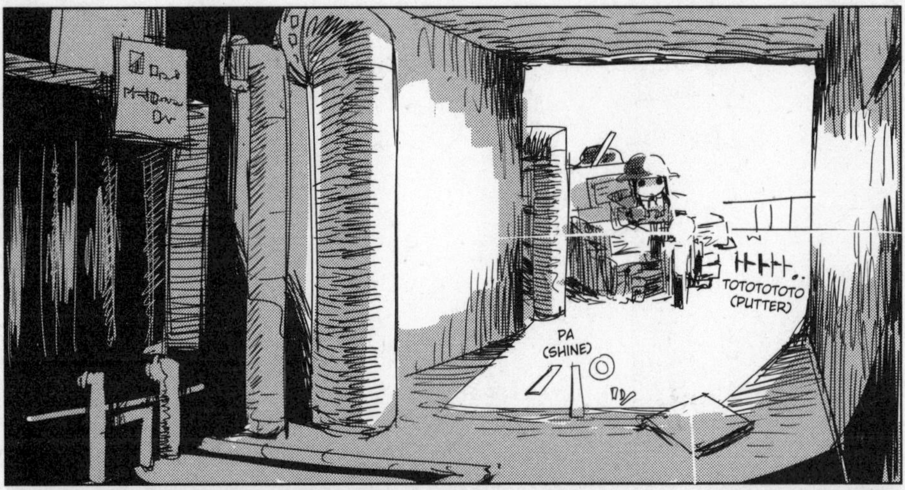
TOTOTOTOTO
(PUTTER)
PA
(SHINE)

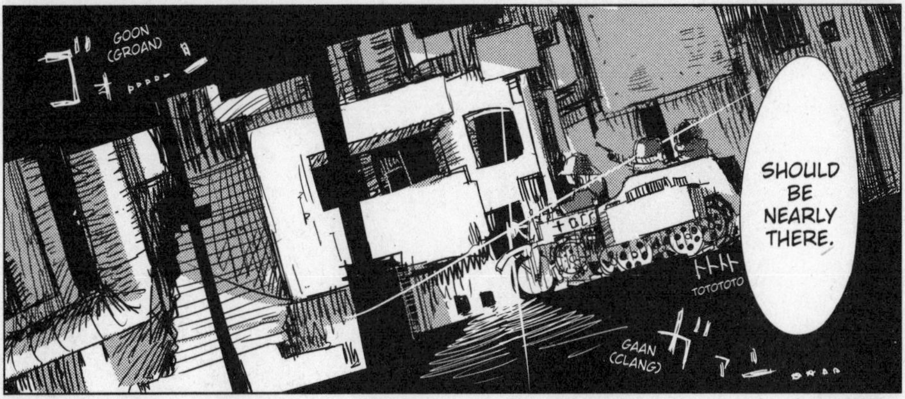
SHOULD BE NEARLY THERE.
TOTOTOTO
GAAN
(CLANG)
GOON
(GROAN)

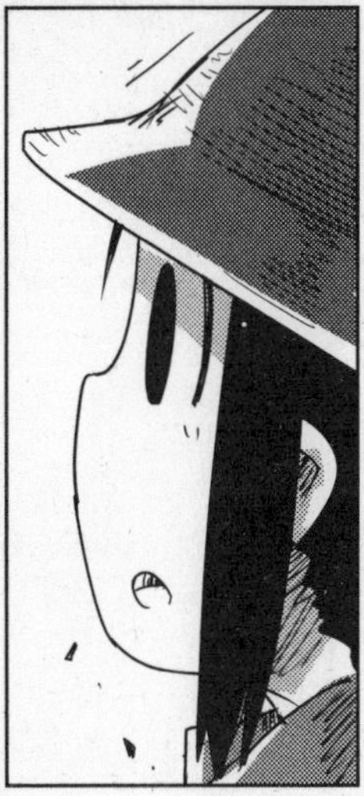

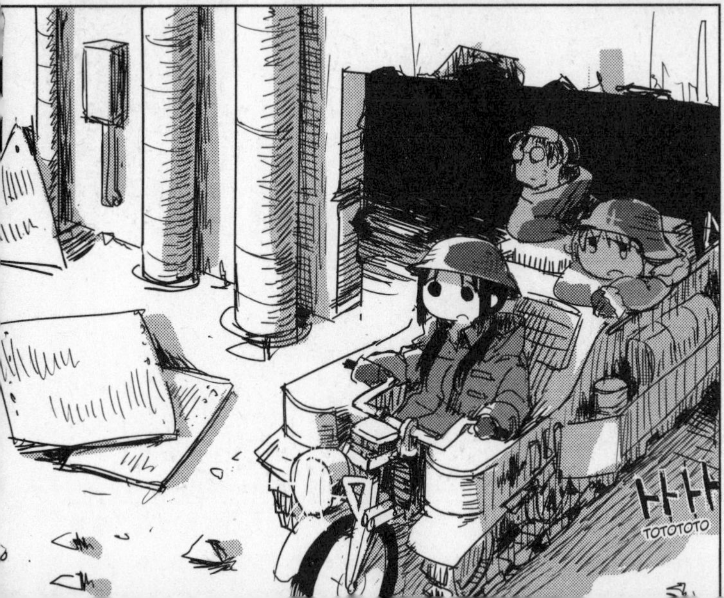
TOTOTOTO

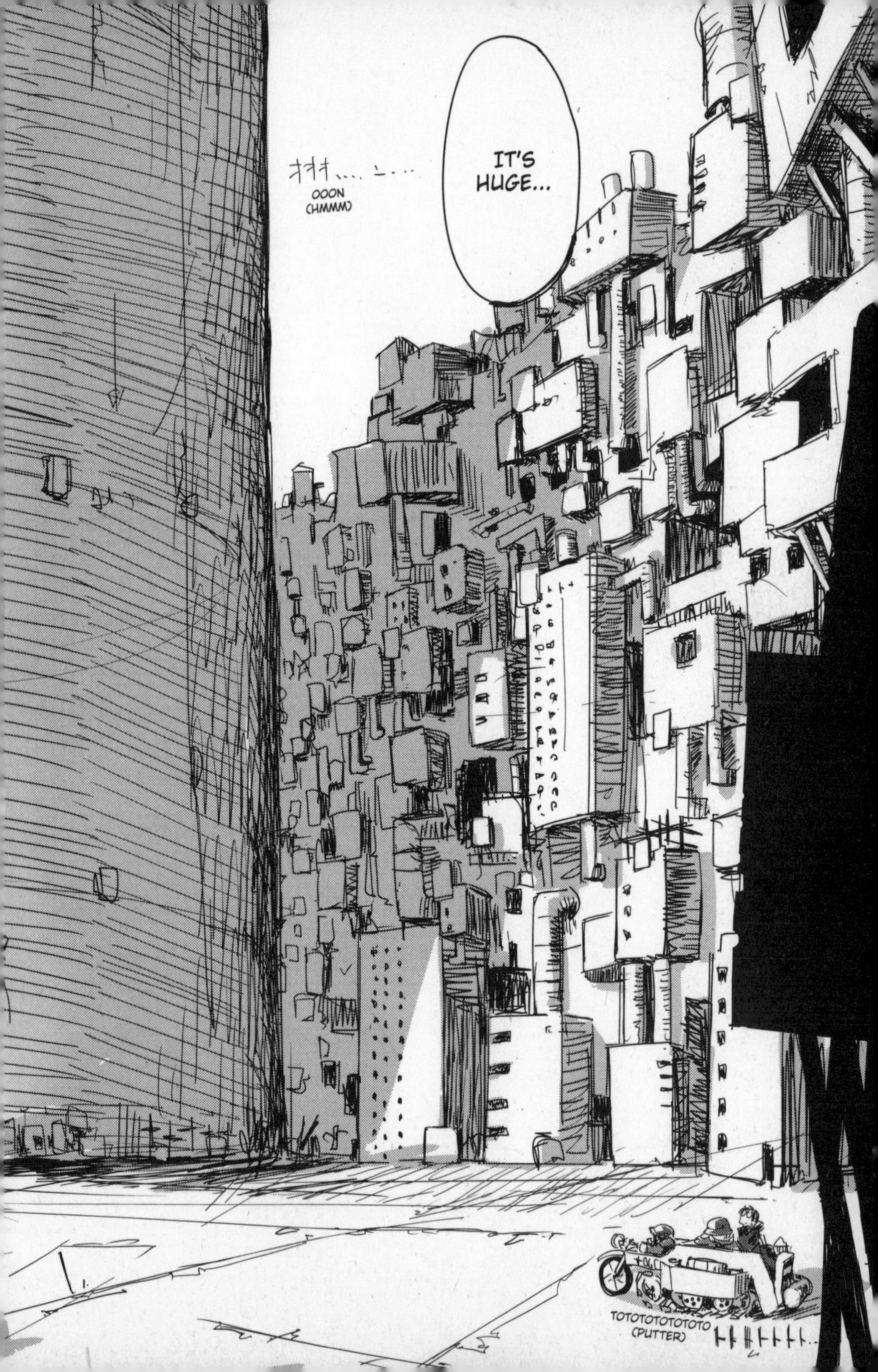
IT'S HUGE...
OOON (HMMM)
TOTOTOTOTOTOTO (PUTTER)

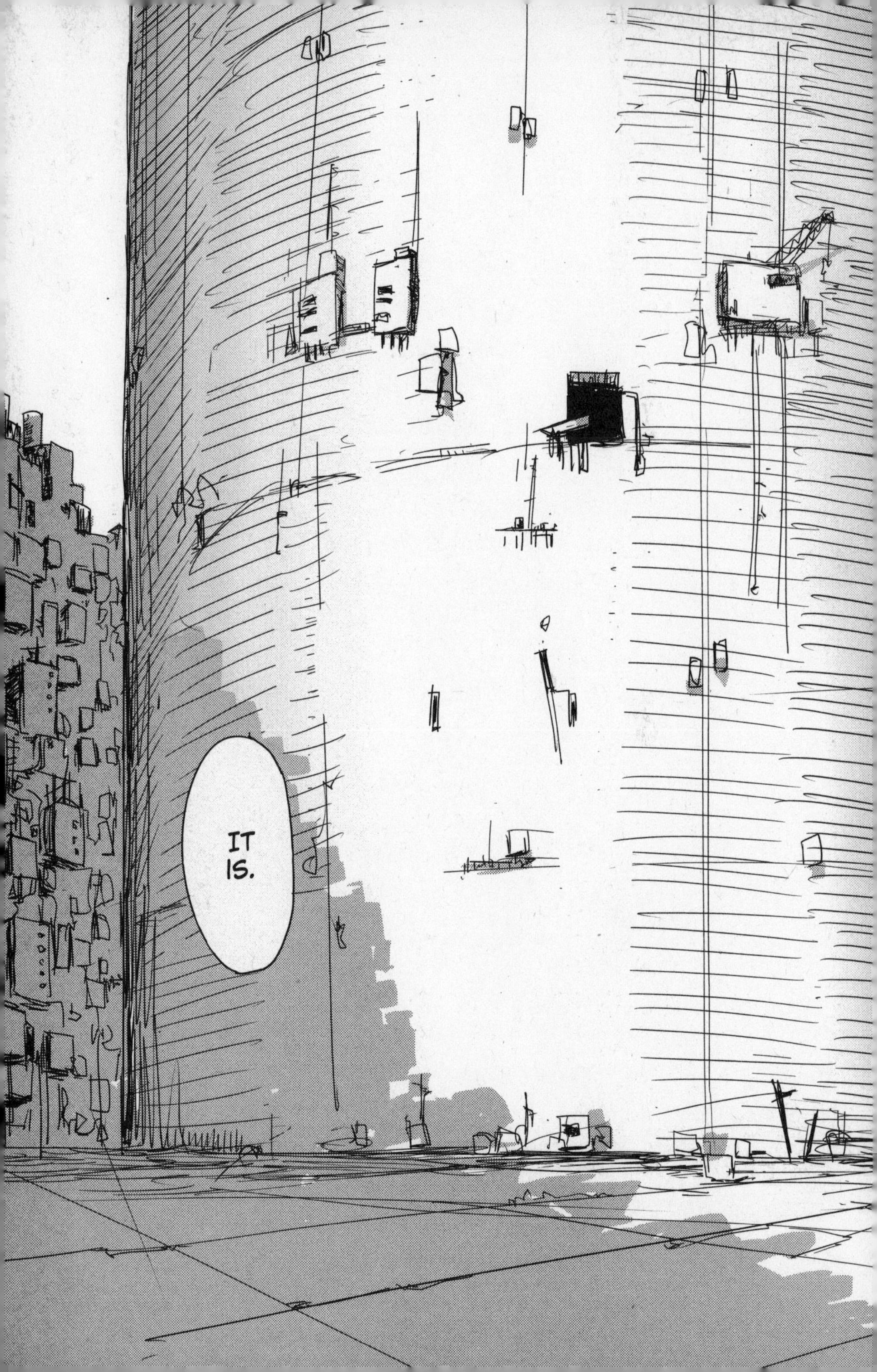
IT IS.

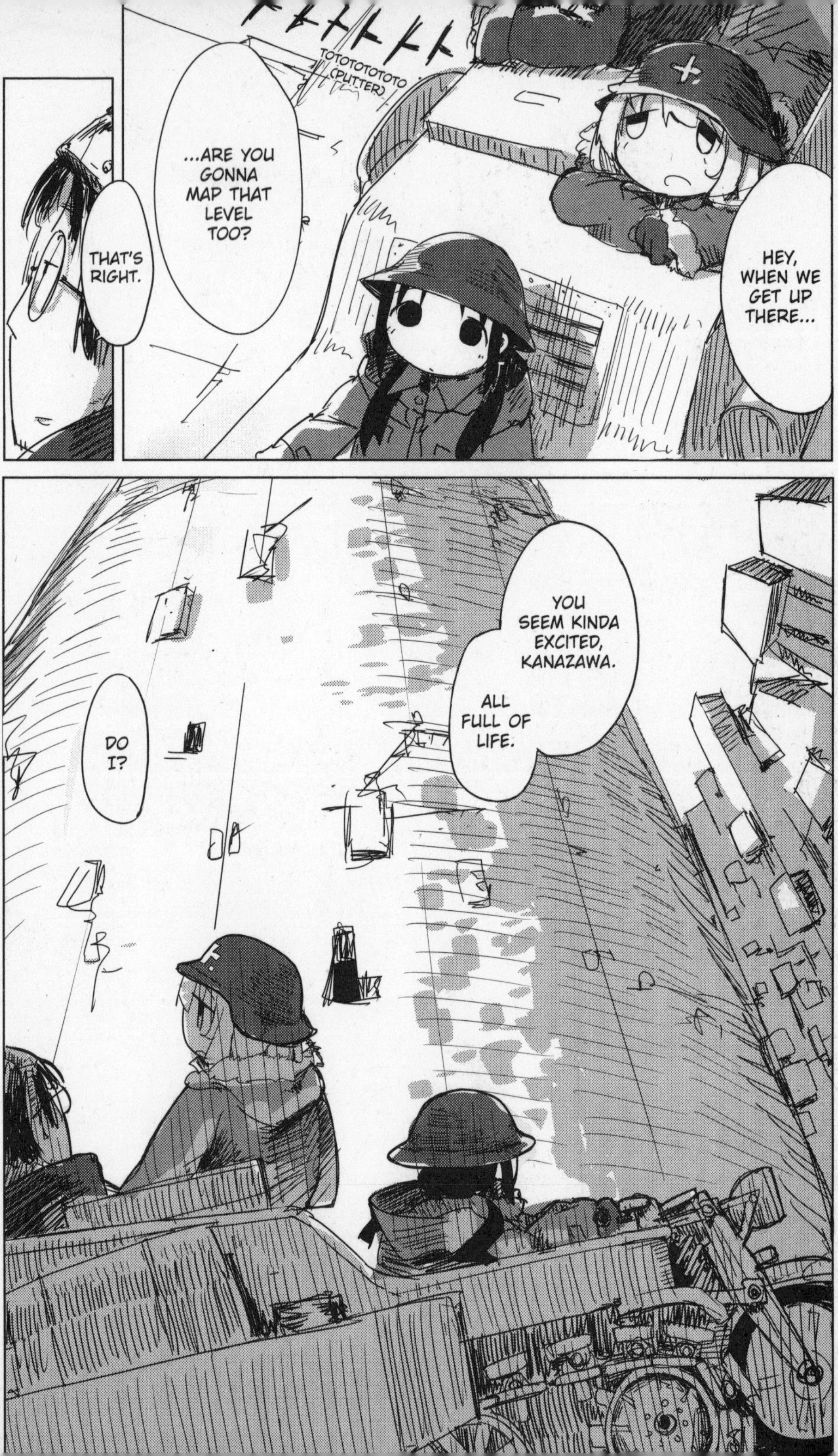
TOTOTOTOTOTO (PUTTER)
HEY, WHEN WE GET UP THERE...
...ARE YOU GONNA MAP THAT LEVEL TOO?
THAT'S RIGHT.
YOU SEEM KINDA EXCITED, KANAZAWA.
ALL FULL OF LIFE.
DO I?

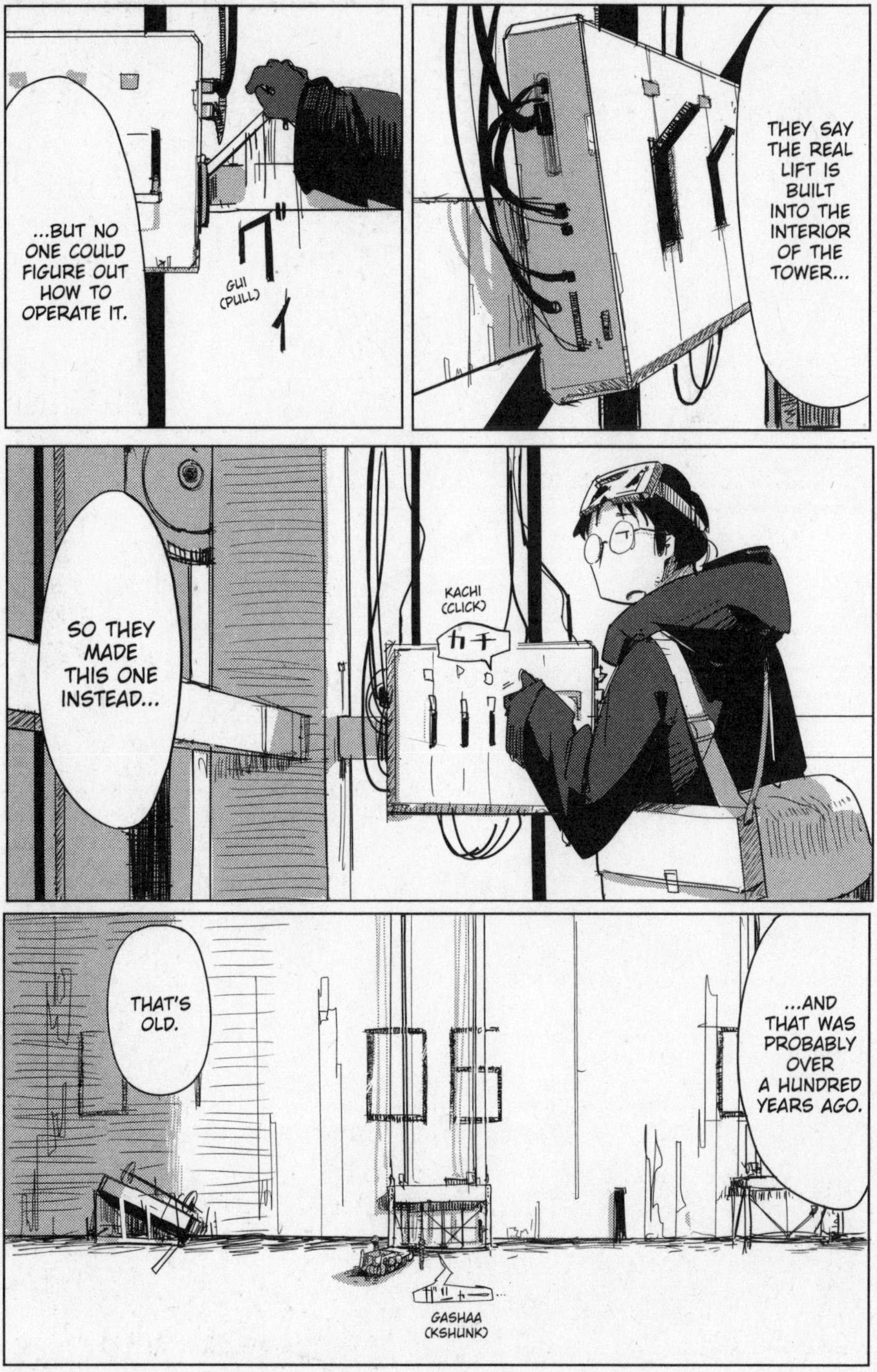
THEY SAY THE REAL LIFT IS BUILT INTO THE INTERIOR OF THE TOWER...
...BUT NO ONE COULD FIGURE OUT HOW TO OPERATE IT.
GUI (PULL)
KACHI (CLICK)
カチ
SO THEY MADE THIS ONE INSTEAD...
...AND THAT WAS PROBABLY OVER A HUNDRED YEARS AGO.
THAT'S OLD.
GASHAA (KSHUNK)

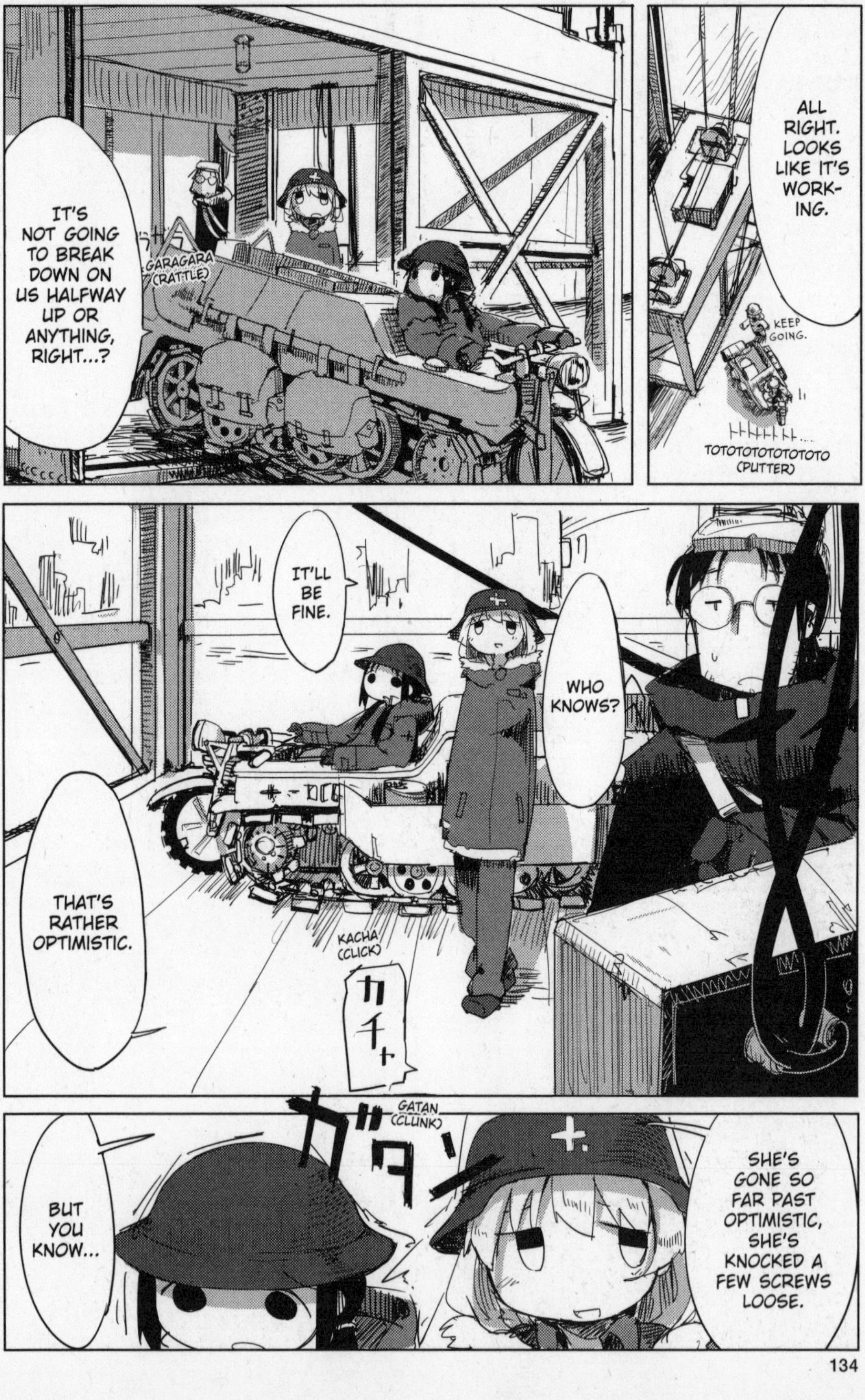
ALL RIGHT. LOOKS LIKE IT'S WORK-ING.
KEEP GOING.
TOTOTOTOTOTOTOTO (PUTTER)
IT'S NOT GOING TO BREAK DOWN ON US HALFWAY UP OR ANYTHING, RIGHT...?
GARAGARA (RATTLE)
IT'LL BE FINE.
WHO KNOWS?
KACHA (CLICK)
カチャ
THAT'S RATHER OPTIMISTIC.
GATAN (CLUNK)
ガタン
SHE'S GONE SO FAR PAST OPTIMISTIC, SHE'S KNOCKED A FEW SCREWS LOOSE.
BUT YOU KNOW...

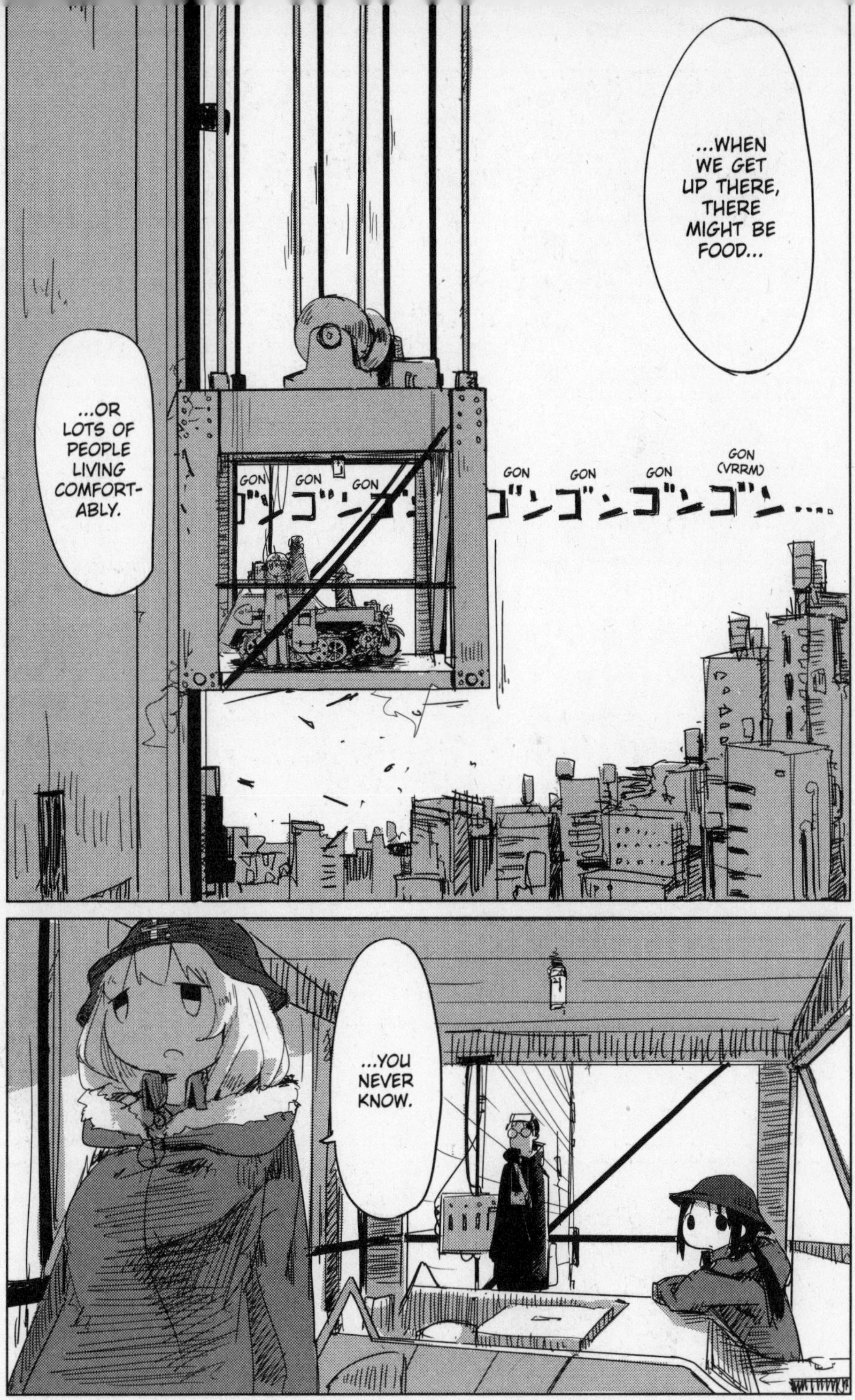
...WHEN WE GET UP THERE, THERE MIGHT BE FOOD...
GON (VRRM)
GON
GON
GON
GON
GON
GON
...OR LOTS OF PEOPLE LIVING COMFORT-ABLY.
...YOU NEVER KNOW.

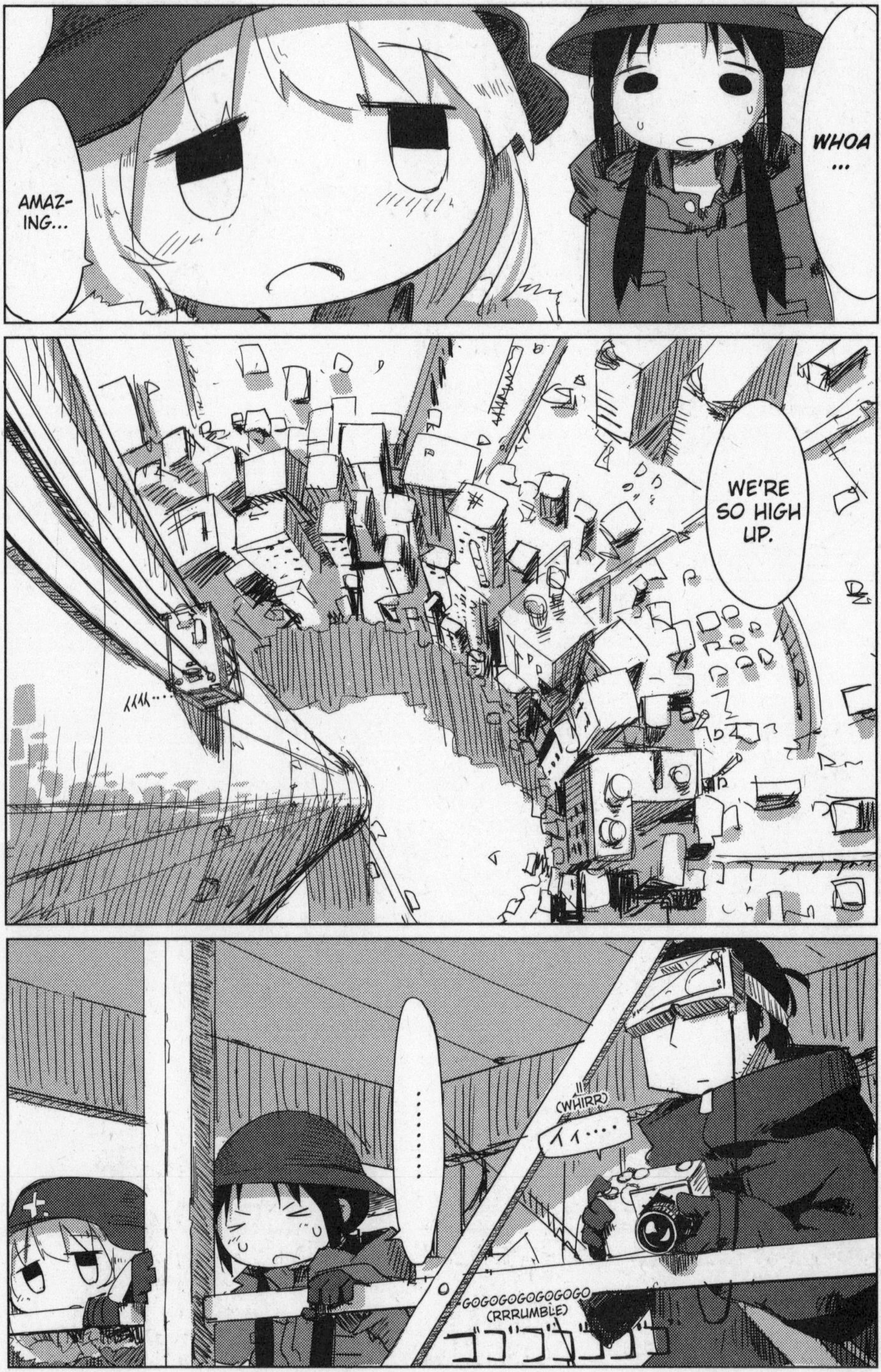
WHOA ...
AMAZ-ING...
WE'RE SO HIGH UP.
(WHIRR)
イィ….
……
GOGOGOGOGOGOGO (RRRUMBLE)
ゴゴゴゴゴゴ

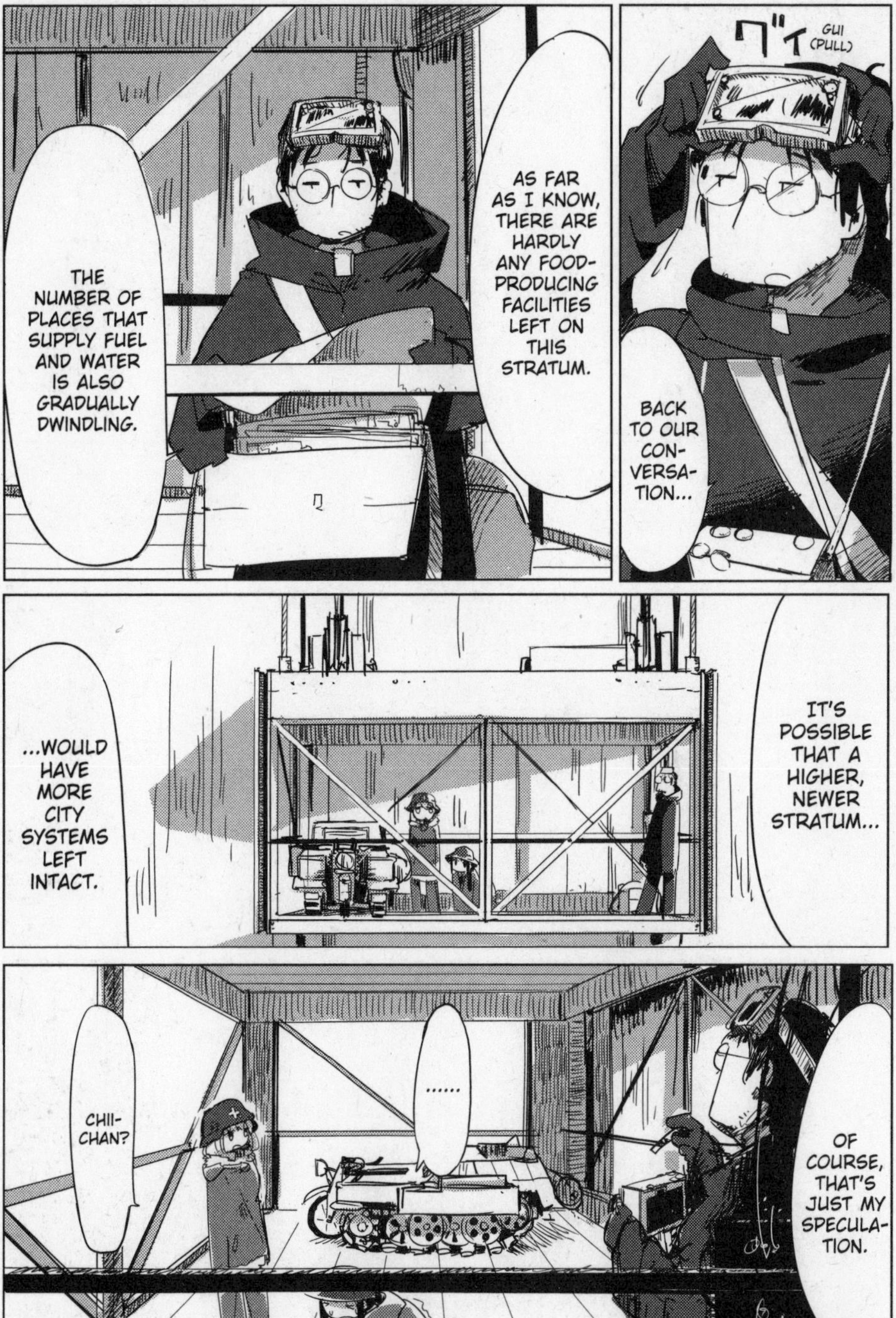
GUI (PULL)
BACK TO OUR CON-VERSA-TION...
AS FAR AS I KNOW, THERE ARE HARDLY ANY FOOD-PRODUCING FACILITIES LEFT ON THIS STRATUM.
THE NUMBER OF PLACES THAT SUPPLY FUEL AND WATER IS ALSO GRADUALLY DWINDLING.
IT'S POSSIBLE THAT A HIGHER, NEWER STRATUM...
...WOULD HAVE MORE CITY SYSTEMS LEFT INTACT.
OF COURSE, THAT'S JUST MY SPECULA-TION.
......
CHII-CHAN?

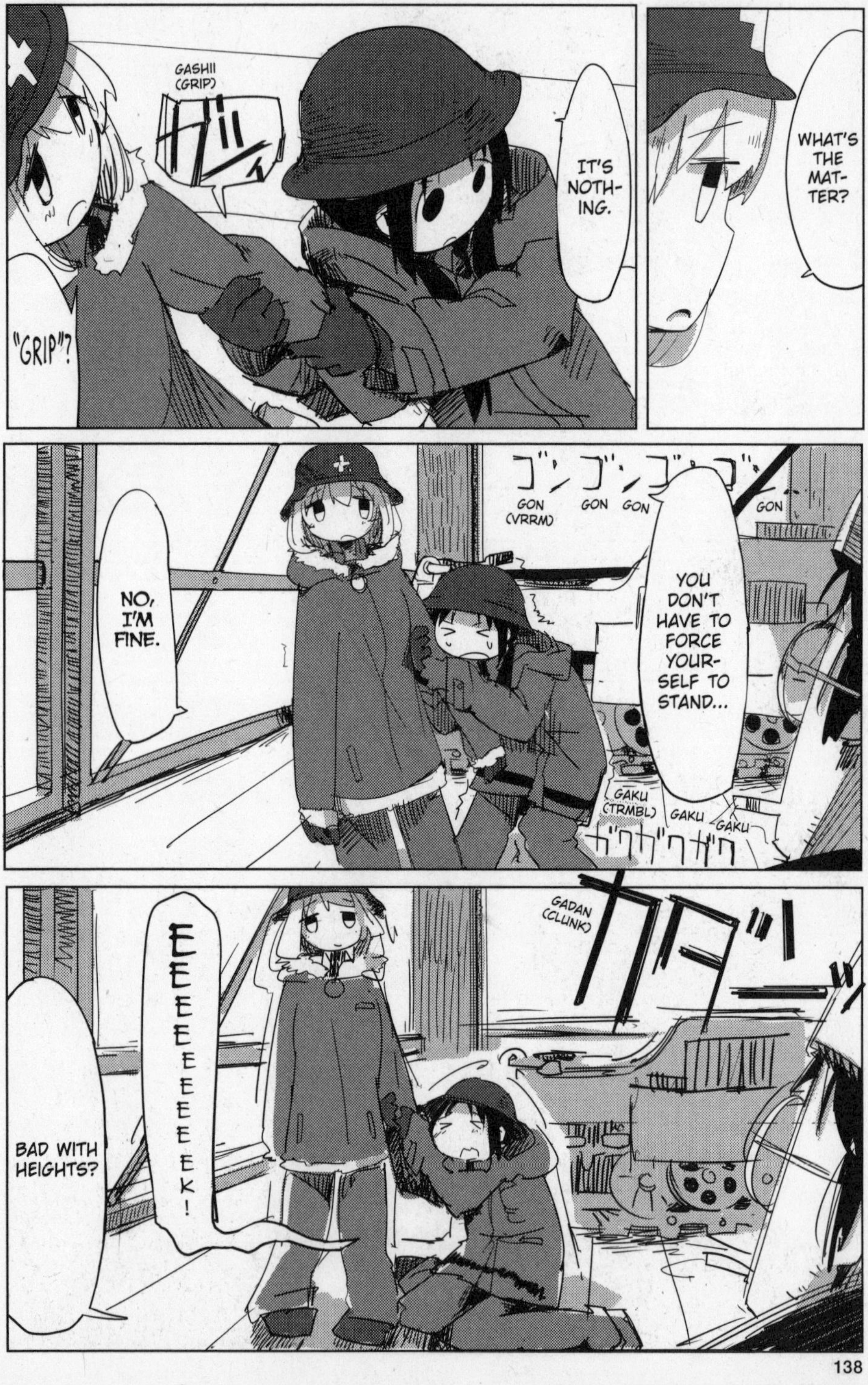
WHAT'S THE MATTER?
IT'S NOTHING.
GASHII (GRIP)
"GRIP"?
GON (VRRM) GON GON GON
YOU DON'T HAVE TO FORCE YOURSELF TO STAND...
NO, I'M FINE.
GAKU (TRMBL) GAKU GAKU
GADAN (CLUNK)
EEEEEEEEEEEK!
BAD WITH HEIGHTS?

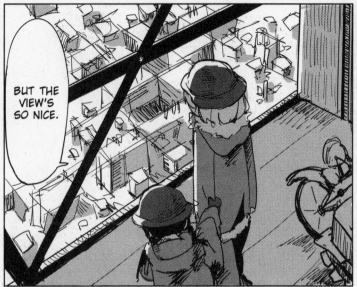

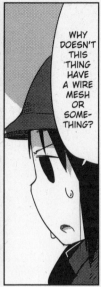

WHY DOESN'T THIS THING HAVE A WIRE MESH OR SOME-THING?
BUT THE VIEW'S SO NICE.
I'M SURE THEY DETERMINED IT WOULD BE A WASTE OF MATERIALS.
BUT WHAT IF IT TILTS AND DROPS?
THESE BARS WON'T CATCH ANY-THING...

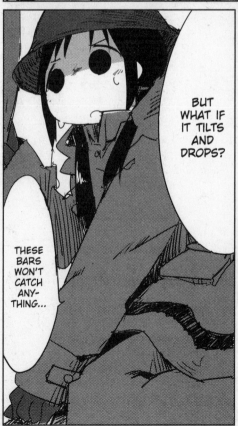

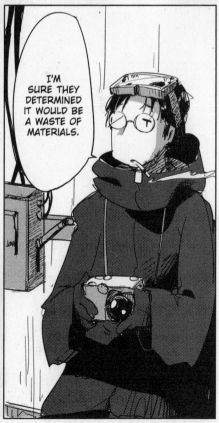

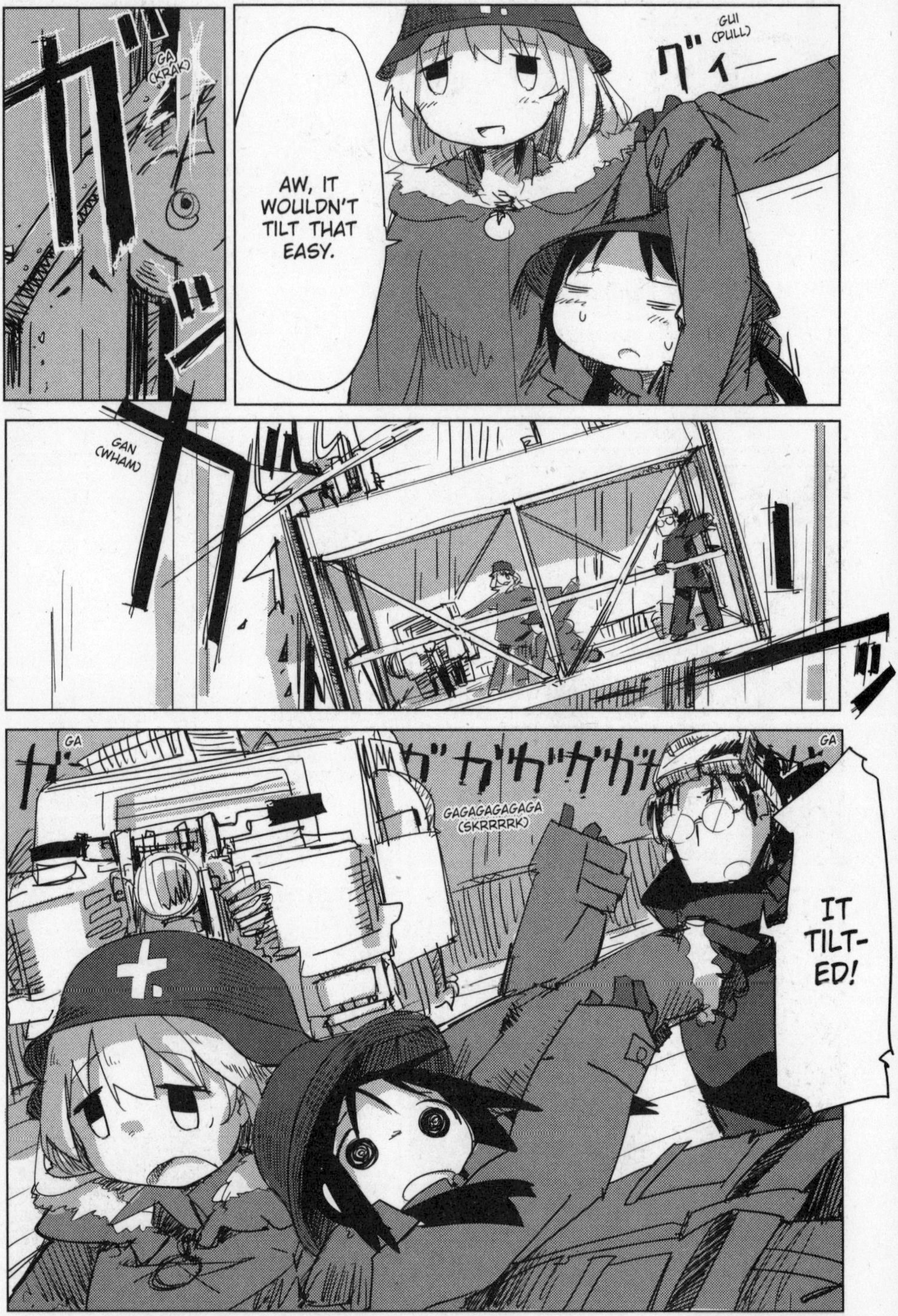
GUI (PULL)
AW, IT WOULDN'T TILT THAT EASY.
GA (KRAK)
GAN (WHAM)
GA
GAGAGAGAGAGA (SKRRRRK)
GA
IT TILT-ED!

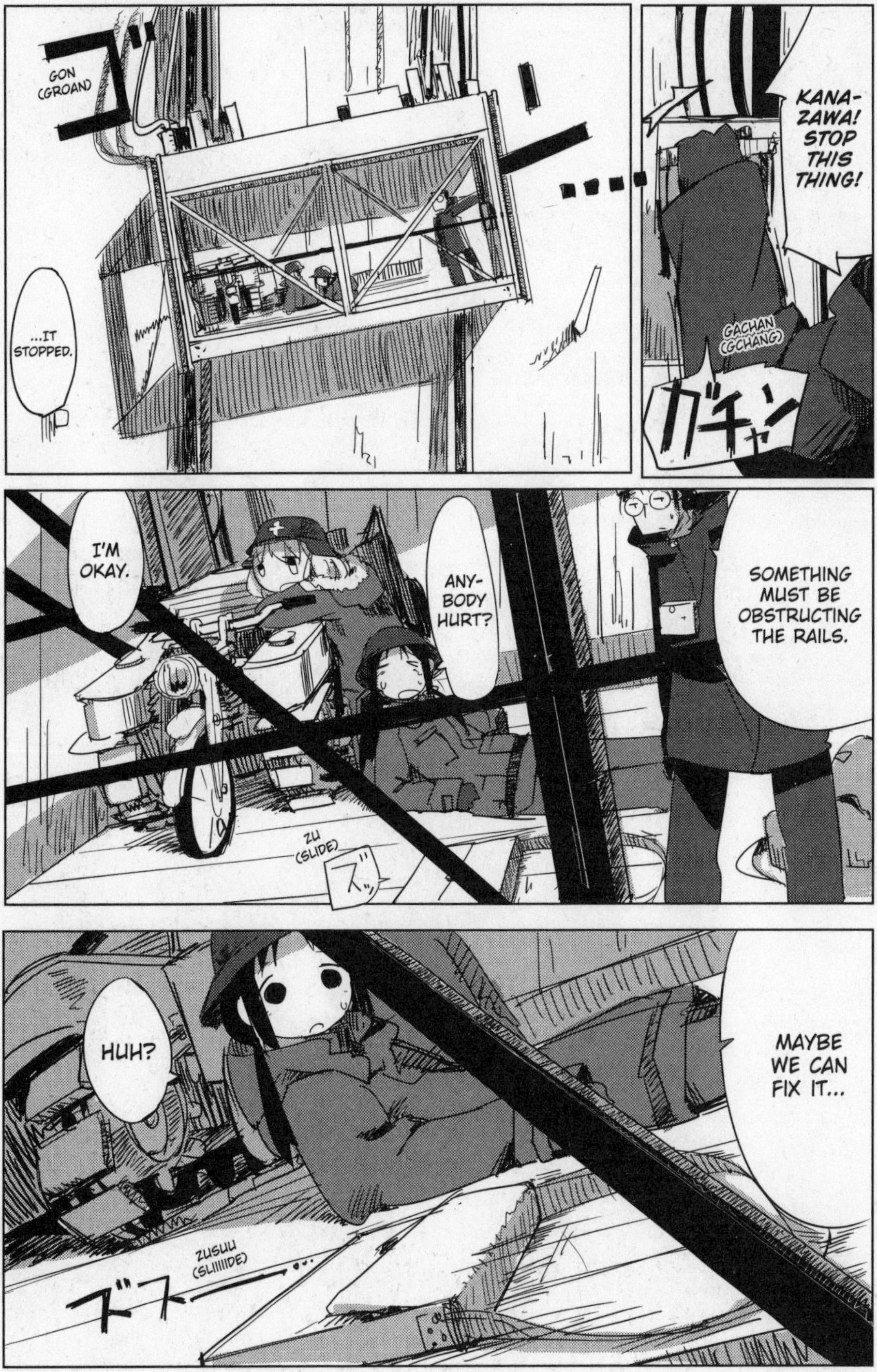
KANA-ZAWA! STOP THIS THING!
GACHAN (GCHANG)
GON (GROAND)
...IT STOPPED.
SOMETHING MUST BE OBSTRUCTING THE RAILS.
ANY-BODY HURT?
I'M OKAY.
ZU (SLIDE)
MAYBE WE CAN FIX IT...
HUH?
ZUSUU (SLIIIIIDE)

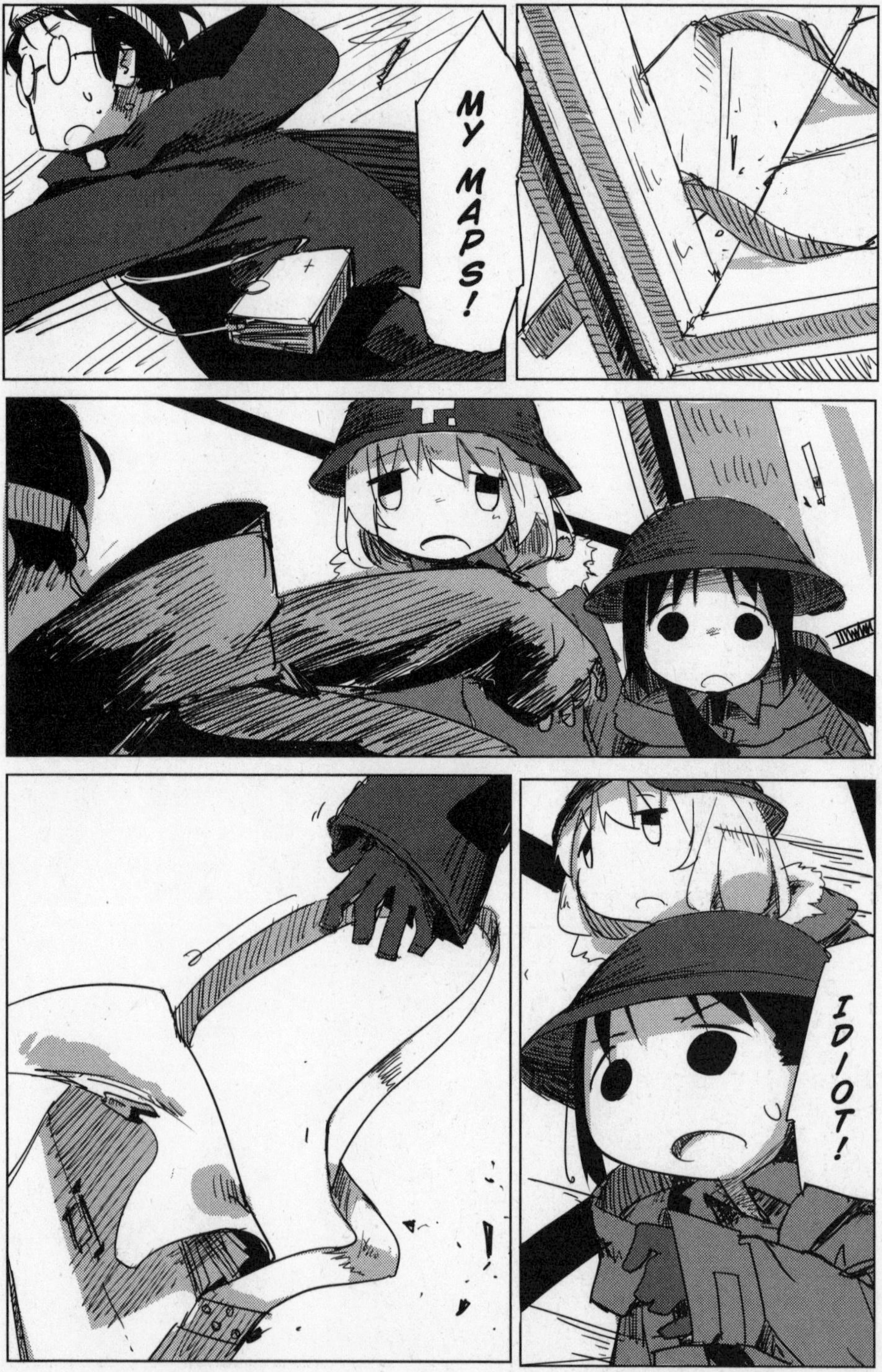
MY MAPS!
IDIOT!

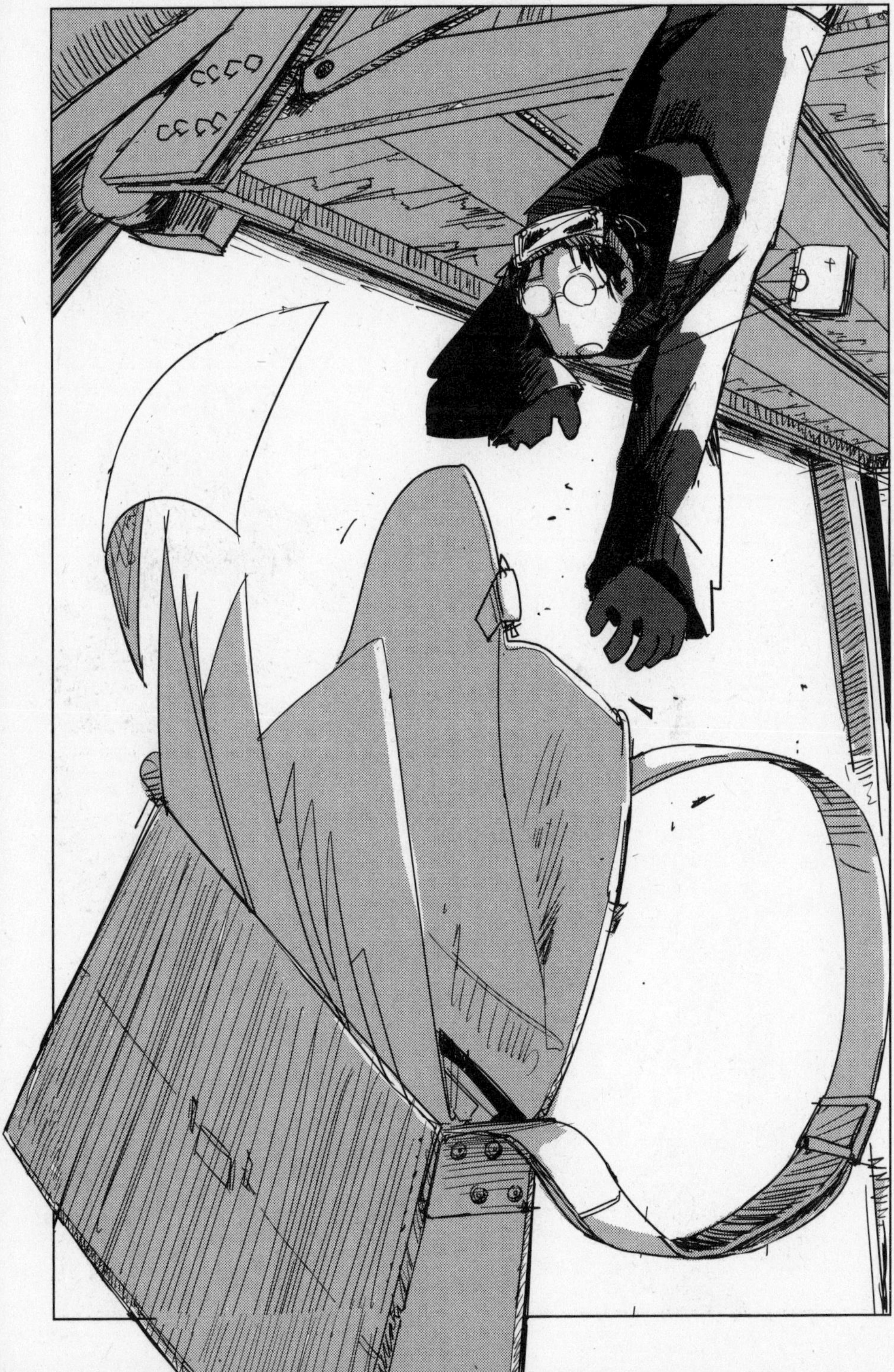

......

...JUST LET ME GO.

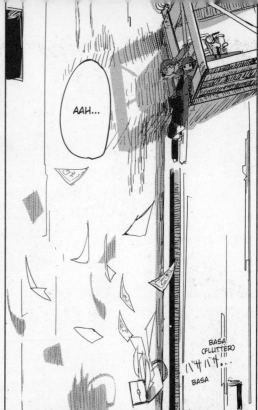

AAH...

BASA
(FLUTTER)
BASA

I MAY AS WELL FALL WITH THEM...

GUI
(TUG)

YOU'VE GOT TO BE KIDDING!

ZURURURU
(DRAAAG)

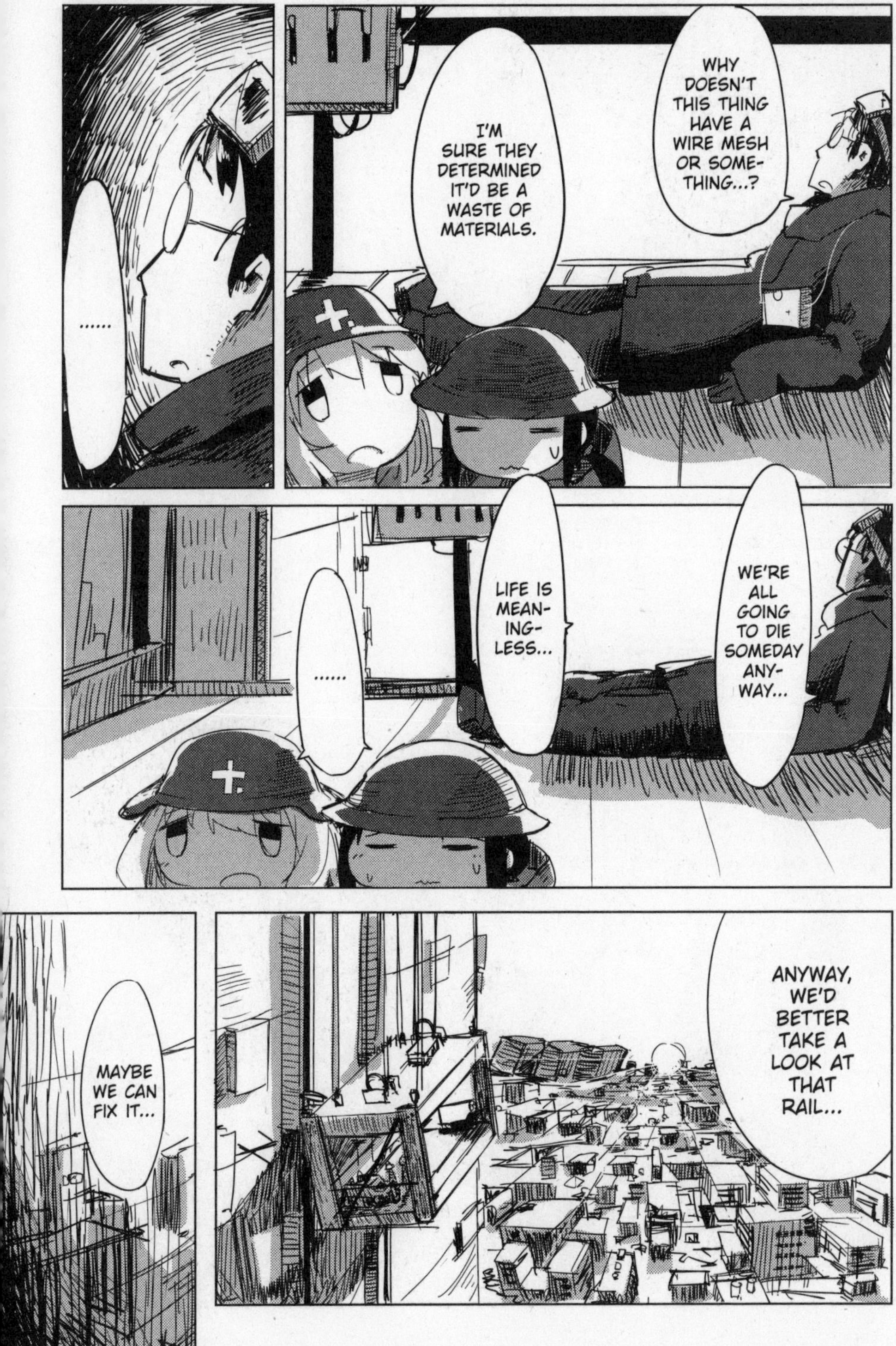
WHY DOESN'T THIS THING HAVE A WIRE MESH OR SOME-THING...?
I'M SURE THEY DETERMINED IT'D BE A WASTE OF MATERIALS.
......
WE'RE ALL GOING TO DIE SOMEDAY ANY-WAY...
LIFE IS MEAN-ING-LESS...
......
ANYWAY, WE'D BETTER TAKE A LOOK AT THAT RAIL...
MAYBE WE CAN FIX IT...

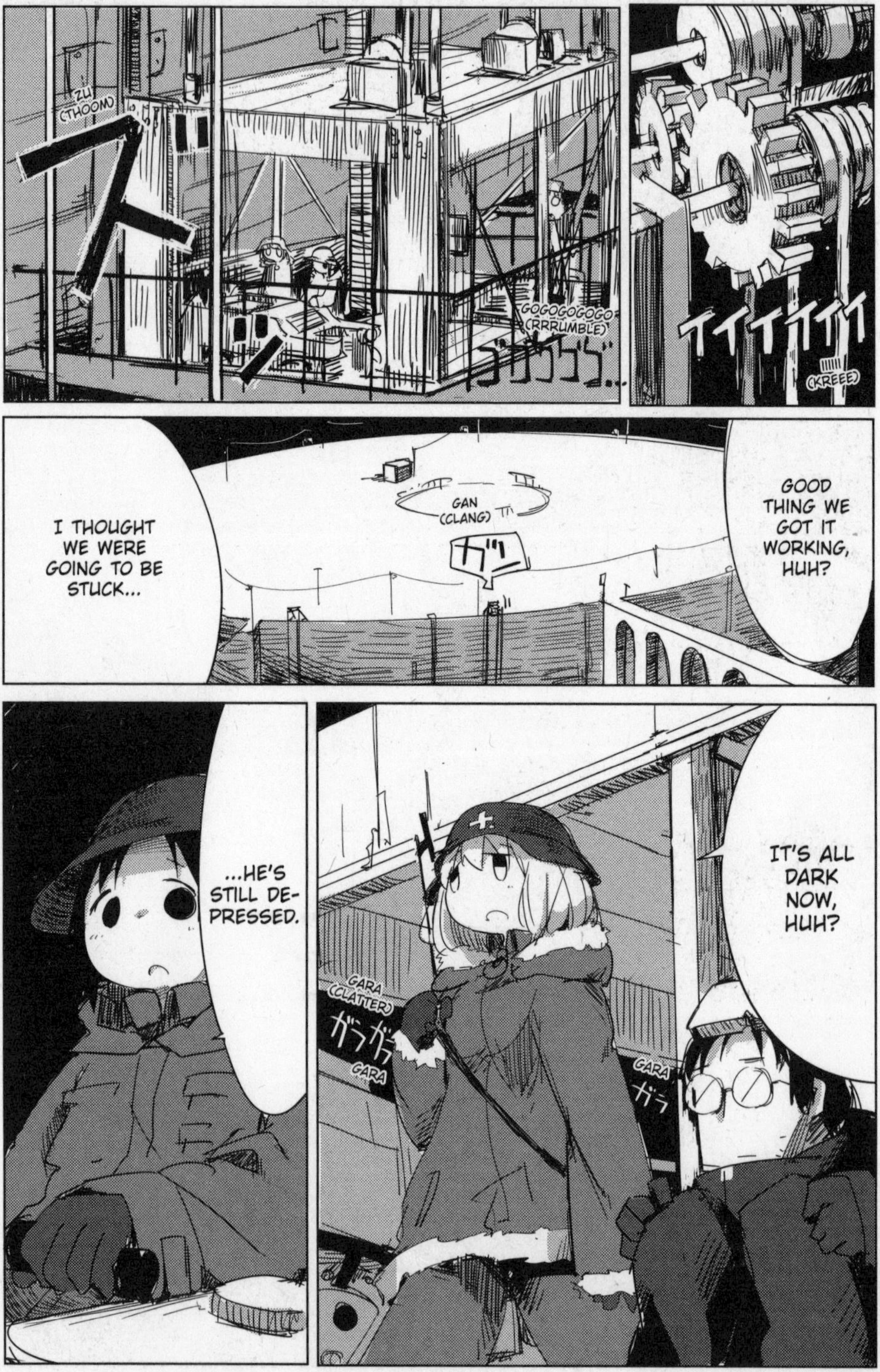
(KREEE)
ZU (THOOM)
GOGOGOGOGO (RRRUMBLE)
GOOD THING WE GOT IT WORKING, HUH?
GAN (CLANG)
I THOUGHT WE WERE GOING TO BE STUCK...
IT'S ALL DARK NOW, HUH?
GARA
GARA (CLATTER)
GARA
...HE'S STILL DE-PRESSED.

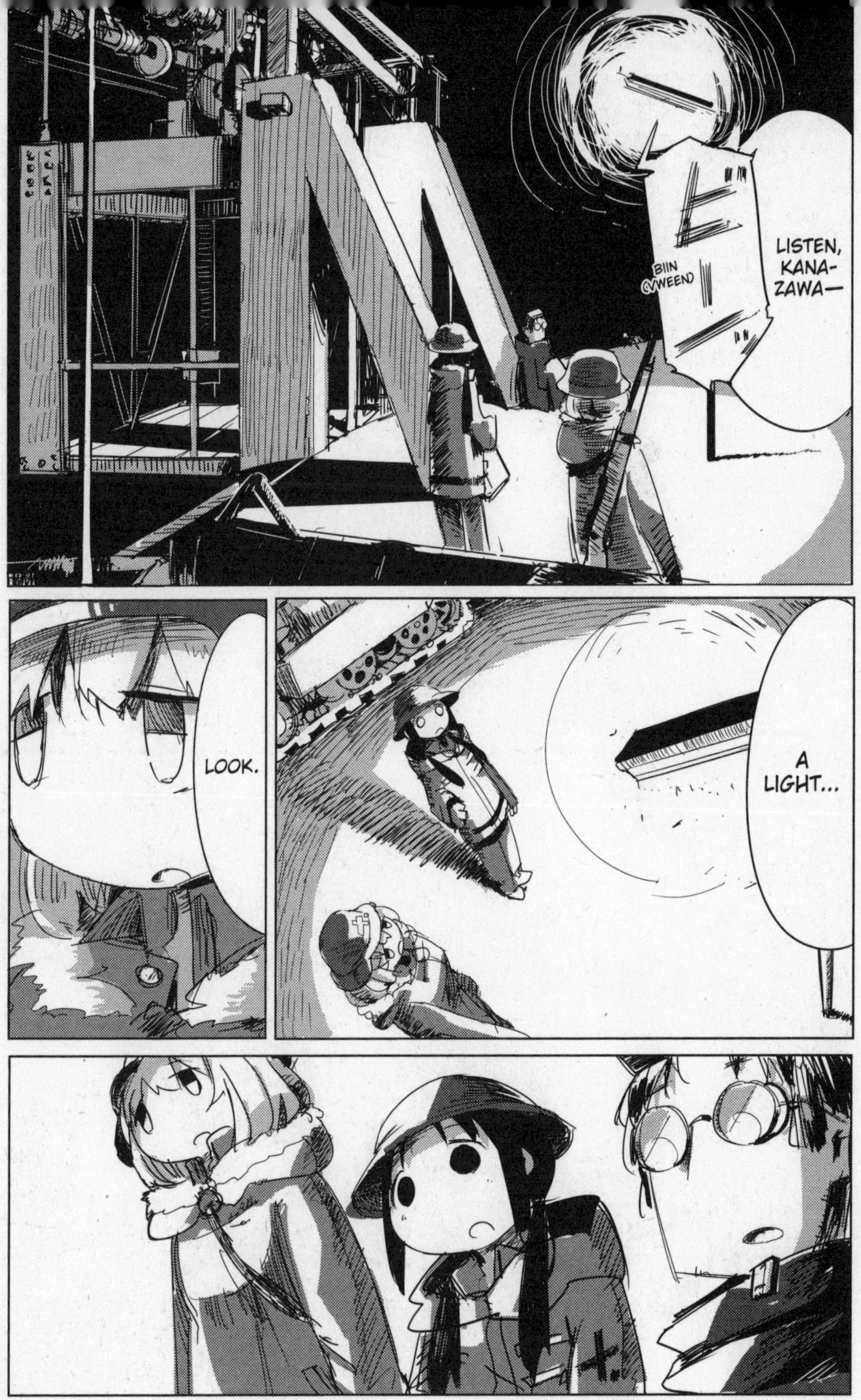
LISTEN, KANAZAWA—
BIIN (VWEEND)
A LIGHT...
LOOK.

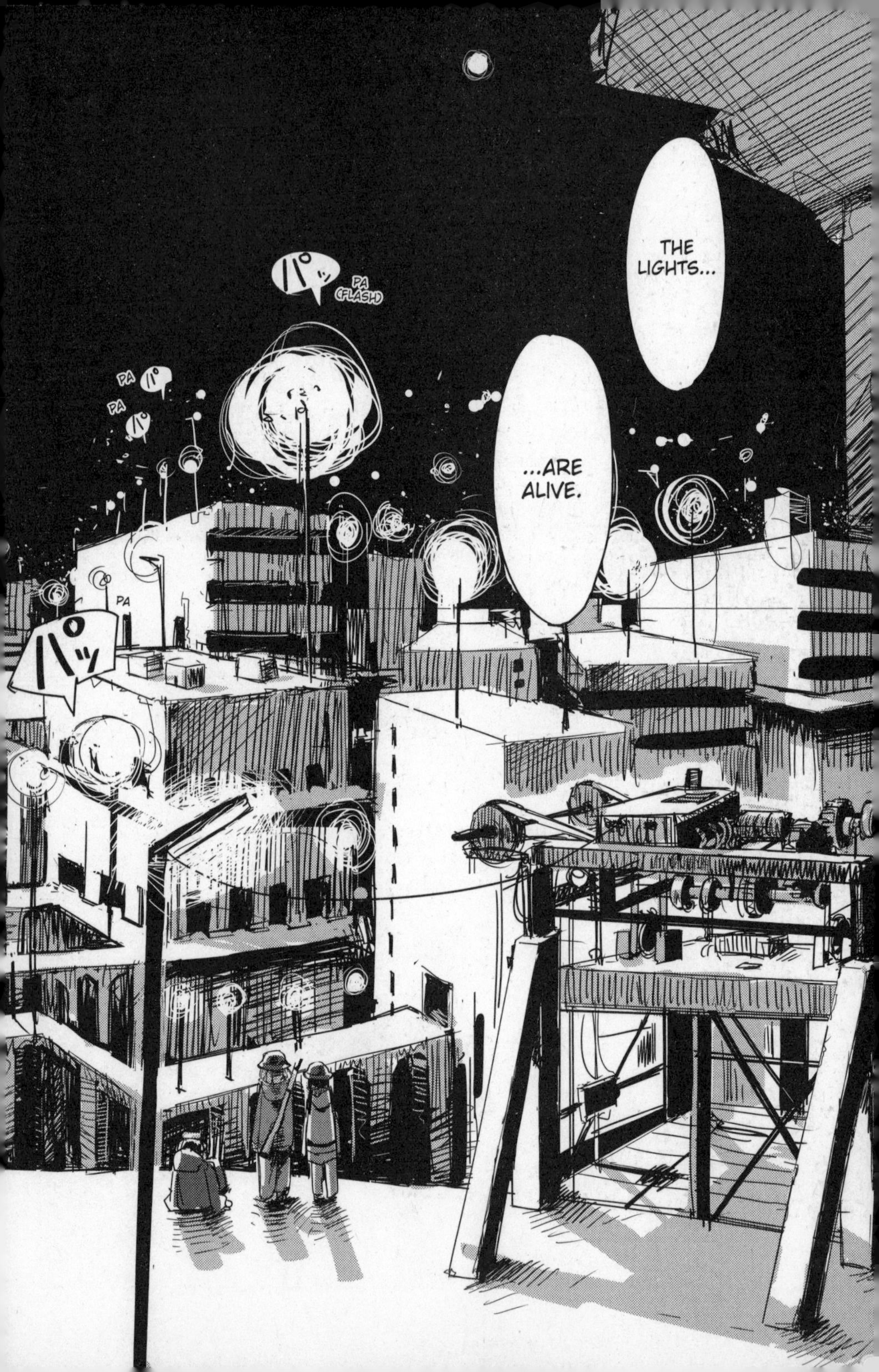
THE LIGHTS...
...ARE ALIVE.
パッ
PA (FLASH)
PA パ
PA パ
PA
パッ

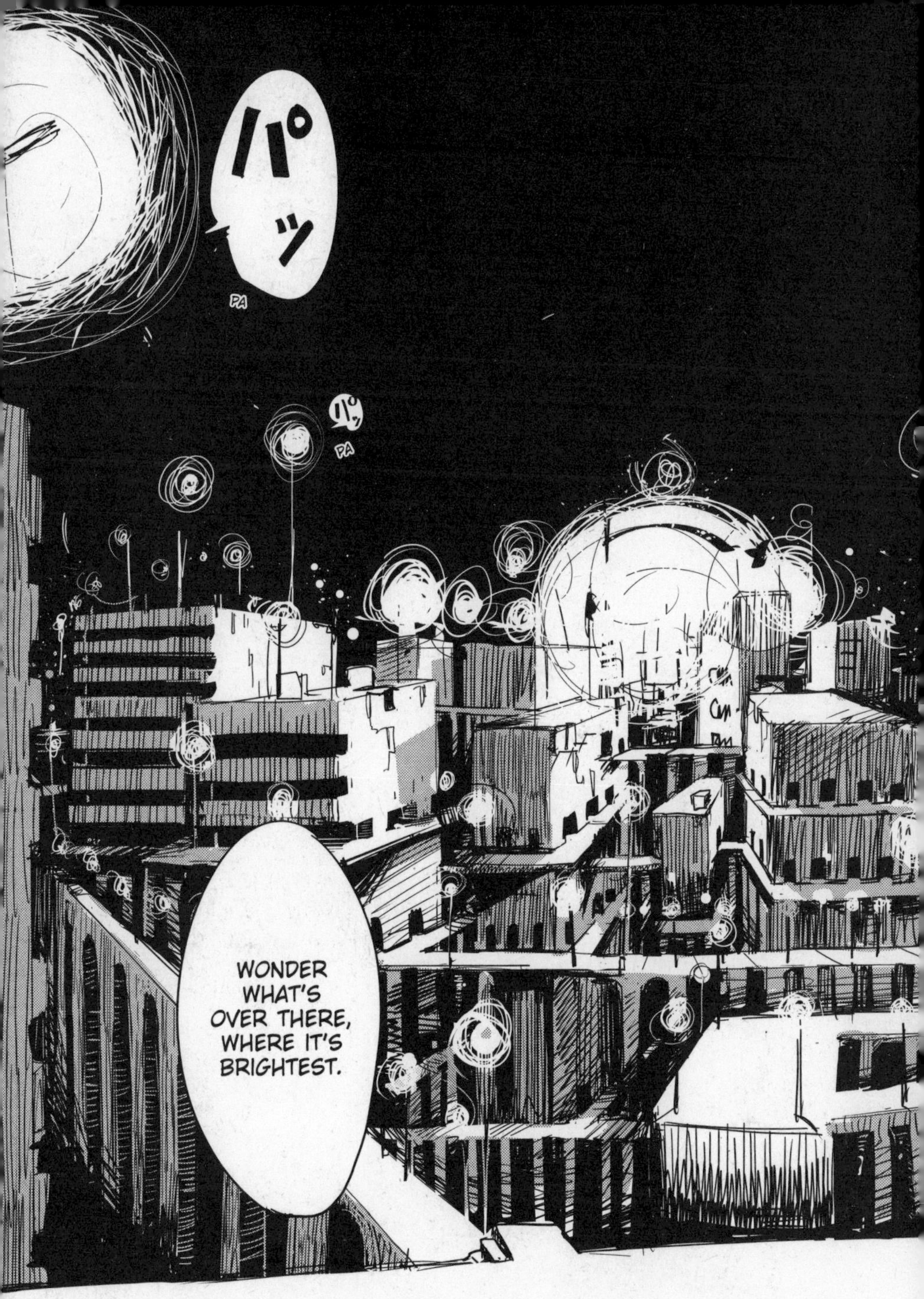
パッ
PA
パッ
PA
WONDER WHAT'S OVER THERE, WHERE IT'S BRIGHTEST.

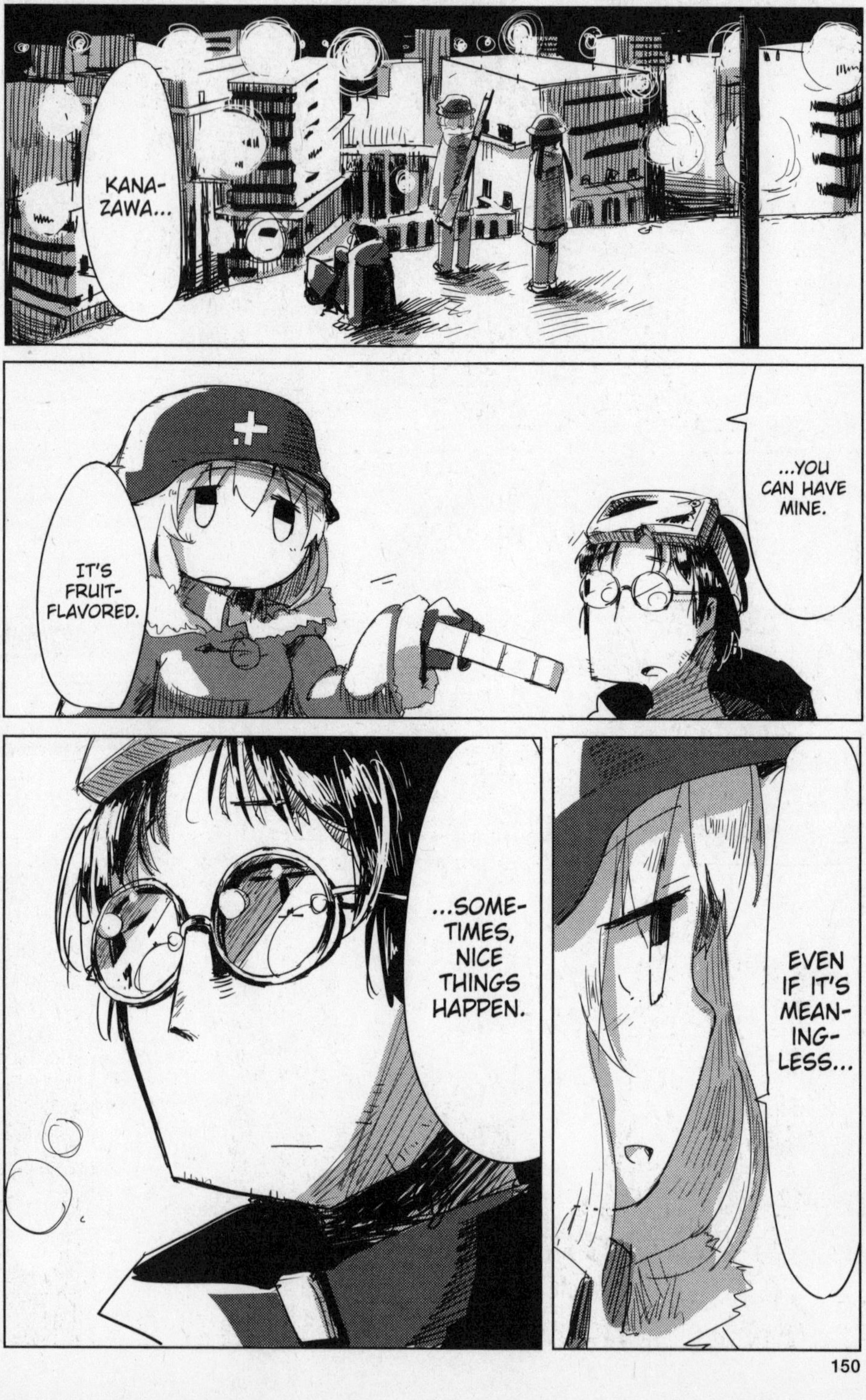
KANA-ZAWA...
...YOU CAN HAVE MINE.
IT'S FRUIT-FLAVORED.
EVEN IF IT'S MEAN-ING-LESS...
...SOME-TIMES, NICE THINGS HAPPEN.

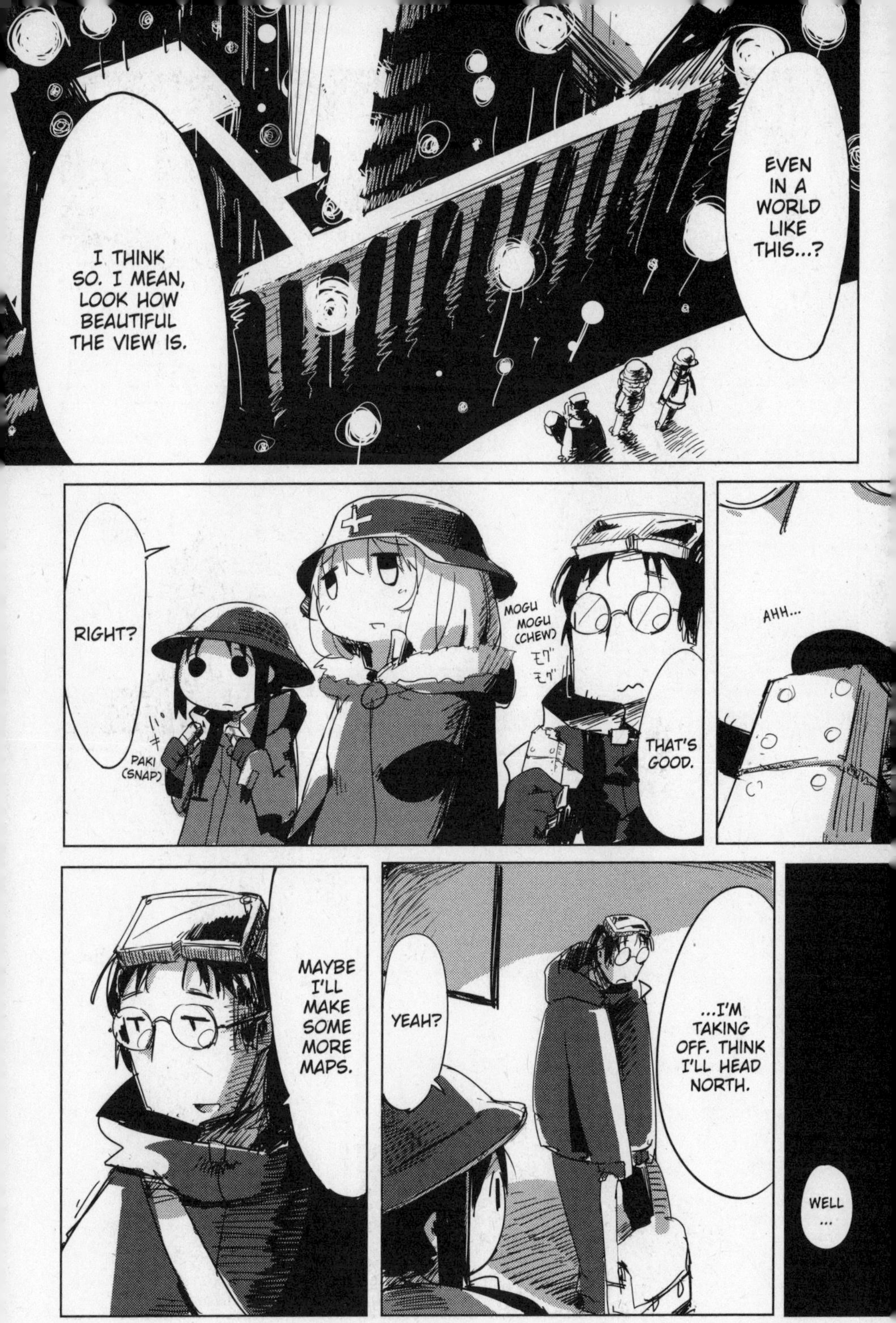

EVEN IN A WORLD LIKE THIS...?
I THINK SO. I MEAN, LOOK HOW BEAUTIFUL THE VIEW IS.
AHH...
MOGU MOGU (CHEW)
モグモグ
THAT'S GOOD.
RIGHT?
パキ
PAKI (SNAP)
WELL ...
...I'M TAKING OFF. THINK I'LL HEAD NORTH.
YEAH?
MAYBE I'LL MAKE SOME MORE MAPS.

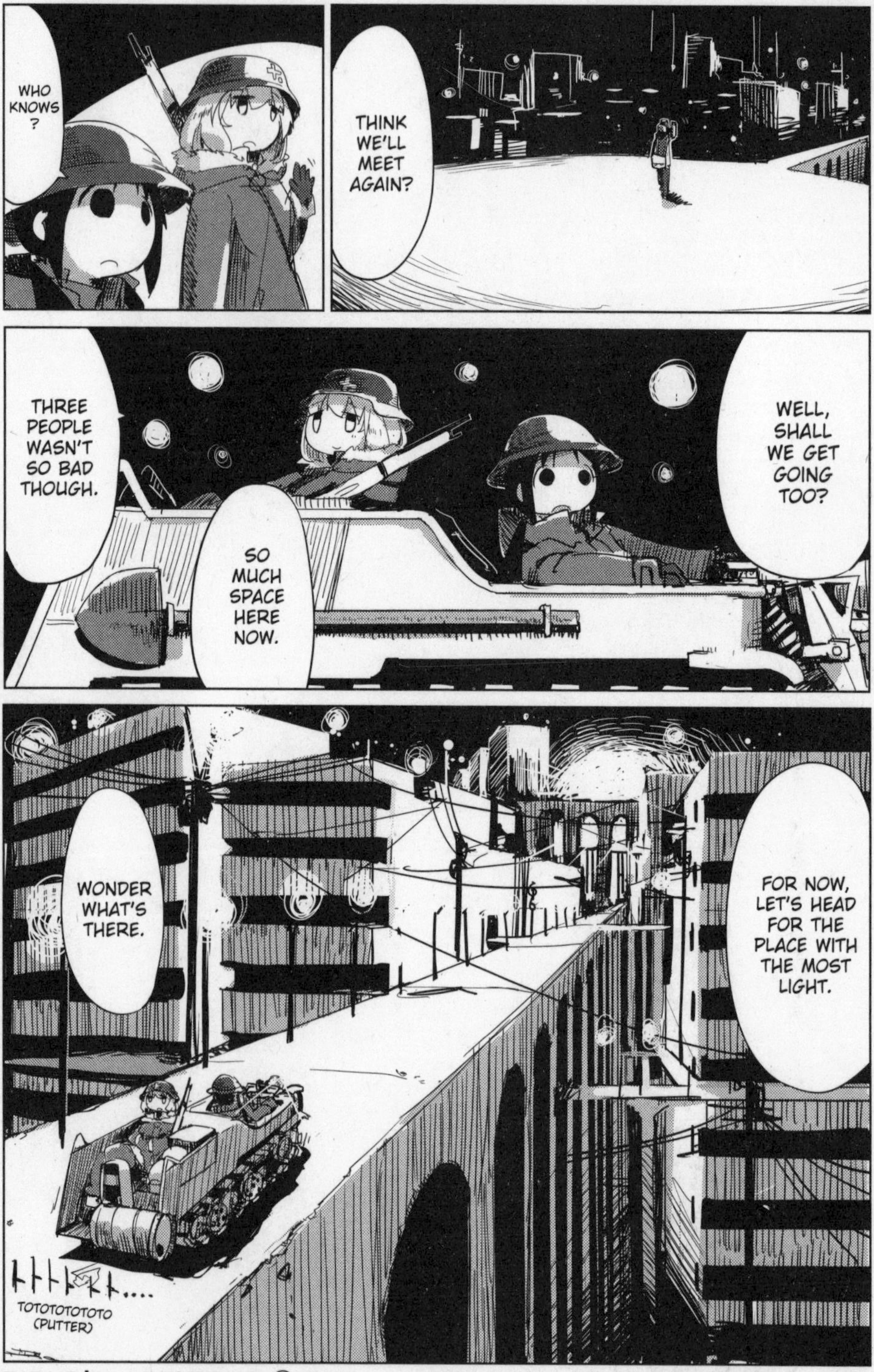
THINK WE'LL MEET AGAIN?
WHO KNOWS?
WELL, SHALL WE GET GOING TOO?
SO MUCH SPACE HERE NOW.
THREE PEOPLE WASN'T SO BAD THOUGH.
FOR NOW, LET'S HEAD FOR THE PLACE WITH THE MOST LIGHT.
WONDER WHAT'S THERE.
TOTOTOTOTOTO (PUTTER)

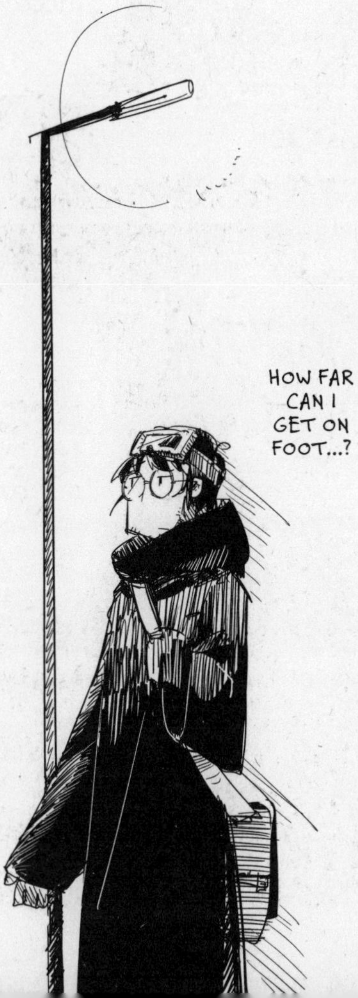
HOW FAR CAN I GET ON FOOT...?

· KETTENKRAD DESIGN ·

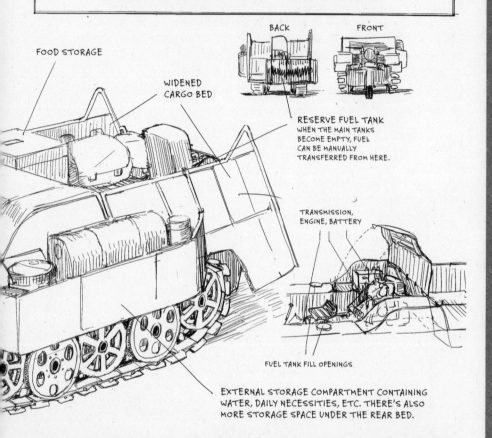

FOOD STORAGE

WIDENED CARGO BED

BACK

FRONT

RESERVE FUEL TANK
WHEN THE MAIN TANKS BECOME EMPTY, FUEL CAN BE MANUALLY TRANSFERRED FROM HERE.

TRANSMISSION, ENGINE, BATTERY

FUEL TANK FILL OPENINGS

EXTERNAL STORAGE COMPARTMENT CONTAINING WATER, DAILY NECESSITIES, ETC. THERE'S ALSO MORE STORAGE SPACE UNDER THE REAR BED.

the KETTENKRAD EXPLAINED

The name "Kettenkrad" is a combination of the German words *Ketten*, meaning "track" or "chain" (in this case referring to continuous tracks), and *Krad* (short for *Kraftrad*), a term for "motorcycle"; it means a tractor-style motorbike. The Kettenkrad is an ultralight half-track (a vehicle with wheels in the front and tracks in the rear) that was first produced in 1939 by German automaker NSU (also known for developing the world's first rotary engine). It was created to be a towing vehicle that could be transported via the Ju 52, Germany's main transport aircraft at the time. In addition to its simple motorbike-like operation, its back tracks allow it to drive through deep mud. Because of this, it first saw heavy use on the Eastern Front and later towed not only artillery as originally intended, but also various kinds of transport, aircraft, etc., and would come to be used everywhere the German army went.

THEIR VEHICLE IS A HALF-TRACK ONCE KNOWN AS THE "KETTENKRAD." THE
DESIGN ITSELF IS RECENTLY OLD, BUT THIS PARTICULAR KETTENKRAD
IS RECENTLY MADE. VARIOUS PARTS OF IT HAVE BEEN CUSTOMIZED, AND IT
DIFFERS FROM THE ORIGINAL DESIGN AT MANY POINTS. AS TECHNOLOGY USED
IN THE WORLD AFTER THE COLLAPSE OF CIVILIZATION IS PREDOMINANTLY
RECONSTRUCTED FROM READING OLD DOCUMENTS, THERE ARE FEW NEW DESIGNS.

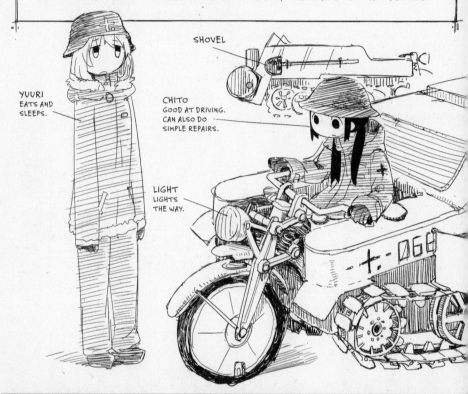

SHOVEL

YUURI
EATS AND
SLEEPS.

CHITO
GOOD AT DRIVING.
CAN ALSO DO
SIMPLE REPAIRS.

LIGHT
LIGHTS
THE WAY.

The Kettenkrad has room for three: the driver and, behind the engine at the center, two passengers facing backward. Its pulling capacity is 450 kilograms (about 1,000 pounds). The Kettenkrad is steered by moving the motorbike-like handlebars connected to the front wheel, but because turning the handlebars toward the track on either side beyond a certain point will engage the brakes on that track, like on a tank, it's possible for the Kettenkrad to be steered without a front wheel. Thus, when off-road conditions were so bad that the front wheel was packed with mud, the Kettenkrad would be used with the wheel removed. According to the designs, its top speed is 70 km/h (43 m/h), but in use, it only reached about about 50 km/h (31 m/h). Including variations built after the war, about 9,000 of these vehicles were produced in total (some sources say 8,345 were built during the war and 550 after the war).

Takaaki Suzuki

Military history adviser, scriptwriter, author. Responsible for developing and directing the settings, military history, and so on for many anime series. Principal works include the *Strike Witches* series (Military History Adviser, World Setting, Scriptwriter) and the *Girls und Panzer* series (Adviser, Supervision, Script).

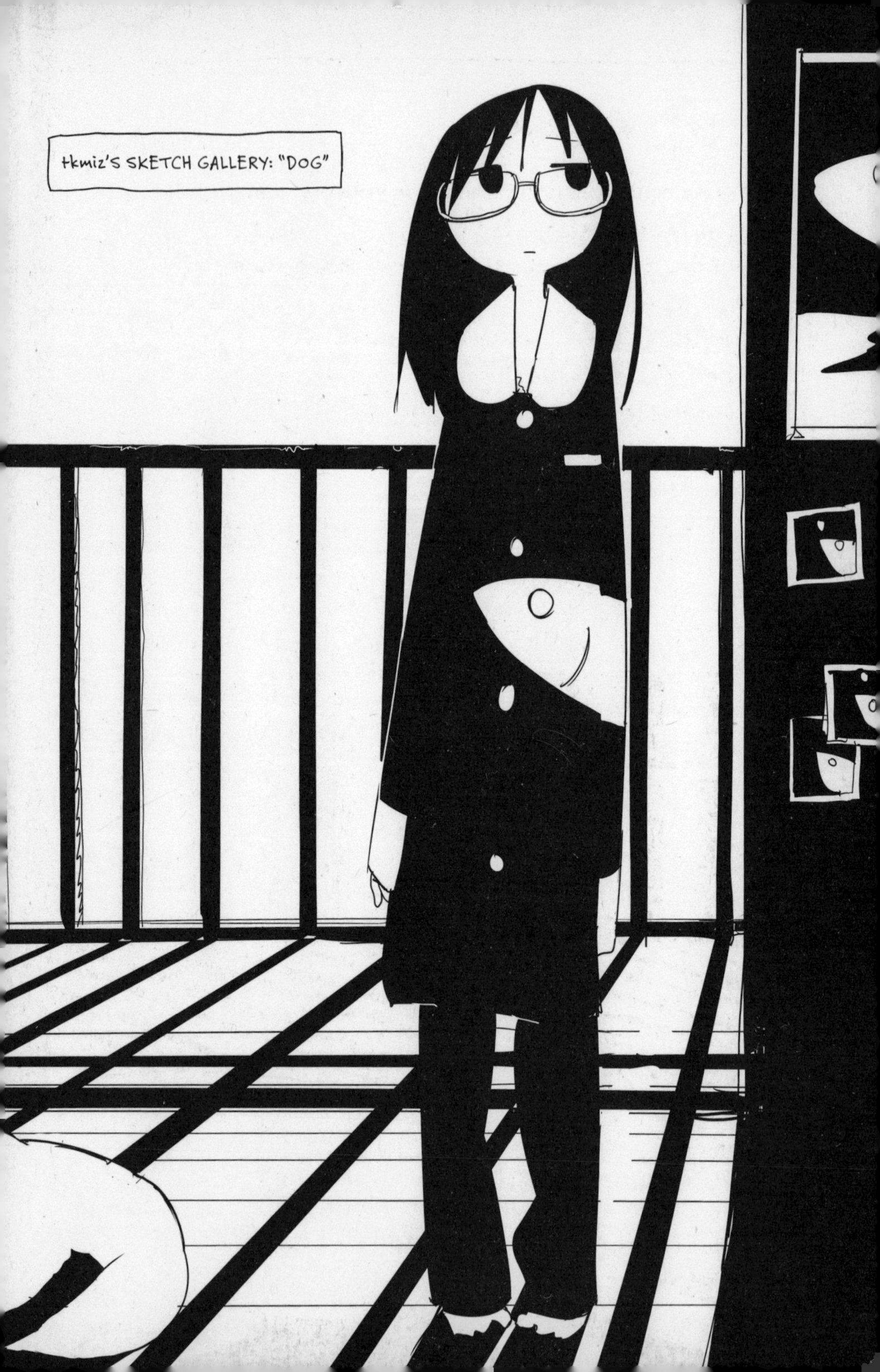
tkmiz's SKETCH GALLERY: "DOG"

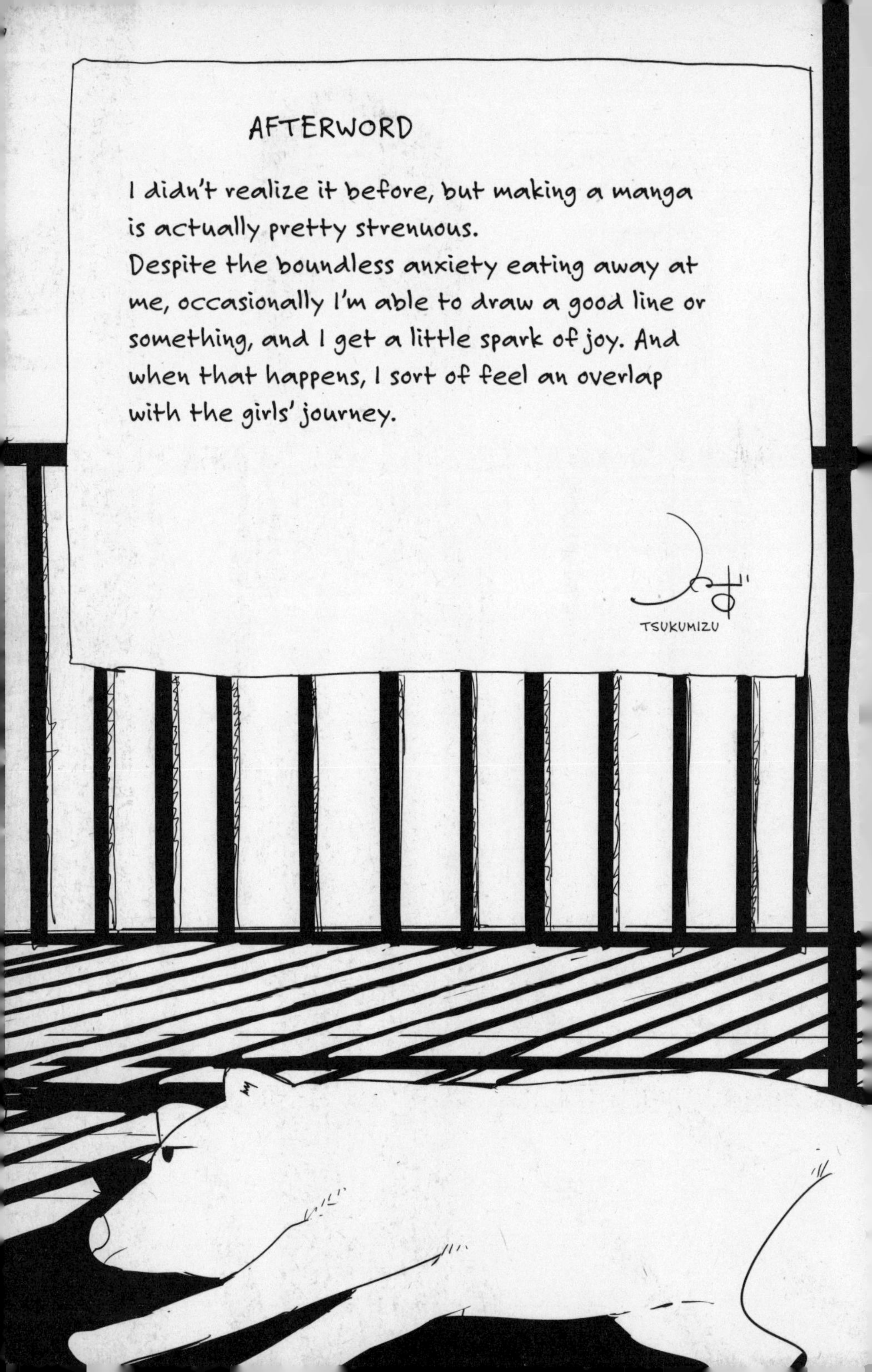
AFTERWORD
I didn't realize it before, but making a manga is actually pretty strenuous.
Despite the boundless anxiety eating away at me, occasionally I'm able to draw a good line or something, and I get a little spark of joy. And when that happens, I sort of feel an overlap with the girls' journey.
TSUKUMIZU

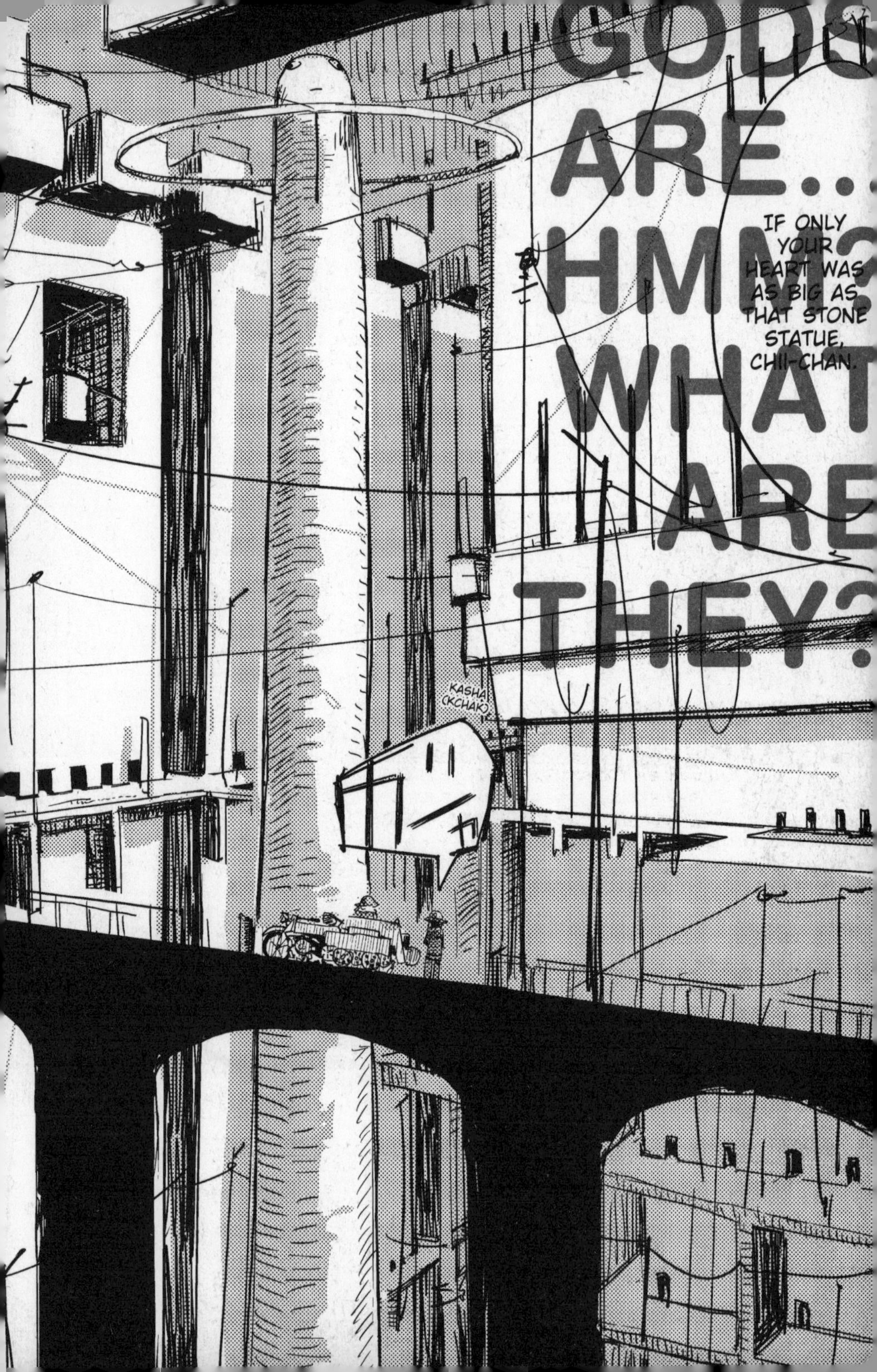
GODS ARE...
HMM? WHAT ARE THEY?
IF ONLY YOUR HEART WAS AS BIG AS THAT STONE STATUE, CHII-CHAN.
KASHA (KCHAK)

GIRLS' LAST TOUR

COMING AUGUST 2017

Chito and Yuuri take their first steps into
the world of the upper stratum. While this
level is just as abandoned as the one below,
a whole new set of places and things to
see stretches out before them. Countless
lights illuminate the darkness of the
night, strange stone statues looming...
Chito and Yuuri hop back onto their beloved
Kettenkrad to continue their journey, but
what will they find at the end of it?

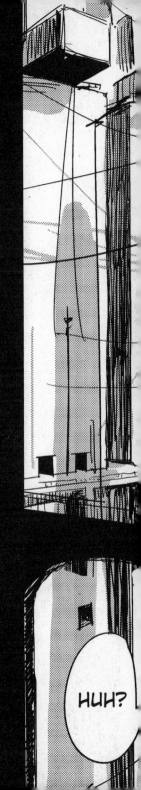

HUH?

GiRLS' LAST TOUR ①

TSUKUMIZU

Translation: Amanda Haley
Lettering: Abigail Blackman

SHOUJO SHUUMATSU RYOKOU Volume 1 © 2014 Tsukumizu. All rights reserved. English translation rights arranged with SHINCHOSHA PUBLISHING CO. through Tuttle-Mori Agency, Inc., Tokyo.

English translation © 2017 by Yen Press, LLC

Yen Press
1290 Avenue of the Americas
New York, NY 10104

Visit us at yenpress.com
facebook.com/yenpress
twitter.com/yenpress
yenpress.tumblr.com
instagram.com/yenpress

First Yen Press Edition: May 2017

Yen Press is an imprint of Yen Press, LLC.
The Yen Press name and logo are trademarks of Yen Press, LLC.

The publisher is not responsible for websites
(or their content) that are not owned by the publisher.

Library of Congress Control Number: 2017932043

ISBNs: 978-0-316-47062-9 (paperback)
           978-0-316-47063-6 (ebook)

10 9 8 7 6 5 4 3

WOR

Printed in the United States of America